Wife and Widow in Medieval England

STUDIES IN MEDIEVAL AND EARLY MODERN CIVILIZATION
Marvin B. Becker, General Editor

Wife and Widow in Medieval England

Edited by Sue Sheridan Walker

Ann Arbor

THE UNIVERSITY OF MICHIGAN PRESS

A CIP catalogue record for this book is available from the British Library.

Library of Congress Cataloging-in-Publication Data

Wife and widow in medieval England / edited by Sue Sheridan Walker.
    p.   cm. — (Studies in medieval and early modern civilization)
    Includes bibliographical references and index.
    ISBN 0-472-10415-2
    1. Husband and wife—England—History. 2. Women—Legal status,
laws, etc.—England—History. 3. Widows—Legal status, laws, etc.—
England—History. 4. England—Social conditions—Medieval period,
1066–1485. I. Walker, Sue Sheridan. II. Series.
KD758.W54   1993
346.4201'34—dc20
[344.206134]   93-30673
                                                                        CIP

In memory of Michael M. Sheehan

Contents

Abbreviations

Guildhall	Guildhall Library, London
	Probate Act Books
PRO	Public Record Office, London
	PRO manuscripts:
C 47	Chancery Miscellanea
C 81	Chancery, Warrants for the Great Seal, ser. 1
C 143	Chancery, Inquisitions *ad quod damnum*
CP 40	Plea Rolls, Court of Common Pleas
E 101	Exchequer, King's Remembrancer, Accounts, Various
E 159	Exchequer, King's Remembrancer, Memoranda Rolls
E 352	Exchequer, Pipe Office, Chancellor's Rolls
E 368	Exchequer, Lord Treasurer's Remembrancer, Memoranda Rolls
E 371	Exchequer, Lord Treasurer's Remembrancer, Originalia Rolls
JUST 1	Plea Rolls, Court of the Justices Itinerant (Eyre Rolls, Assize Rolls, etc.)
KB 26	Curia Regis Rolls
KB 27	Plea Rolls, Court of King's Bench
SC 1	Special Collections, Ancient Correspondence
SC 8	Special Collections, Ancient Petitions
York	Borthwick Institute manuscripts:
Cons. AB. 2	Consistory Court Act Books
CP. E.	Ecclesiastical Cause Papers: The Court of York (14th-c. files)
CP. F.	Ecclesiastical Cause Papers: The Court of York (15th-c. files)
York Minster	Fragment of Act Books, 1371–1375

Bracton	Henry de Bracton, *Bracton on the Laws and Customs of England,* ed. G. E. Woodbine, trans. and rev. Samuel E. Thorne, 4 vols. (Cambridge, Mass., 1968–77)
BNB	*Bracton's Note Book,* ed. F. W. Maitland, 3 vols. (London, 1887)
Britton	*Britton,* ed. Francis Morgan Nichols, 2 vols. (1865; reprint, Holmes Beach, Fla., 1983)
CIPM	*Calendar of Inquisitions Post Mortem*
Fleta	*Fleta,* ed. H. G. Richardson and G. O. Sayles, Selden Society (several vols. and series continuing)
Foedera	*Foedera, Conventiones, Literae, etc.,* ed. T. Rymer, 10 vols. (The Hague, 1739–45)
Glanvill	*The Treatise on the Laws and Customs of the Realm of England Commonly Called Glanvill,* ed. G. D. G. Hall (London, 1965)
HEL	W. S. Holdsworth, *History of the English Law,* 16 vols., 7th ed. (London, 1956)
PCC	Public Record Office, Wills of the Prerogative Court of Canterbury
Provinciale	William Lyndwood, *Provinciale seu Constitutiones Angliae* (Oxford, 1679)
RS	Rolls Series
Statutes	*Statutes of the Realm,* 11 vols., in vol. 12, Record Commission (London, 1810–28)
TE	*Testamenta Eboracensia,* ed. James Raine and James Raine, Jr., Surtees Society, vols. 4, 30, 45, 53 (1836–69)
X	*Liber extra* (= Decretales Gregorii IX) (in *Corpus juris canonici*)

Introduction

Sue Sheridan Walker

The frequency with which women used the law courts and bureaucratic tribunals of the king, the church, and the town is one of the striking features of medieval England. Utilizing a vast array of archival and printed material, the authors in this volume reconstruct important aspects of what being a woman meant between the twelfth and the fifteenth centuries in England or rebellious Scotland. The richness of detail offers new understanding of the life struggles of wives and widows, while the various interpretive frameworks situate women more securely in their sociolegal setting. Medieval law and administration were complex, but evidently both were understandable to the women who actively exploited them. Behind the public avenues of redress and defense we can discern the networks and power relationships that women used to secure their rights and defend them from challenge.

The wives and widows discussed here varied in age, personality, wealth, and status. The eight essays in this volume seek to define important aspects of the relationship of medieval Englishwomen to the law of the church and the state. Our findings often suggest gender parity in that women acted very much like men in similar situations, such as their increasing use of attorneys in the royal courts. Gender distinctions have been found, however, in church court proceedings and testamentary practice. A recent scholar has tartly remarked that "medieval England did not have even a lurking suspicion that women as persons might be equal to men."[1] This may well be true, but the authors of these essays do not wish to belabor the constraints that might have limited feminine agency. Nevertheless, the peculiarities of English law touching women are central to the plot of *Wife and Widow* because we explore what women could and did do as wives, as widows, and again as wives. We stress what women accomplished when circumstances and their own determination empowered them to act for themselves. Individual choice within a given range of options was essential for them and for our appreciation of the freedom inherent in medieval English society.

There are undoubtedly subtle differences in the authors' perceptions of the degree of freedom enjoyed by individuals, especially women, in medieval England. Two areas in which there was a tension between "free choice" and "possible constraint" concern property matters and the choice of a marital partner. The theory and practice of land law are drawing more attention from scholars.[2] Quantitative studies are necessary to refine our understanding of the ability to acquire, enjoy, and resettle real property. Despite certain restraints upon the disposition of freehold and customary tenures, the land law permitted, and individuals actively used, the ability to make a variety of inter vivos transfers of land.[3] Charters, in large part unexplored by medieval scholars, offer evidence of widespread personal initiative in the manipulation of real property.[4] Court records give copious examples of often disputed consequences of extensive resettlement of property. This "return to the land" by legal, social, and economic historians is very important, especially because this work holds the promise of transcending the somewhat artificial division of late medieval property holders into peasants or freeholders. The more we know about the land, the more we will know about women's participation in property and the economy. Because land transactions were increasingly committed to written record, we can see the variety of persons active in both the peasant and free-land market.

About marital choice canon law proclaimed and church courts, when asked by one of the parties, enforced the view that the free consent of both parties was necessary for a valid marriage.[5] This meant that neither family nor seignorial lords could "force" someone to marry against his or her will. We recognize that force and influence are not the same thing. Though still the subject of some controversy, in general "control" over marriage by either feudal or manorial lords seems to have been reduced to a fine roughly equivalent to a "marriage tax."[6] By the mid-thirteenth century the king came to accept a fine from tenants-in-chiefs' widows who married without royal license. Lesser feudal lords seem to have abandoned the attempt to profit from the remarriage of their tenants' widows.[7] The king and other feudal lords continued, however, to collect a fine for "forfeiture of marriage" from wards—minor heirs to feudal property—of both sexes who refused suitable marriages.[8] Public records indicate much about "feudal" and "manorial" involvement in marital choice. The considerable number of widows in "the king's gift" or feudal wards who were willing to pay a fine to please themselves about marriage are recorded. Those who accepted, or even welcomed, the offer of a marital partner usually appear in neither the administrative nor litigation records. Family influence is harder to document, but experienced researchers catch glimpses of it. Then and now, practical parameters help to define choices made by both men and women.[9] This is especially true about decisions touching marriage. The current interest in gender is very useful in emphasizing the necessity of comparing what men and women of the same group could and did do in similar situations. Our essayists focus on situations in which property and marriage are involved.[10] Law and biology placed medieval women in a "peculiar" but not powerless position. The legal and bureaucratic consequences of their choices, demands, and actions form the evidence for our study.

Wife and *widow* are related but opposite terms. *Wife* corresponds to the legal description of *feme covert,* one whose legal existence is "covered" by her spouse; *widow* denotes an autonomous status equivalent to the legal term *feme sole,* a woman who enjoyed full legal personality. The legal disabilities of married women in medieval England were nearly all encompassing,[11] yet many widows remarried. Thus, they left the independent status of "free widowhood" to return to the legally confining rules of coverture. An unmarried adult woman could, for example, hold property, sue and be sued, and borrow or lend money. When she married, however, her land ordinarily came under the control of the husband: he did homage for the holding and could make disposition of it, although she might be able to recover the land after his death. The husband and wife had to be joined in any legal action touching the property, including pleas for dower of a previous husband; credit transactions, for example, had to be in the name of both spouses.

John Baker has described the unity of person in marriage as a legal fiction. "The origin of the doctrine, and its one-sidedness, may be found in the earlier customary treatment of women as inferiors and the power which social custom gave the husband over his wife."[12] *Feme sole* had another meaning in medieval law, whereby a married woman could maintain an independent status for trading purposes.[13] Loengard has observed that, without husbands, some adult women enjoyed a capacity—similar to men—to hold and deal with property, although women were, of course, at a disadvantage for inheritance purposes.[14] R. M. Smith, in discussing women's property rights under customary law, has suggested that, "although males were generally preferred heirs, demographic realities ensured that women would be found in a sizeable minority of instances as the residual heirs."[15] While women also inherited feudal land,[16] the women's property most discussed in this volume is dower. In terms of property dower is the chief marital entitlement.

Common lawyers, and to a lesser extent canon lawyers, agreed that in the eyes of the law husband and wife (*baron* and *feme*) were one person, and that person was the husband. In the rigid formulation of *baron* and *feme* the legal reality of the wife is largely subsumed by that of the husband and only revived upon his death. Thus, there is a quicksilver quality about the experiences of wives who are most often known as "Alice wife of John" or, on occasion, as the "heiress of William." This volume is entitled *Wife and Widow* because many of our essays utilize the extensive historical documentation of the woman "uncovered" by the death of her husband. A widow might have been bereaved and vulnerable, but legally she was at her most competent: She had full legal power. By studying the public acts of medieval women as they pass between the states of being married, widowed, and remarried, we can focus upon the evidential reality of women's lives.

Single women also appeared before the English tribunals, such as heiresses yet unmarried as they attempted to defeat the widow's bid for dower or as plaintiffs who brought a claim to enforce a marriage in a church court. An heiress had something upon which to live. A "spurned" bride, if she had means of supporting herself, probably preferred to remain single to marriage to a reluctant spouse. The woman identifiable as single in one set of records may have married quickly thereafter. While many widows remarried, the converse is also true: many did not or at least waited until the outcome of their dower litigation. Thus, many of our "facts" are capable of an alternative explanation: Potential husbands might want to be sure about the dower land, but the women might also not accept any marital partner if they received enough from a previous spouse to support themselves. Some of the women remaining widows must have been advocates of the single life at least for a time. Of course, these alternative "possibilities" confronted medieval women as well as their late-twentieth-century historians.

Long ago Eileen Power wrote of women that their "position in theory and law is one thing, their practical position in every day life another."[17] The new historiography confirms what common sense suggests: that there often were significant disjunctions between status and actual functioning in society, between moral dictate and behavior, between legal pronouncements and practice in the courts.[18] These important anomalies will be discussed in terms of the dynamic world of late medieval Britain. We explore the lives of women when their circumstances were dramatically altered and major decisions confronted them. The evidence used here reveals women at a time when they moved from the more private sphere of the home to the public forums of administrative request and litigation. Medieval women were caught in the tension between the customary and the possible, the morally commended and the merely licit alternative. Their lives were changed by the death of a landholder, marital breakdown, or the thought of their own mortality. Their fortunes were at risk in the world of local and sometimes international politics.

All the authors in this volume are working in aspects of medieval research that have long interested them. Indeed, in various ways all have expanded the "canon" of their special branches of traditional legal, political, social, and economic history to include women, family, and gender. Collectively, we talk more of "evidence" available to answer our questions, more of the subtlety required to discover feminine agency within formulaic records, than of theoretical approaches. Yet we have all learned from theorists: feminist, literary, economic, and the anthropological and sociological approaches to law and society. We are testing, on the basis of new evidence from documents of practice,[19] what roles medieval women played against the limited roles allotted to them in legal and moral treatises and the custom of a patriarchal society. The sharp dichotomy between "public" and "private" sphere has already been modified by other scholars in their recognition of the public dimensions—economic, legal, and political—of the private sphere.[20] These essays show that the public courts of law and administrative tribunals often were, at decisive events in family life, an inevitable extension of the private.

So many women went to law in courts of various jurisdictions and petitioned the king and lesser lords for redress that the English public records, when looked at from our perspective, are filled with the demanding voices of women. When women were victorious in their claims they were in a better position both to live without a husband or to marry again. Secure in the property rights that flowed from marriage, women were also in a position to balance their involvement in the public sphere with a return to a private one in order to rebuild their lives and their property until the next challenge. Their possession of land and capital meant, of course, some continuing public involvement. Energetic recourse to the public forum by the recently widowed was often necessary to preserve the private sphere for these women and for those who depended upon them.

Because most of our sources are legal, it is important to remember that litigation, while frequent, is never normative. A widow should have been able to enter her dower without a lawsuit, although many dower pleas came before the courts. Derek Hall has observed that 20 percent of the pleas on the royal court roll for Michaelmas term 9–10 Henry III (1225) were for dower.[21] There continued to be a large number of dower pleas, but we know little about the larger number of instances in which the widow entered her land without dispute. It has been estimated that 10 percent of the population went to law in a year, which leaves 90 percent that did not.[22] There is also far more to law than litigation. While women were neither judges, jurors, nor lawyers, they participated in the pervasive legal culture as plaintiffs, defendants, and warrantors. Quarrels over family property touched the lives of a larger group than just the parties to the action. More routine than litigation were regular procedures such as probate of a will; involvement with the controlled land market and agrarian regulation of a manorial court;[23] the supervision of wardship and apprenticeship by a town; or the frequent claims of the royal bureaucracy. In terms of the lives of medieval people—men and women—it is the exceptional moments in their lives that caused the majority of our documents to be created.

Wife and Widow in Medieval England begins with two essays that set the scene for the experiences of medieval Englishwomen by discussing the moral, practical, and emotional framework in which they made their choices. In the opening essay James Brundage discusses the role of international canon law in shaping the moral universe in which widows decided whether or not to remarry. Although remarriage was a fact in medieval society, the teaching of the Church offered contradictory models of behavior for good Christians that affected the decisions of medieval women. He delineates two competing strands in canon law: one that strongly urged the morally higher path of consecrated celibacy instead of remarriage, while the other defended the sanctity of marriage even for the second or third time. Brundage shows the reconciliation of these sharply divergent views about sanctity and sexuality by the teachers of canon law in the High Middle Ages. The academic study of matters relating to marriage and morals had an impact on the laity through the pulpit, the confessional, and the church courts. The actual choices made by the widows in these essays as a whole seem to mirror the mixed tradition that declared, on the one hand, that good Christian widows had a perfect right to remarry while, on the other, maintained the opposite view that emphatically discouraged remarriage of widows and, as Brundage argues, "hinted strongly that remarriage signified shameless slavery to the voluptuous enticements of sexual passion."

Joel Rosenthal analyzes the emotive process by which widows recovered from grief, rebuilt their lives, and were reintegrated into their community, often through remarriage. His materials show bereavement and recovery of women of varied socioeconomic status and the influence of religion, friends, and family in their experiences. Rosenthal observes that different sources offer different pictures of widows and widowhood. While manorial and legal records often push forward the sad tale of the dispossessed and the impoverished, urban materials argue more strongly for independence and involvement in civic and economic life. The wills of widows often depict a world of some substance, if not affluence, and wills can convey the reassurance of family as well as networks of support such as the Church and personal piety. The emotional universe is the hardest to reconstruct, but the widows' choices, survival strategies, and utilization of their newly independent status are seen in part as a reflection of their response to the death of their spouse.

Medieval women, especially widows, had to have considerable knowledge of law and the functioning of various courts and bureaucratic tribunals in order to secure their property rights and defend them from challenge. The more complex the law or the problem, the greater was the need for expert information; seeking advice was part of a woman's intelligent response. The next four essays see the law through the eyes of women actively involved in litigation before the royal or other secular courts or in quest of redress from the monarch. These court-centered struggles were often interfamilial, involved close neighbors, made demands upon feudal lords as well as resisted feudal demands upon the women, and could either have invoked or resisted the moral and marital supervision of the Church. At the outcome—victory, defeat, or compromise—the parties usually had to go on living in close proximity.

While a medieval woman could both buy and inherit land, the most common form of landholding enjoyed by her was a cumulative life interest in a portion of her late husband's land known as dower. No litigation should have been necessary, but a large number of widows had to go to

law to secure this valuable right to a third or a half of the estate, depending upon the tenure. Dower provided the essential support for the widow
and any children not heirs to their father's property. Because dower was
usually not forfeited upon remarriage, its possession made the widow
very attractive in the "marriage market." Securing dower often was an
arduous process that brought widows and remarried women with their
new spouses into court in a variety of legal jurisdictions. Husbands who
survived wives with landed property were also entitled, under certain
circumstances, to what may be thought of as "male dower," a life interest called curtesy. Dower rights are at issue in the essays of Janet Loengard, Sue Sheridan Walker, Cynthia Neville, and Barbara Hanawalt.

Two essays study dower proceedings in the royal common law courts.
Janet Loengard describes how "reasonable dower," the widow's fair
share, was computed in the early thirteenth century. This approach gives
us a fuller picture of the kinds of material resources that were part of the
widows' entitlements. The opportunity to choose and the ability to provide for themselves and their children depended upon this financial base.
Dower was indeed the widow's insurance policy, but there were often
costs associated with securing it. Furthermore, dower was not a static
concept but, rather, evolved over time; a crucial issue was that of
defining what measure would be used to determine what of the husband's
land would provide dower. A wide-reaching alteration of common law
dower in the thirteenth century lay in the amendment of the class of
property subject to the widow's share to include in the computation of
dower lands and tenements acquired by the husband at any time during
the marriage. Loengard describes the period after Magna Carta as one
of significant transition in the law of dower. The situation of the feudal
doweress improved amid protest from the family of her former spouse.

Walker examines the large number of pleas decided in the royal courts
in the late thirteenth and fourteenth centuries to understand the personal
experience involved in going to law to secure dower. The central focus
is the contest between the widow claimant and the defendant who tried
to deny the widow her dower. Walker argues that suing for dower was
a compelling personal quest that exposed the widow, whether she had
an attorney or not, to assertions such as that she was not validly married
to the man from whom she claimed dower, that her husband never held
the land in question in such a way as to provide dower, or accused her
of adultery, which, if true, would bar her claim. From initial writ to the
end of the lawsuit one aspect of her experience was shaped by court

dates, defendant recalcitrance, as well as by an intricate and changing legal procedure. By the end of the thirteenth century the professionalization of the royal courts was distancing dower plaintiffs—like other common law litigants—from the course of their own lawsuit. The focus here is not on strict legal history but, rather, explores the personal impact on plaintiffs of the substantive and procedural aspects of the common law of dower. Despite the different time span and emphasis, both Loengard and Walker discuss a large number of female litigants who sought dower in the royal courts. The widows of tenants-in-chief of the Crown down to very small freeholders were part of a group undergoing a shared experience in going to law. Though plaintiffs differed and the law evolved, a large number of widows still brought suits for dower in the royal courts.

Some situations, however, were beyond the remedies of the regular courts. Women's struggles, legal and extralegal, all had a political dimension to them in that they usually involved both allies and advice, composing a peace after the dispute was resolved, just as men would do in similar circumstances. Civil war carried heavy penalties of treason and forfeiture. Cynthia Neville describes the embattled women of Scotland at a time of national revolt against their English overlord, Edward I. Edward, the most legalistic of kings, denied them the traditional protections afforded to women and other noncombatants by medieval laws of war on the ground that it was a feudal revolt, not a just war. Some of the women were true widows of men killed on the battlefield, but others were "political widows," wives of men taken prisoner in the struggle against the English king. These wives and widows who sought redress came from a broader group than the upper classes of Scotland. Neville's research combines diplomatic, administrative, and legal sources, for the women of Scotland used all those avenues in their attempts to secure from the English Crown their dower or commensurate support for themselves and the families they now headed. Edward's curious view of the equality of women in war meant that a few Scottish widows of war even sought release from *"durance vile."*

Far happier options were available to Englishwomen of both town and countryside—in their share of marital lands and goods and their exercise of the related opportunity to remarry advantageously. Barbara Hanawalt draws upon her new research in legal and administrative archives of London to contrast the situation of urban and peasant widows. Emphasizing material about the greater and lesser London merchants, she describes widowhood and remarriage against the background of family agreements and disagreements. Hanawalt proposes a new model for marriage choice in England that undermined the strength of patriarchy. She sees London women, in particular, as having a considerable control over the structure of London society. She argues that "generous dowers together with widows' freedom to choose a new husband combined to emphasize horizontal, nonkin ties rather than vertical, patrilineal ones." Using their freedom and securing their entitlements brought both rural and urban widows before a variety of legal and administrative tribunals. Women's triumphs in the public forums of courts and guilds, together with their independence about remarriage, were damaging to patrilineal ideas.

Medieval women had as well to be familiar with canon law rules and procedures. The last two essays concern wives, widows, and single women in their dealings with the ecclesiastical courts. English church courts long retained jurisdiction over the probate of wills. Richard Helmholz examines the question about whether women had the legal right to make a will. Previous scholarship has indicated that English widows made wills and that a married woman could make a will with her husband's permission. Helmholz's intriguing findings indicate that, although married women may once have possessed testamentary capacity, by the fifteenth century they had lost it. He demonstrates the erosion of the right of a married woman to make a will in the late Middle Ages and explores various explanations for this development. Rejecting as too simple the argument that a rise in the hard-heartedness of men deprived married women of a right that once belonged to them, Helmholz also rejects the explanation that a substantive change took place in ordinary legal practice on the grounds that the judges of England's ecclesiastical courts did not change their minds about women's rights. He then looks beyond the ecclesiastical lawyers to account for the change, but a study of the practitioners of the English common law fails to solve the problem. His tentative solution is to suggest that the change grew out of the evolution of testamentary freedom for married men during the fifteenth century and also the rise of the use. What personal property married women did have would be held for them in trust. Otherwise, women were regarded as having nothing to will.

The history of women is not the story of continuously improving conditions; modernity meant a decline in status and function for English women. The last medieval century may, however, have offered greater opportunities for women to support themselves outside of marriage. On the basis of extensive evidence from the archiepiscopal court of York in the fourteenth and fifteenth centuries, Charles Donahue, Jr., analyzes women's behavior and their success rate as litigants in marriage cases. Many of the women were trying to enforce a marriage contract; some of the others, especially widows—probably of proven wealth and fertility—were trying to escape from men who claimed them as their wives. The nature of marital consent is central to the cases. Donahue's statistical analysis shows that women went to court more often than men and were more persistent in that they carried on more suits to judgment, while men, faced with a losing situation, were more inclined to drop it or make a compromise. The outcome appears to have been more crucial to the female litigant than to her male counterpart. A large portion of the suitors were women of middle and upper peasant stock and other middling types for whom wage labor or entrepreneurial activities were possible. In a later period many of that group would have been described as yeomen or copyholders. The findings for the two centuries are different and suggest that changes in social and economic conditions altered female behavior as litigants. While marriage was still desirable, it may have been less essential in the fifteenth century, especially in the north of England. Donahue's evidence and approach make it possible to examine gender parity in medieval ecclesiastical court litigation. The material reveals some independent-minded women, especially widows, but it also suggests that some of the women may have been influenced by their relatives.

Much recent research has focused upon the widow, and our volume is part of that new direction. It is natural that historians would devote themselves to the period in a woman's life when she was most clearly identifiable as an independent agent and full legal person. The death that "liberated" her from coverture left many formal records. Widows in charge of their own destinies, however, often gave up independence for remarriage, and, accordingly, their "legal" and "documentary" separateness was submerged in a new marital relationship. Although women's perception of self vis-à-vis both the law and marriage is difficult to ascertain, the authors of this volume have pierced the curtain of coverture at several key points. "Free choice" for widows and other women—indeed, for everyone—was undoubtedly conditioned by all sorts of practical and emotional considerations. Nevertheless, it is noteworthy that so many chose to remarry. Understanding their capabilities, their access to avenues of redress and economic opportunity, we can better see the new matches in the light of free choice, rather than acceptance of a desperate necessity because women could not function in their world without male protectors. Of course, we do not ordinarily know what pressure motivated them to marry or remain single, to go to court with what might be known to be a weak case, or to settle out of court. More apparent in our sources is the person who tried to block her by denying her dower, disputing her guardianship of the heir, or interfering with her practice of a craft governed by a guild. Naturally, not all these attempts were successful. The loss of testamentary capacity of married women involved not simple interference with their individual acts but, rather, basic changes in the settlement of property.

Our conjoint search for clearer understanding of the medieval wife as well as the widow and the recognition that choice is affected by limits falling far short of coercion leads us to the scholar to whom *Wife and Widow* is dedicated. The publication of Michael M. Sheehan's article on "The Influence of Canon Law on the Property Rights of Married Women in England" in 1963 marked a decisive stage in the scholarship concerning medieval women.[24] His volume on English wills from the Anglo-Saxon period through the thirteenth century enabled historians to make more effective use of wills as historical sources.[25] Sheehan's 1971 analysis of a fourteenth-century Ely register to determine patterns concerning the formation and stability of marriage urged medievalists toward the use of quantitative methods.[26] His cycle of articles on the question of free consent to marriage became an essential part of the dialogue that stimulated both our essayists and the profession at large.[27] Sheehan's learning has influenced many areas of scholarship, and it has been invaluable for the study of the impact of law on medieval women and the family.

Sheehan never claimed too much for his evidence, and his sensitive understanding of human nature always enabled him to recognize factors that influence the actors in history as well as the very creation of the documents historians use. Friendship with Michael has been a very special part of the lives and work of the authors. We owe him our gratitude for all the wisdom and affection that he has given to his colleagues in the scholarly world. Michael Sheehan had many students in the formal sense, but we, and many others, have been his pupils too. We designed *Wife and Widow in Medieval England* as a gift for him in the hope that he would both appreciate our efforts and remain an active part of our shared enterprise for many years to come. Sadly, we must now dedicate it to his memory. Michael's teaching and writing are a living tradition of what is best in our craft. They will continue to inspire and instruct those who work in the many areas that interested him. We are very grateful to have been enriched by his life as well as his learning.

NOTES

1. Robert C. Palmer, *The Whilton Dispute, 1264–1380: A Social-Legal Study of Dispute Settlement* (Princeton, 1984), 147.
2. Feudal landholding has lately drawn less interest than that of peasants. Important works, however, include S. F. C. Milsom, *The Legal Framework of English Feudalism* (Cambridge, 1976); Palmer, *Whilton;* and J. M. W. Bean, *The Decline of English Feudalism, 1215–1540* (Manchester, 1968). Valuable works include A. W. B. Simpson, *A History of the Land Law,* 2d ed. (Oxford, 1986); J. H. Baker and S. F. C. Milsom, *Sources of English Legal History: Private Law to 1750* (London, 1986); and, forthcoming in the monograph series of the American Society for Legal History, Eileen Spring, *Law, Land, and Family: Aristocratic Inheritance in England, 1300–1800.*
3. See, e.g., the recent article by L. Bonfield and L. R. Poos, "The Development of the Deathbed Transfer in Medieval English Manor Courts," *Cambridge Law Journal* 47 (1988): 403–27. Manorial court proceedings contain frequent references to surrenders of property and subsequent resettlement or record the admission fine from a new tenant, often after a sale of the land by a previous tenant. See R. M. Smith, "Some Thoughts on 'Hereditary' and 'Proprietary' Rights in Land under Customary Law in Thirteenth and Early Fourteenth Century England," *Law and History Review* 1 (1983): 95–128. Anne and Edwin de Windt, jointly and severally, have contributed much to this subject.
4. Paul R. Hyams, "The Charter as a Source for the Early Common Law," *Journal of Legal History* 12 (1991): 173–89, has discussed charters as "a source for the legal historian that proceeds neither from the legal system itself or the needs of lawyers" and examined them as "some of the records of medieval property transactions written for the actors themselves." Discussing the daunting bulk of surviving charters, which could not be mastered without computers, he observed that "charters offer a route into what might be called preventive law, an aspect of legal history that has yet to receive due attention" (173). Hyams's article sets charter studies in clear perspective.
5. See the previously published work of Brundage, Donahue, Helmholz, and Sheehan, all of which are cited in this volume.
6. For the lively debate, see Jean Scammell, "Freedom and Marriage in

Medieval England," *Economic History Review* 2d ser., 27 (1974): 523–37, "Wife-Rents and Merchet," *Economic History Review* 2d ser., 29 (1976): 487–90; and Eleanor Searle, "Freedom and Marriage in Medieval England: An Alternative Hypothesis," *Economic History Review* 2d ser., 29 (1976): 482–86. Searle's "Seignurial Control of Women's Marriage: The Antecedents and Function of Merchet in England," *Past and Present* 82 (1979): 3–43, has provoked further discussion; see, e.g., Paul A. Brand and Paul R. Hyams, untitled contribution to "Debate: Seignurial Control of Women's Marriage," *Past and Present* 99 (1983): 123–33; and Searle's rejoinder on 148–60.

7. J. C. Holt, *Magna Carta* 2d ed. (Cambridge, 1992), (rights of widows), 54, 199, 308, and 452–53; Sue Sheridan Walker, "Feudal Constraint and Free Consent in the Making of Marriages in Medieval England: Widows in the King's Gift," *Historical Papers,* ed. Terry Cook and Claudette Laceke (Ottawa, 1979), 97–109.

8. See, e.g., Sue Sheridan Walker, "Free Consent and the Marriage of Feudal Wards in Medieval England," *Journal of Medieval History* 8 (1982): 123–34; and other Walker studies cited in chapter 4 of this volume.

9. See Robert C. Palmer, "Contexts of Marriage in Medieval England: Evidence from the King's Court circa 1300," *Speculum* 59 (1984): 42–67. Elaine Clark ("The Decision to Marry in Thirteenth- and Early Fourteenth-Century Norfolk," *Mediaeval Studies* 49 [1987]: 496–516) observes that while not "minimizing the web of customary constraints that impinged on the decision to marry during years when lordship was strong and manorial obligations at their heaviest"; her evidence suggests that "the realities of choice in English society can be better understood when viewed in relation to the customs and changing political traditions of a countryside where peasants indeed had a well-defined sense of their own capacity to make decisions and plan for the future" (510–11).

10. Judith M. Bennett (*Women in the Medieval English Countryside: Gender and Household in Brigstock before the Plague* [Oxford, 1987]) consistently employs gender comparisons; see her index for "Litigation" and "Marriage."

11. See the bibliographical and historical discussion in Janet Senderowitz Loengard, "Legal History and the Medieval Englishwoman: A Fragmented View," *Law and History Review* 4 (1986): 161–77: this article is now updated in " 'Legal History and the Medieval Englishwoman' Revisited: Some New Directions," in *Medieval Women and the Sources of Medieval History,* ed. Joel T. Rosenthal (Athens, Ga., and London, 1990), 210–36.

12. J. H. Baker, *An Introduction to English Legal History,* 3d ed. (London, 1990), 551–52.

13. That privilege was not universal and was frequently abridged by borough custom in late medieval England. See examples of the *feme sole* in *Borough Customs,* ed. Mary Bateson, 2 vols., Selden Society 18 (1904): 226–27, and 21 (1906): cxii–cxiii. "The Exeter courts upheld this juristic distinction; several

husbands successfully declined legal responsibility for their wives' trading debts"
(Maryanne Kowaleski, "Women's Work in a Market Town," in *Women and
Work in Preindustrial Europe,* ed. Barbara A. Hanawalt [Bloomington, 1986]
146). Kowaleski continued: "Under common law, by contrast, women were
mere adjuncts of their husbands. Thus, Exeter husbands generally brought suit
on behalf of their wives, especially in cases of assault or unpaid salaries. In
several instances, married women who sued on their own in the Exeter courts
were accused of failing to appear with their husbands."

14. Loengard, "Legal History," 215.

15. R. M. Smith, "Women's Property under Customary Law: Some Developments in the Thirteenth and Fourteenth Centuries," *Transactions of the Royal
Historical Society,* 5th ser., 36 (1986): 165–94.

16. For a discussion of the law of inheritance and women in Angevin England,
see S. F. C. Milsom, "Inheritance by Women in the Twelfth and Early Thirteenth
Centuries," from the Thorne festschrift, now reprinted in *Studies in the History
of the Common Law* (London, 1985), 231–60; J. C. Holt, "Feudal Society and
the Family in Early Medieval England," Vol. 4: "The Heiress and the Alien," in
Transactions of the Royal Historical Society, 5th. ser., 35 (1985): 1–28; and
Palmer, *Whilton Dispute,* which describes a property dispute lasting from 1264
to 1380 and involving women of several generations.

17. Eileen Power, "The Position of Women," in *The Legacy of the Middle
Ages,* ed. C. G. Crump and E. F. Jacob (Oxford, 1926), 401.

18. See, e.g., R. H. Helmholz, *Marriage Litigation in Medieval England* (Cambridge, 1974), regarding the persistence of the "idea that people could regulate
marriages for themselves" (4–5). See also the references to the canon law concerning clandestine or informal marriages in the work of Brundage, Donahue,
and Michael M. Sheehan. Concerning the common law, see, e.g., Paul A. Brand,
"Legal Change in the Later Thirteenth Century: Statutory and Judicial Remodel-
ing of the Action of Replevin," *American Journal of Legal History* 31 (1987):
43–55; on the nonenforcement of the penal sanctions, see Sue Sheridan Walker,
"Punishing Convicted Ravishers: Statutory Strictures and Actual Practice in
Thirteenth- and Fourteenth-Century England," *Journal of Medieval History* 13
(1987): 237–50.

19. Susan Stuard uses this terminology in her useful article on "Sources of
Medieval Women in Mediterranean Archives," in Rosenthal, *Medieval Women,*
in which she remarks that the "Medievalists' undoubted advantage over our
colleagues in ancient historical studies lies in the availability to us of a largely
unexplored literature . . . and medievalists may compare what women did with
what was said about women in a substantial number of cases" (342).

20. This subject, with excellent references to the authorities, is found in the
important introduction by Mary Erler and Maryanne Kowaleski to their *Women
and Power in the Middle Ages* (Athens, Ga. and London, 1988), 1–17. Many of

the works they cite have conditioned the thinking of medievalists in a variety of fruitful ways.

21. G. D. G. Hall, review of *Curia Regis Rolls of 9 to 10 Henry III* (London, 1957), *English Historical Review* 74 (1959): 107–10.

22. Palmer, *Whilton Dispute;* see discussion in chapter 4 of this volume. Palmer, for sound legal reasons, counted husband and wife as one person. In attempting to recognize women's understanding of legal matters, however, the exclusion of wives from suits in both their names is misleading. It also undercounts the number of human beings involved in litigation in medieval English royal courts.

23. See Bennett, *Women in the Medieval English Countryside,* a study that uses the exceptional evidence of the coroner's inquests to draw out the normal picture of family life; see Barbara A. Hanawalt, *The Ties That Bound: Peasant Families in Medieval England* (Oxford, 1986).

24. *Mediaeval Studies* 25 (1963): 109–24.

25. Michael M. Sheehan, *The Will in Medieval England,* Pontifical Institute for Mediaeval Studies, Studies and Texts ser. 6 (Toronto, 1963).

26. Michael M. Sheehan, "The Formation and Stability of Marriage in Fourteenth-Century England: Evidence of an Ely Register," *Mediaeval Studies* 33 (1971): 228–63.

27. Michael M. Sheehan, "Marriage and Family in English Conciliar and Synodal Legislation," in *Essays in Honour of Anton Charles Pegis,* ed. J. Reginald O'Donnell (Toronto, 1974), 208–14; "Marriage Theory and Practice in the Conciliar Legislation and Diocesan Statutes of Medieval England," *Mediaeval Studies* 40 (1978): 408–60; "Choice of Marriage Partner in the Middle Ages: Development and Mode of Application," *Studies in Medieval and Renaissance History,* n.s. 1 (1978): 3–33; "The Wife of Bath and Her Four Sisters: Reflections on a Woman's Life in the Age of Chaucer," *Medievalia et Humanistica,* n.s. 13 (1985): 23–42; and "Theory and Practice: Marriage of the Unfree and the Poor in Medieval Society," *Mediaeval Studies* 50 (1988): 457–87.

Chapter 1

Widows and Remarriage: Moral Conflicts and Their Resolution in Classical Canon Law

James A. Brundage

Canonists of the classical period (ca. 1140–1375) found in their patristic sources an abundant but ambivalent tradition concerning the remarriage of widows. Eminent authorities of impeccable orthodoxy had declared repeatedly that good Christians could both marry and go to heaven, that disparagement of Christian marriage constituted heresy, and that a widow had a perfect right to remarry after the death of her first husband. But other, equally eminent, canonical authorities strongly deprecated remarriage of widows, discouraged them from doing so, hinted pointedly that remarriage signified shameless slavery to the voluptuous enticements of sexual passion, and lauded, sometimes in quite extravagant terms, the virtue of women who spurned remarriage in order to cultivate in widowhood a second career of consecrated chastity.

Those who taught fledgling canon lawyers in university law faculties faced the challenge of making sense out of this heritage, of finding ways to harmonize the contradictory viewpoints of earlier authorities and the disjunction between patristic exhortation and current practice. The essays in this volume by Joel Rosenthal, Sue Sheridan Walker, and Barbara Hanawalt discuss instances of remarriage of medieval English widows. This chapter will analyze the canonists' efforts to grapple with both the practical and theoretical issues involved in the remarriage of widows and the conclusions that eventually emerged from their discussions.

It may seem strange, at first glance, that the issue even arose. Had not Saint Paul, after all, confronted the question and answered it directly? "A woman is bound by law," he had said, "so long as her husband lives;

but if her husband dies, she is freed: let her marry whom she will in the Lord" (1 Cor. 7:39).[1] Apostolic authority might seem to have settled the matter once and for all. True, Paul strongly encouraged widows and widowers to remain single after their first spouse's death (1 Cor. 7:40), and dicta that passed under his name could be interpreted to mean that the twice-married thereby became ineligible for the office of bishop.[2] Nonetheless, the apostle had clearly stated that widows could properly remarry.

Still, some early Christians held strong reservations about the morality of remarriage. Tertullian, for example, had called the remarriage of widows an obstacle to faith and then, as his views became more extreme, had declared that no Christian could decently remarry, that remarriage was as grave a moral delinquency as fornication, adultery, or murder. Remarriage, according to him, was absolutely forbidden for a Christian man or woman.[3] But Tertullian's opinions lay outside the mainstream of early Christian belief, and in his later years, when he voiced his harshest denunciations of the twice-married, Tertullian had joined the Montanist sect, whose teachings mainline Christians rejected as heretical.[4] The Manichaean sect also condemned remarriage of widows and excluded remarried persons from communion on the grounds that they were adulterers.[5] But the Manichaeans, too, were heretics.

Conventional Christian authorities in the West had early sought to distance themselves from such views as these. The first general council of the Christian Church explicitly declared that widows and widowers who remarried should be admitted to communion in the Church and condemned those who taught otherwise.[6] But at the same time Christian leaders actively discouraged remarriage.[7] The Council of Laodicaea, for example, cautioned widows and widowers not to remarry hastily and advised them to dedicate themselves to prayer and fasting before committing themselves to a second marriage.[8] The Second Council of Braga in the sixth century went even further and required those who remarried to do penance for lascivious conduct, a measure reiterated by other councils, then by penitential writers and in the eleventh century by Church reformers.[9] Moreover, clerics who married widows thereby forfeited their chances of ecclesiastical advancement.[10]

The ecclesiastical status of widows thus remained a shade ambiguous. Widows who did not remarry often exercised considerable influence in Christian communities and were in a sense assimilated to the clergy. Indeed, many leaders of the early Church were drawn from the ranks of widowed men and women who had chosen not to remarry.[11] There was also a feeling that remarriage showed disrespect to the memory of the first spouse. For this reason, among others, Roman law forbade widows to remarry within a year following the death of their first husbands, a practice approved by both Christians and pagans.[12] Romans also considered it inappropriate for widows beyond childbearing age to remarry at all,[13] and they held that men who had been widowed then remarried should be ineligible for the more important priestly functions in pagan worship, a view that the Christian establishment also adopted almost as soon as Constantine assured the Church a settled place within the political structure of the Roman Empire.[14]

As medieval canon law began to reach maturity in the mid-twelfth century, canonists remained aware of the reservations concerning the remarriage of the widowed that had been current in late antiquity and felt obliged to take account of them in their treatments of the law of marriage. Gratian, whose *Concordia discordantium canonum,* or *Decretum* (written about 1140), became the fundamental textbook in the canon law faculties of medieval universities, accordingly found it necessary to address these issues. Although he cited one ancient authority of impeccable orthodoxy who had maintained that the remarriage of a widow was a type of fornication (albeit an "honest" one),[15] and another who described the remarried widow as not much different from a prostitute,[16] Gratian made it clear that he disagreed with these unpleasant characterizations. These statements, Gratian maintained, must be understood as efforts to persuade widows to practice continence, rather than as condemnations of second and subsequent marriages,[17] and he then cited other authorities who taught that widows had every right to remarry.[18]

Twelfth- and thirteenth-century teachers of canon law, when they dealt with these passages, elaborated on Gratian's reading of the law on this matter. Rolandus (fl. ca. 1150), Rufinus (fl. ca. 1130–92), and the anonymous *Summa Parisiensis* (ca. 1160) recalled that early Christian communities had punished those who married a second time.[19] Rufinus added that remarriage was once considered a great sin[20] and that third marriages had been forbidden altogether in the primitive Church, although this policy, he noted, was no longer operative.[21] Later canonists generally denied that there was any distinction between second and subsequent marriages beyond the first. The eminent thirteenth-century authority, Cardinal Hostiensis (ca. 1200–1271), for example, declared that it made no difference in principle how often a widow remarried; she could remarry a thousand times, he declared, and the last of her marriages would be just as valid and legitimate as the first.[22]

Commentators on Gratian's *Decretum* nevertheless questioned the value of second marriages in the scheme of salvation. Both Rufinus and Rolandus agreed, for example, that only first marriages were fully sacramental and that subsequent marriages, although nowadays permitted, were merely tolerated as concessions to human frailty.[23] This position seemed inconsistent with Saint Paul's statements (1 Cor. 7:39 and Rom. 7:2), as Johannes Teutonicus briefly noted in his *Ordinary Gloss* on the *Decretum,* but other commentators largely ignored this difficulty.[24]

Gratian left certain important aspects of the remarriage of widows unclear and still unresolved. There was, for one thing, the matter of the nuptial blessing. Although canonists generally agreed that a priestly blessing was not required for a valid marriage, nonetheless it had been usual since the fifth century for Christian couples to receive such a blessing when they married for the first time.[25] But it was also common for the blessing to be denied if one of the couple had previously been married. Gratian provided no clear guide to the legal basis for this practice or the reasoning that supported it. He also neglected to deal with the question of how soon a widow was entitled to remarry after the death of her first husband, nor did he furnish much guidance for resolving the problems that arose when feudal lords and others forced widows to remarry and limited their choice of partners when marrying a second time. Both popes and law teachers addressed these difficulties during the second half of the twelfth century and the first half of the thirteenth.

Pope Alexander III (1159–81) confronted the matter of the nuptial blessing in two decretals that were eventually incorporated in the *Liber Extra* (1234), the principal thirteenth-century collection of the post-Gratian canons. The nuptial blessing must not be repeated, Alexander ruled in the decretal *Vir autem.* If one party had received the blessing in a previous marriage, then his or her second marriage could not be blessed.[26] Moreover, Alexander held in another decision, reported in the decretal *Capellanum,* that a priest who bestowed the nuptial blessing on a second marriage committed a canonical offense and should be punished: he was to be suspended from all ecclesiastical offices and benefices until he had made satisfaction for this misdeed.[27]

Alexander failed to articulate a rationale for these two decisions, and canonists found them difficult to account for. One problem that underlay both *Capellanum* and *Vir autem* centered around the problematic relationship between the nuptial blessing and the sacrament of marriage.[28] If marriage was a sacrament, as many believed it was, then was a priestly blessing required to impart it? Or did the couple themselves create a sacramental union through the exchange of consent and consummation by sexual union? Opinions on these questions varied, and authoritative answers were in short supply. Alexander III's decretals did little to resolve the problem; arguably, they even made resolution less easy.

Commentators on both decretals muddied the waters further. Bernard of Parma in his *Standard Gloss* (or *Glossa ordinaria*) to the Decretals, for example, suggested that the reason why it was forbidden to give the nuptial blessing in a second marriage might be that a sacrament could not be repeated.[29] But that reasoning would not work, as Bernard himself acknowledged. For one thing, some sacraments certainly could be received more than once, most obviously the sacrament of penance and, some would add, extreme unction as well. Bernard was no doubt drawing here upon the comments of Geoffrey of Trani (d. 1245), whose list of sacraments that could be repeated also included ordination and the laying on of hands.[30] Geoffrey concluded that the prohibition of the nuptial blessing for second marriages must have been intended to encourage widows and widowers to commit themselves to a life of sexual continence when their first spouses died.

Bernard of Parma noted that identifying the nuptial blessing as the constitutive act in conferring the sacrament of marriage raised serious problems, both legal and theological. If the nuptial blessing was essential to marriage, then it might seem to follow that Mary and Joseph, the earthly parents of Jesus, had not been married, and that seemed quite an unacceptable consequence.[31] Moreover, a requirement that marriages be blessed by a priest contradicted other papal pronouncements, including several of Alexander III himself.[32] Beyond that, and even more fundamental, if the nuptial blessing was essential to sacramental marriage and if that blessing could be received only once, it would then follow that second and subsequent marriages were not sacramental marriages, as some commentators on the *Decretum* in fact maintained.[33]

Thirteenth-century canonists seemed reluctant to commit themselves on this issue. What Innocent IV thought about this provision of the law, for example, is not clear: he simply passed over *Capellanum* and *Vir autem* in silence when he wrote his massive *Apparatus* on the *Liber*

Extra, perhaps because he found them anomalous or difficult to account for. Innocent's contemporary, Cardinal Hostiensis, likewise refrained from committing himself on the relationship between the blessing and the sacrament. In his *Golden Summa,* an early work (completed in 1253), Hostiensis argued that the crucial element in accounting for the ban on repetition of the nuptial blessing might be sexual relations between the couple. To illustrate the point he posed a hypothetical problem. Suppose that a couple, having married and received the nuptial blessing, then divorced before consummating their union. If they subsequently remarried, could they then receive the nuptial blessing a second time? In his discussion of this problem, Hostiensis made a strong case that they could but eventually concluded that priests and couples must comply with the ruling in *Vir autem.*[34] He did not, however, deal with the relationship between the nuptial blessing and the sacramental character of marriage. In his *Lectura,* a systematic commentary on the Gregorian Decretals finished at the end of his career, Hostiensis merely reported the opinion of others that the prohibition was intended to discourage second marriages.[35]

Thirteenth-century theologians had little more success than the canonists in accounting for the prohibition of the nuptial blessing. Saint Bonaventure, for example, maintained that, since the pope forbade the nuptial blessing to be given to second marriages, those marriages were sacramentally incomplete—although he evaded the issue of whether the blessing was an essential element of marriage or not.[36] Thomas Aquinas adopted a similar approach but attempted a fuller and more nuanced analysis than Bonaventure provided. A second marriage, Aquinas argued, is sacramentally complete in itself (*in se consideratum*), but it is less complete than a first marriage because it is not a singular relationship between one man and one woman, signified by the relationship of Christ with the Church. For this reason, he continued—and here Aquinas introduced a distinction foreign to the canons—the nuptial blessing is forbidden when both parties are marrying for the second time or if a woman marries for a second time. But the blessing may be given if a man is entering a second marriage with a previously unmarried woman.[37] Aquinas grounded this exception on an analogical argument: although Christ had only one Church as His spouse, He was betrothed to many persons within that one Church. Similarly, Aquinas argued, a man who contracted a second marriage with a virgin was entering a singular relationship with her and could therefore receive the nuptial blessing a second time, but a woman who had had an earlier husband was not contracting a singular relationship when she married a second husband and therefore was ineligible to receive the blessing again.[38] The reasoning here seems murky and perhaps does not represent Aquinas at his most lucid. The analogical comparison between a second human marriage and the union of Christ and the Church seems forced, and the rationale underlying the distinction between the second marriage of a widower and the second marriage of a widow is not one of his more elegant arguments.

While academic canonists and theologians had the luxury of debating or ignoring these issues in the relative calm of their lecture rooms,[39] priests charged with the cure of souls had to cope with the practical reality that their parishioners often did marry two or three times and that many of them wanted, or even demanded, that their priest bless their most recent union. Since the pope forbade priests to repeat the nuptial blessing and was prepared to punish those who defied the ban, priests needed to find ways to deal with the prohibition. Many, perhaps even most, simply ignored it and gave the blessing despite the prohibition. For this reason the commissions given to papal legates and nuncios regularly included the power to dispense clerics from the irregularity contracted by giving the nuptial blessing at second marriages.[40] Others found means of evading the letter of the law while still responding to the needs and wishes of their parishioners: they confected different blessings to replace the forbidden one and recited the new benediction at a different point in the ritual.[41] Thus, they could argue, if the question arose, that they were in technical conformity with the papal prohibition, while the couples whom they blessed were presumably satisfied that they were properly married.

The interval that elapsed between the death of one spouse and the remarriage of the other was a matter of legal concern only when the survivor was a woman. Ancient Roman custom permitted a man to remarry at any time after the death of his former spouse but required a woman to wait for a considerable period before remarrying, both out of respect for her first husband and—what particularly concerned lawyers and lawmakers—to avoid uncertainty about the paternity of a child born after the death of the previous spouse.[42] Postclassical Roman law established one year as the mandatory period of mourning and prescribed the penalty of *infamia* for widows who remarried during that time.[43] In his decretal *Super illa* Pope Alexander III declared that this restriction no longer applied and abrogated the penalty of *infamia* in these situations. Pope Innocent III reaffirmed Alexander III's ruling in the decretal *Cum secundum* in 1201.[44] Western canon law thus allowed widows to remarry at any time without suffering *infamia*.[45] Both pontiffs, in support of their rulings, cited Saint Paul's statement "Let her [a widow] marry whom she will in the Lord" (1 Cor. 7:39).

Canonists commented at some length on both decretals but addressed their remarks principally to the issue of the conflict of jurisdictions raised by papal abrogation of imperial law. Johannes Teutonicus, commenting on *Cum secundum,* read the decretal expansively and maintained that the ruling exempted widows not only from *infamia* but also from other penalties that civil law visited upon those who married during the mourning period.[46] Both Hostiensis and Innocent IV argued, however, that *Super illa* and *Cum secundum* should be interpreted narrowly: although the two decretals freed widows who remarried within the prescribed period from the penalty of *infamia,* they left intact the other penalties that civil law imposed on women who remarried in haste.[47] Hostiensis noted, moreover, that the decretals suggested a loophole in civil law for widows whose husbands died while away from home: if a woman first learned of her husband's death 364 days after the event, Hostiensis argued, she could, if she pleased, remarry the following day, since a year would then have elapsed between her first husband's death and her second marriage.[48]

Canonists' discussions of the remarriage of widows during the period of mourning were not just academic speculations. Secular law in the thirteenth century continued to impose penalties and disabilities on widows who remarried within the prescribed year of mourning, as canonists were well aware.[49] The laws of the Latin Kingdom of Jerusalem, for example, mandated a mourning period that must elapse before a widow (but not a widower) could remarry.[50] Similar provisions appeared in civil laws elsewhere.[51] The laws of the Latin kingdom were peculiar, however, in that they not merely permitted widows to remarry after the mandatory waiting period had elapsed but also positively required them to do so, on pain of forfeiture of their fiefs.[52] The requirement to remarry was also subject to an unusual limitation, for it applied only to widows prior to the age of sixty. Once past their sixtieth year widows might remarry but could no longer be compelled to do so. The widow who chose not to remarry, however, must promise to remain chaste and undertake not to use her freedom to lead a life of licentious sensuality.[53]

Legal and theological discussions of the remarriage of widows assumed, as a matter of course, that widows and widowers enjoyed a free choice of whether to remarry or not. For most widows and many widowers the reality was entirely different. The severe dislocation of the family economy that resulted from the death of a male head of household made it a practical necessity for the majority of medieval widows to remarry if they possibly could and to do so at the earliest available opportunity.

Academic lawyers and their colleagues in theology faculties focused their discussions of remarriage on the continued sexual opportunities it afforded. They also tended to discuss remarriage in terms of problems that faced members of the more affluent sectors of society. How the widowed felt about the sexual implications of remarriage is not easy to discover, but the urgency and speed with which widows whose social and economic resources were modest remarried strongly suggests that economic necessity rather than lust may have been foremost in the minds of many. This was especially true for widows, who often desperately needed help in order to keep their households intact, particularly if they had young children to care for.

The social situation of widows was typically far more precarious than that of widowers. As adult single women, widows were vulnerable to threats, both against their property and their persons, while men in a comparable situation rarely had much to fear.[54] But widows typically experienced much greater difficulty than widowers in finding second spouses: they remarried less frequently than their male counterparts, and the time elapsed between the death of the first spouse and marriage to the second was appreciably greater for women than for men. Widows who held land had notably greater success in finding a second partner than their more impoverished sisters, and this also suggests that economic considerations, rather than sexual opportunities, were the principal driving forces behind many second marriages.[55]

The long history of ecclesiastical ambivalence concerning the remarriage of the widowed suggests that the authorities who made Church law and the lawyers who translated it into practice were attempting without great success to accommodate the necessities of economic and social life among the majority of the widowed with the ascetic sexual ideals of the clerical elite. The result was an intellectually untidy and practically unworkable patchwork. On the one hand, churchmen told widows that they could remarry, but they also told them that they should not. Social and economic necessity required most widows to remarry if they could possibly do so, but some ecclesiastical authorities refused to bless their marriages. Widows of modest means were better advised not only to remarry but also to do so speedily. But at the same time civil authorities threatened to punish them if they did so within a year, while Church officials promised to nullify the civil penalties.

The confusion and distress that resulted from these disjunctions between policy and practice, I submit, served few well and many poorly. Since the law so inadequately served the needs of those to whom it was directed, a great many of them, very sensibly, seem to have ignored it.

NOTES

1. Cf. Rom. 7:2. Jesus, when confronted with a related question, however, artfully dodged the issue of remarriage altogether; Mark 12:18–25.

2. 1 Tim. 3:2; Titus 1:6. Modern New Testament specialists generally agree that Paul himself wrote neither of these, but they probably originated in his circle and may well have reflected his views.

3. Tertullian, *Ad uxorem* 1.7.4, in *Corpus Christianorum, series Latina,* ed. A. Kroyman (Turnhout, 1953–), 1:381 (hereafter CCL); *De exhortatione castitatis*, 9.1, in CCL 2:1027; and *De monogamia*, 4.3, 10.7, 15.1, in CCL 2:1233, 1243, 1250.

4. See, generally, James A. Brundage, *Law, Sex, and Christian Society in Medieval Europe* (Chicago, 1987), 68–69.

5. Brundage, *Law, Sex, and Christian Society*, 97.

6. 1 Council of Nicaea (315) c. 8, in *Conciliorum oecumenicorum decreta,* 2d ed. by Giuseppe Alberigo et al. (Freiburg, 1962), 9. On the far more negative views of remarriage current among Slavic Orthodox churchmen, see Eve Levin, *Sex and Society in the World of the Orthodox Slavs, 900–1700* (Ithaca, 1989), 105–14.

7. Although prominent churchmen over a long period of time certainly discouraged remarriage, as we shall see, I nonetheless find it difficult to agree with the argument that this policy was predicated primarily or even in significant part upon the hope that widowed men and women would in the end be constrained to leave most or all of their property to the Church; see Jack Goody, *The Development of the Family and Marriage in Europe* (Cambridge, 1983), 94–95, 154–56, and passim. But cf. David Herlihy, *Medieval Households* (Cambridge, Mass., 1985), 11–13; and Brundage, *Law, Sex, and Christian Society*, 606–7.

8. Council of Laodicaea (ca. 360) c. 1, in *Sacrorum conciliorum nova et amplissima collectio,* ed. Giovanni Domenico Mansi, rev. ed., 60 vols. (Paris, 1901–27) 2:564; Brundage, *Law, Sex, and Christian Society*, 98.

9. 2 Braga (572) c. 26, 80; 2 Seville (619) c. 4, in *Concilios Visigóticos e Hispano-Romanos,* ed. José Vives, España Cristiana, vol. 1 (Barcelona and Madrid, 1963), 94, 105, 165; Brundage, *Law, Sex, and Christian Society,* 142, 164, 196.

10. I have dealt with this matter elsewhere in an article entitled "Bigamy, Spiritual and Carnal: A Study in Legal Theology" (forthcoming).

11. Peter Brown, *The Body and Society: Men, Women and Sexual Renunciation in Early Christianity,* Lectures on the History of Religions, n.s., no. 13 (New York, 1988), 148–50.

12. Cod. *5.9.1* pr. (380), *5.17.8.4b* (449); Dig. 3.2.11.2 (Ulpian). Citations of the texts of the *Corpus iuris civilis* refer throughout to the critical edition by Paul Krueger, Theodor Mommsen, Rudolf Schoell, and Wilhelm Kroll, 3 vols. (1872–95; reprint, Berlin, 1963–65). References to the civilian *Glossa ordinaria* are to the Iuntas edition (Lyon, 1584). See also Jean Gaudemet, *Le mariage en Occident: Les moeurs et le droit* (Paris, 1987), 42.

13. They could, however, become concubines; Gian Carlo Caselli, "Concubina pro uxore: Osservazioni in merito al C. 17 del primo concilio di Toledo," *Rivista di storia del diritto italiano* 37–38 (1964–65): 165–68.

14. Marjorie Lightman and William Zeisel, "*Univira:* An Example of Continuity and Change in Roman Society," *Church History* 46 (1977): 19–20.

15. Gratian, *Decretum* C. 31 q. 1 c. 9, citing Saint John Chrysostom; citations throughout to Gratian and other texts of the *Corpus iuris canonici* refer to the standard edition by Emil Friedberg, 2 vols. (1879; reprint, Graz, 1959).

16. Saint Jerome, cited in C. 31 q. 1 c. 10.

17. C. 31 q. 1 d.p.c. 10: "Verum hoc eum ad exhortationem uidualis continentiae, non in condempnationem secundarum et deinceps nuptiarum dixisse, quam multorum auctoritatibus constat licitas esse."

18. C. 31 q. 1 c. 11–13.

19. *Die Summa Magistri Rolandi nachmals Papstes Alexander III* to C. 31 q. 1 c. 8, ed. Friedrich Thaner (Innsbruck, 1874), 155–56; Rufinus, *Summa decretorum* to C. 31 q. 1 c. 8, ed. Heinrich Singer (1902; reprint, Aalen, 1963), 471; *The Summa Parisiensis on the Decretum Gratiani* to C. 31 q. 1 c. 8 v. *De his qui frequenter,* ed. Terence P. McLaughlin (Toronto, 1952), 238.

20. Rufinus, *Summa* to C. 31 q. 1 c. 10 v. *quantum distat in crimine,* ed. Singer, 473.

21. Rufinus, *Summa* to C. 31 q. 1 c. 11 v. *trigamos,* ed. Singer, 473; likewise, Johannes Teutonicus, *Glossa ordinaria* to C. 31 q. 1 c. 11 v. *trigamos.* The *glos. ord.* to the *Decretum* and to other texts in the *Corpus iuris canonici* will be cited throughout from the edition published at Venice in 1605.

22. Hostiensis, *Summa aurea,* lib. 4, tit. 33, *De secundis nuptiis* §§1–2, (1537; reprint, Aalen, 1962), fol. 224va–vb. For similar opinions among theologians, see Saint Bonaventure, *Commentaria in quatuor libros Sententiarum* 4.42.3.1 in

28 Wife and Widow in Medieval England

his *Opera omnia* (Quaracchi, 1882–) 4:876–77; Pierre de la Palude, *Lucubrationum opus in quartum Sententiarum* 42.3.1 (Salamanca, 1552), 436.

23. Rolandus, *Summa* to C. 31 q. 1 c. 10 v. *esse desistit*, ed. Thaner, 156; and Rufinus, *Summa* to C. 31 q. 1 c. 10 v. *esse desistit*, ed. Singer, 472.

24. Johannes Teutonicus, *Glossa ordinaria* to C. 31 q. 1 d.p.c. 10 v. *verum:* "Magister hoc capitulum intelligit de secundis nuptiis licitis, sed competentius intelligitur de illicitis, aliter exemplum de Lamech non congrueret; quare tam aspera proponeret Hieronymus, cum auctoritate Apostoli licita sint, non video."

25. Brundage, *Law, Sex, and Christian Society,* 88; Gaudemet, *Mariage en Occident,* 265–66.

26. *Liber extra* (= Decretales Gregorii IX), in *Corpus juris canonici* (hereafter X), 4.21.3: "Vir autem vel mulier, ad bigamiam transiens, non debet a presbytero benedici, quia, quum alia vice benedicti sint, eorum benedictio iterari non debet."

27. X 4.21.1: "Capellanum nihilominus, quem benedictionem cum secunda tibi constiterit celebrasse, ab officio beneficioque suspensum cum literarum tuarum testimonio appellatione cessante ad sedem apostolicam nullatenus destinare postponas."

28. The belief that marriage was a sacrament, although still debated among theologians, was by Alexander III's day beginning to be generally accepted; see Brundage, *Law, Sex, and Christian Society,* 254, 431–32; Philippe Delhaye, "The Development of the Medieval Church's Teaching on Marriage," *Concilium* 55 (1970): 83–88; Christopher N. L. Brooke, *The Medieval Idea of Marriage* (Oxford, 1989), 273–80.

29. Bernard of Parma, *Glos. ord.* to X 4.21.1 v. *cum secunda:* "Secunde nuptie benedicende non sint, infra eodem vir autem [X 4.21.3]; et secundam accipere secundum veritatis rationem, vere fornicatio est, 30 q. 3 hac ratione [*recte:* C. 31 q. 1 c. 9]. Sed illud intelligitur prima viuente, et non debent benedici secunde nuptie ad exhortationem continentie, sic et sacerdos interesse non debet nuptiis clandestine contractis, supra de cland. matrimonio, cum inhibitio § sane [X 4.3.3 §2]; multo minus debet illas benedicere, et alia ratio est quia sacramentum iterari non debet, infra eodem vir autem [X 4.21.3] ubi haec ratio notatur."
Glos. ord. to X 4.21.3 v. *iterari:* "Sacramenta enim iterari non debent, 1 q. 1 hanc regulam [C. 1 q. 1 c. 57] et c. hi [C. 1 q. 1 c. 51], ne fiat eis iniuria, 1 q. 1 quidam [C. 1 q. 1 d.a.c. 1] et de consecr. dist. 4 ostenditur [D. 4 de cons. c. 32], 33 q. 7 quemadmodum [*recte:* C. 32 q. 7 c. 10], et C. ne sanc. baptiste. l. 1 et 2 [Cod. 1.6.1–2]. Videretur enim quod sacramentum huiusmodi non fuisset collatum, vel quod inefficax fuisset omnino, et sic fieret iniuria ei, 1 q. 1 sacramenta [C. 1 q. 1 c. 34]. Tamen penitentia bene iteratur, de pen. dist. 3 adhuc instant [D. 3 de pen. c. 32]. Fallit etiam secundum quosdam in extrema vnctione. Quid enim impediret hanc iterari, cum non sit sacramentum, sed oratio super hominem, 1 q. 1 manus [C. 1 q. 1 c. 74], et solemnis penitentia non iteratur, 50 dist. quam his et c. in capite [D. 50 c. 62, 64]. Gratianus tamen dicit quod iteratur

secundum consuetudinem quorundam, de pen. distinc. 3 § ex persona [D. 3 de pen. d.p.c. 21], et benedictio ista cum aliquis secundam duxit virginem iteratur secundum consuetudinem quorundam locorum et hoc si Papa sciat talem consuetudinem, alias non licet."

30. Geoffrey of Trani, *Summa super titulis decretalium,* to X 4.21 pr. (1519; reprint, Aalen, 1968), 390–91.

31. Penny S. Gold, "The Marriage of Mary and Joseph in the Twelfth-Century Ideology of Marriage," in *Sexual Practices and the Medieval Church,* ed. Vern L. Bullough and James A. Brundage (Buffalo, N.Y., 1982), 102–17.

32. Brundage, *Law, Sex, and Christian Society,* 331–37; and "Marriage and Sexuality in the Decretals of Pope Alexander III," in *Miscellanea Rolando Bandinelli Papa Alessandro III,* ed. Filippo Liotta (Siena, 1986), 59–83.

33. See n. 22.

34. Hostiensis, *Summa aurea,* lib. 4, tit. 33, *De secundis nuptiis* §3, 1537 ed., fol. 224vb. See also the detailed analysis of this situation in Charles Donahue, Jr., "The Case of the Man Who Fell into the Tiber: The Roman Law of Marriage at the Time of the Glossators," *American Journal of Legal History* 22 (1978): 1–53.

35. Hostiensis, *In quinque decretalium libri commentaria [Lectura]* to X 4.21.1 v. *secunda,* 5 vols. in 2 (1581; reprint, Turin, 1965), vol. 4, fol. 48ra: "Magistri tamen dicunt utrumque dictum ad exhortationem castitatis, alias non vident quare haec benedictio iteranda non sit, quia benedictio quae super homines fit non prohibetur iterari, i. q. i. manus [C. 1 q. 1 c. 74]." He added in his remarks on X 4.21.3 v. *benedici* (fol. 48rb) that the nuptial blessing was treated as quasisacramental but failed to specify just what that meant.

36. Saint Bonaventure, *Comm. to Sent.* 4.42.3.2, in his *Opera omnia,* 4:877–78: "Resp. ad arg. dicendum quod dupliciter est loqui de secundis nuptiis: aut in se, aut in relatione ad primas; si in se, cum sit ibi consensus expressus inter legitimas personas, est utique ibi sacramentum, nec est ibi carnis divisio, sed unio carnis viri et mulieris; si autem loquamur in comparatione ad praecedentes, sic manet in eis sacramenti ratio incompleta propter carnis divisionem, quia in primis carnem suam univit cum uno, in secundis cum alio, et talis divisio tollit de plenitudine significationis."

37. For a similar practice in Eastern Orthodoxy, see Levin, *Sex and Society,* 108.

38. Saint Thomas Aquinas, *Summa Theologiae,* Supp. q. 63 a. 2 resp. ad 2, in his *Opera omnia, iussu edita Leonis XIII* (Rome, 1882–) 12/2:129: "Ad secundum dicendum, quod secundum matrimonium, quamvis in se consideratum sit perfectum sacramentum, tamen in ordine ad primum consideratum habet aliquid de defectu sacramenti, quia non habet plenam significationem, cum non sit una unius, sicut est in matrimonio Christi et Ecclesiae. Et ratione hujus defectus benedictio a secundis nuptiis subtrahitur. Sed hoc est intelligendum, quando secundae nuptiae sunt secundae et ex parte viri et ex parte mulieris, vel ex parte

mulieris tantum. Si enim virgo contrahat cum viro qui habuit aliam uxorem, nihilominus nuptiae benedicuntur; salvatur enim aliquo modo significatio etiam in ordine ad primas nuptias, quia Christus, etsi unam Ecclesiam sponsam habeat, habet tamen plures personas desponsatas in una Ecclesia. Sed anima non potest esse sponsa alterius quam Christi, quia alias cum daemone fornicatur; nec est ibi matrimonium spirituale. Et propter hoc quando mulier secundo nubit, nuptiae non benedicuntur propter defectum sacramenti." Hostiensis (*Summa aurea,* lib. 4, tit. 33, *De secundis nuptiis* §3 [1537 ed., fol. 224vb–225ra]) also refers to this practice but describes it as a *consuetudo prava.*

39. Although jurists' treatments of remarriage problems were not wholly theoretical: Bulgarus' students found it hilarious when, on the morning after his marriage to a widow, the master began lecturing on Cod. 3.1.14, which begins "Rem non novam" (Accursius, *Glos. ord.* to Cod. 3.1.14 pr. v. *rem non novam*).

40. G. Mollat, "La bénédiction des secondes noces," in *Etudes d'histoire de droit canonique dédiées à Gabriel Le Bras,* 2 vols. (Paris, 1965), 2:1337–39.

41. Jean-Baptiste Molin and Protais Mutembe, *Le rituel du mariage en France du XIIe au XVIe siècle,* Théologie historique, vol. 26 (Paris, 1974), 243–44.

42. J. A. C. Thomas, *Textbook of Roman Law* (Amsterdam, 1976), 423; Eva Cantarella, *Pandora's Daughters: The Role and Status of Women in Greek and Roman Antiquity,* trans. Maureen B. Fant (Baltimore, 1987), 122.

43. Cod. 5.9.1 pr. (380), 5.17.8.4b (449). On *infamia,* see, generally, Peter Landau, *Die Entstehung des kanonischen Infamiebegriffs von Gratian bis zur Glossa Ordinaria,* Forschungen zur kirchlichen Rechtsgeschichte und zum Kirchenrecht, vol. 5 (Cologne, 1966), and Elisabeth Vodola, *Excommunication in the Middle Ages* (Berkeley and Los Angeles, 1986), 71–81, 124–25.

44. X 4.21.4–5.

45. Byzantine and South Slavic canon law followed the Roman model; Russian canon law did not and stipulated no mandatory waiting period before remarriage (Levin, *Sex and Society,* 109–10).

46. Johannes Teutonicus, *Apparatus* to 3 Comp. 4.16. un., v. *iacturam,* ed. Kenneth J. Pennington, Jr., in *A Study of Johannes Teutonicus' Theories of Church Government and of the Relationship between Church and State, with an Edition of His Apparatus to Compilatio Tertia* (Ph.D. diss., Cornell University, 1972), 646.

47. Innocent IV, *Apparatus toto orbe celebrandus super V libris decretalium* to X 4.21.5 v. *infamia* (1570; reprint, Frankfurt am Main, 1968), fol. 485rb: "<Nota> [Non] solum non teneri infamia, sed nec alijs poenis, quae irrogantur, quia nupsit intra tempus luctus. . . . Ratio diuersitatis est, quia poenae impositae nubentibus intra tempus luctus sunt merae poenae, et ideo omnes poenas a legibus propter hoc inflictas, tolli credimus, sicut infamiam, sed poena quae imponitur secundo nubentibus non est mera poena, imo est prouisio illorum, et ideo non tollitur haec poena per canone, sic etiam non credimus tolli poenas

impositas illi qui contra proprium iuramentum nubit, recepta tutela filij non reddita ratione, C. ad Tertul. omnem [Cod. 6.56.6], in Authent. de nup. § sin autem tutelis [Nov. 22.40 = Auth. 22.4.1.]." Likewise, Hostiensis, *Lectura* to X 4.21.5 §2 v. *sustinere iacturam* (1581 ed., vol. 4, fol. 48ra–vb): "Hoc notauerunt quidam quod quamuis infamia sit remissa per apostolum, non tamen aliae poenae reales, in quibus punitur haec mulier per leges humanas de quibus no. e.c. proxi. super verbo 'tempus luctus [*Lectura* to X 4.21.4 §1], dicentes quod haec mulier videtur dehonestasse primum virum et quasi quamdam causam ingratitudinis contra virum praemortuum commississe, ut innuit dictum Auth. de rest. § unum siquidem [Nov. 39.1.1 in C. = Auth. 41.4.6], ideo tanquam ab ingrata res donatae auelluntur, ar. supra de do., propter [X 3.24.10], nec unquam fuit intentio apostoli quod talis poena remitteretur, et si hoc fuisset, non haberet in talibus potestatem, cum iurisdictiones diuisae sint."

48. Hostiensis, *Lectura* to X 4.21.4 §2, 1581 ed., fol. 48va.

49. E.g., Hostiensis, *Summa aurea,* lib. 4, tit. 33 *De secundis nuptiis* § 5 (1537 ed., fol. 225rb–va).

50. *Livre au Roi* 30 and *Assises des bourgeois* 166–67, in *Recueil des historiens des croisades,* Lois, 2 vols. (Paris, 1841–43) 1:626–27 and 2:113–14 (hereafter RHC, Lois).

51. E.g., in Spain, *Las Siete partidas del rey don Alfonso el Sabio, cotejadas con varios codices antiguos por la Real Academia de la Historia,* 4.12.3, 3 vols. (1807; reprint, Madrid, 1972), 3:83.

52. *Livre au Roi* 30, in RHC, Lois, 1:627; and see, generally, James A. Brundage, "Marriage Law in the Latin Kingdom of Jerusalem," in *Outremer: Studies in the History of the Crusading Kingdom of Jerusalem Presented to Joshua Prawer,* ed. B. Z. Kedar, H. E. Mayer, and R. C. Smail (Jerusalem, 1982), 270–71.

53. *Livre de Jean d'Ibelin* 228, in RHC, Lois, 1:362–64.

54. Jacques Rossiaud, "Prostitution, Youth, and Society in the Towns of Southeastern France in the Fifteenth Century," in *Deviants and the Abandoned in French Society,* ed. Robert Forster and Orest Ranum, trans. Elborg Forster and Patricia M. Ranum (Baltimore, 1978), 12, 15–17; and *Medieval Prostitution,* trans. Lydia G. Cochrane (Oxford, 1988), 27–30; Natalie Zemon Davis, "The Reasons of Misrule: Youth Groups and Charivaris in Sixteenth-Century France," *Past and Present* 50 (1971): 41–75.

55. David Herlihy, "Marriage at Pistoia in the Fifteenth Century," *Bullettino storico pistoiese* 74 (1972): 3–21; "The Medieval Marriage Market," *Medieval and Renaissance Studies* 6 (1976): 3–27; and *Medieval Households* (Cambridge, Mass., 1985), 100–103, 124–25, 135, 154–55; Barbara Hanawalt, *The Ties That Bound: Peasant Families in Medieval England* (Oxford, 1986), 220–26; Roderick Phillips, *Putting Asunder: A History of Divorce in Western Society* (Cambridge, 1988), 367–69.

Chapter 2

Fifteenth-Century Widows and Widowhood: Bereavement, Reintegration, and Life Choices

Joel T. Rosenthal

"The husband dies first."[1] In this lapidary fashion Maitland opens his discussion of the legal rights of the surviving partner. With four words he sets us upon a bedrock of social reality about widowhood and the widow's future life from which we can go forward but upon which all that follows must be built.

The scholarship of recent years has given us a wealth of sympathetic and sanguine discussions examining and championing the legal rights, the social and economic opportunities, the new potential for status and independence, and the matriarchal possibilities and multigenerational family role of the widow.[2] Part of the attraction of such work is its vindication of the rights and privileges of so many medieval women and the way it highlights the greater reach and power now within the survivor's grasp, were she of good fortune and sufficiently resilient to cope on her own in a gender-biased and patriarchal world.

Maitland's sober words, however, are deeply engraved. Widowhood may have been a gateway to opportunity, for some at least: The modern politician's claim that "you never had it so good" can serve as the appropriate subtext for our lesson. Nevertheless, or simultaneously, we must note that widowhood began with a wrench, a sharp turn in the road of life's journey: the husband had indeed died first. That the wrench was neither an unlikely one in a woman's life nor statistically improbable, in a study of any given universe of women, may spread a coating of protective fatalism over a life experience that, for many, ushered in a frightening day of bereavement and anomie. Regardless of what was to come, and whether, in the long run, we deem her to be ahead or behind by virtue of his departure, the tale of the widow opens to a bleak page in the life story.

Proceeding from this sober prologue, we offer an overview of options and alternatives available to *her,* from the moment of *his* death onward. There are some salient characteristics of widowhood worth setting out at the start. One, as we have said, is that it opens with a closing; from an ending came a beginning. Furthermore, the closure was accompanied by isolation, loss, and vulnerability. The second point is that in widowhood she could open doors of choice, perhaps for the first time in her life. She could contemplate a menu with an array of alternatives: remarriage, widowhood until the end, or some form of ecclesiastically sanctioned withdrawal from the secular and sexual world. Nor did her choices have to be mutually exclusive, at least not across the full span of her remaining days. A woman's life—certainly a widow's life—is composed of stages or segments. As she exercised her newly acquired right to choose, she could perhaps go back and forth—to new marriages, thence to new widowhoods, perhaps ultimately to vows of chastity or to the cloister, or to some mix and variation of these alternatives.

In some ways widowhood is a status created by events of a moment; like entropy, it seems irremediable and irreversible. It separates everything before from everything afterward. The data indicate that the new choice, the step toward the next segment of life—the leftover life, if we wish—was often made very quickly. Within a short interval she might approach and cross new lines of demarcations. Life not only went on, but sometimes it went on with but little pause.

Most societies allow some measure of and duration for grief and bereavement following a spouse's death. When the surviving partner is a widow, there is the question of her particular future—usually in a social framework wherein men hold the purse, the sword, and the plow handle—and of the general phenomenon of widowhood, of women free of direct male control. After the mourning period, the interval in which isolation and bereavement are enjoined, most societies have mechanisms for some sort of reintegration, prescribed steps toward the resumption of a normalized (and controlled) life pattern. Though the spectrum of historical and anthropological literature displays tremendous latitude regarding the rate at which she is reintegrated, and the extent to which she is called upon to resume a life consonant with her class, status, and past, there is space for mobility (in both directions) and for independence or autonomy. Though freedom is always a relative matter, English widows rarely had a future as neatly predetermined as it was, elsewhere, by the levirate or the suttee.[3] The potential for power and separateness embedded in her new status might allow her to disrupt the flow of wealth, social control, and ideology that normally ran unchecked in masculinized channels of expression and transmission.

I focus these comments, truisms of social science, upon widows and widowhood in late medieval England. I am not attempting a synthesis of recent historiography, nor am I trying to cover the full scope and breadth of a woman's new roles, after widowhood, nor to enlarge upon the opportunities of her new persona. Rather, this chapter proposes a quick survey of the stages of life as they stretched before her, after "the husband died first." I emphasize both the segmentary nature of her life and the links that could be forged between the segments: different chapters of the biography that unfolded before her (and that she helped unfold). As her life contained its mix of good and bad news, so it contained elements of the involuntary—as in widowhood itself—and the voluntary, the choices she could now make. The taste of her new freedom might be soured by the fashion of her entry into her new status, but for many it was, nevertheless, an intriguing taste.

In this essay I will pick and choose statistical and anecdotal material to offer suggestions about life choices and the life course. There are firm patches of quantitative and precise data, as there are stretches of uncertain trekking across the shifting sands of emotion, of intentions, and of each woman's need—perhaps under great pressure and at a time of vulnerability and isolation—to make choices about life courses. Nor was she just choosing for herself; the fate of children, the future of baronial estates or artisan's shops or manorial shares, plus questions of burial, of last wills and their execution, and, many times, no doubt, of how to put bread and ale on the table, were frequently items on the agenda we call getting on with life.

Methods of inquiry and the nature and value of our sources run hand in hand. As with so many excursions into women's lives, much of what we know is only by way of sources more sensitive to an administrative transaction than to women's lived experience, confined as it was by a patriarchal worldview and a hierarchical social order. A widow's petition to recover her dower share or to assume guardianship of her minor children is exactly that, a *petition;* the very name of the proceeding highlights her dependency: former wife, now suppliant. Could we know more of widows' feelings about choices—why and when they chose from among their alternatives—we might have a key to unravel the complex dialectic of behavior and *mentalité*. But, whether we concentrate on words or actions, we probe a personal and private world, unlikely to be fully explicated in the idiom of our sources. Individual reticence, in the context of cultural norms that mute self-expression, sets barriers against the intrusion of even the most sympathetic curiosity.

On the other hand, it ill behooves the historian to grow deferential when confronted with individuality and eccentricity. If the emotional and volitional range of a widow is invariably beyond recapture, we know that culture conditions us so that, in some aggregate fashion, common stimuli are acknowledged in terms of common response. We mostly act within predictable channels and not particularly wide ones. The articulation of grief and loss is likely to be confined, in outward voice, to a smallish range of expressions and behaviors. Beyond this range (and the period of behavioral dispensation during which it can be freely indulged) unchecked outbursts are read as indications of a failure to reengage, as excessive and self-indulgent. Our tolerance, despite conventions of sympathy and the need to give vent to sorrow and alienation in a mourning period, is fairly limited. Not only did one have to get on with the business of life, but the evidence is that a great many widows—whatever life choice they wound up making and whatever their satisfaction with the choice—followed this practical wisdom with considerable dispatch.

Remarriage was always a popular choice; widowhood was too common, its dilemmas too familiar, and the convenience if not the pleasure of marital partner too obvious for much explanation or apology. Marriage to a widow of property, as we see at every turn, was an avenue upward for prospective husbands, be they young or old, just entering the world of marriage or themselves carrying the scars of a lost spouse.

Reintegration through remarriage was the modal path for those with the common experience of having buried a husband. Where we can isolate a particular group, such as the peeresses, we find the option of remarriage chosen by about half the women (including those now widowed for a second or third time, to complicate our categories and tallies). Probably something over half the younger widows remarried; henceforth remaining unmarried became a more popular choice as we move toward older women with neither young children to rear nor long and uncertain futures to plot. For the fifteenth-century peeresses 89 of 162 widows chose not to remarry (54 percent), while 73 had at least one subsequent marriage.[4] For a smaller subgroup within the peerage—those younger at the moment of widowhood than the total group—21 remarried, against 20 who remained single.

Though few other groups can be analyzed in this fashion, the impression based on studies of bourgeois or rural society is that upper-class behavior was much in line with that of women a bit down the social scale. At the commensurate level expectations were probably similar, as were social pressures. Eileen Power speculated that, if anything, the incidence of remarriage for aristocratic widows was lower than for burgesses' wives, as upper-class affluence could subsidize independence, if one so chose.[5] Recent studies of rural, urban, and small-group aggregations support these unexceptionable findings. The Wife of Bath was unusual in terms of the number of husbands and the frankness of her discourse on strategems and sexuality, along with her haste to get on with it, but the remarrying widow was a commonplace of literature *and* of society; Barbara Hanawalt's detailed examination of London women (in the present volume) is further confirmation, offering a precision of detail that has been hard to establish.

To determine that a good half of widowed women moved on to remarriage certainly tells us something fairly concrete about how they dealt with their life options, the choice now thrust upon them by widowhood. Motives behind behavior are probably not hard to assess; if an explicit statement is rare, it is rarely needed. The new marriage might enlarge her scope for control, for independence. In other instances remarriage was perhaps semi-forced, given the stress of her new status and the uneasy balance between material resources and psychological and emotional ones. The call of independence could be the siren song of the fair deceiver.

The quality of remarriage, like that of first marriage, is an obscure issue, whether it had been arranged by others for youngsters or freely contracted between adults with buried spouses among their life baggage. Marriage contracts and similar diplomatic agreements focus on property, with an emphasis on division and transmission. Such documents are tight-lipped, at best, on domesticity, shared decision making, and the intimacies of chamber and bed. It would be nice to say that women looked more at daughters' futures, husbands at sons', and that a mutual-assistance treaty took care of the stepchildren. But there is little evidence for this picture of a homey bifurcation of responsibility, whether along gender or progenitary lines. Sometimes stepchildren blended comfortably, and in other instances we can imagine the range of second-class citizenships that were offered, if not happily received.

When a woman married she recast her identity: a new surname, a new family of primary obligation, a new male cover figure. Remarriage did the same, once again. Against her greater element of control and independence we can set the greater complications of the new marriage contracted, against the emotional backdrop of widowhood and coming atop ties of a first marriage that might continue through life. Even terms and definitions can bedevil us; "widowhood" itself was not as clear a life distinction as it would seem. Remarried women were widows and wives. A study of aristocratic widows reveals that the first marriage was often a short-lived affair, while the second or third might be the one that stamped her with a more lasting identity, determined both by longevity and childbearing. And for some women—wives and widows and back again—three or four marriages, not just two, constituted the full biography. Length of marriage was a factor of demography, not of compatibility; would that we could plot a correlation between length of marriage and self-identification.

When we turn to the social and economic side of remarriage we are on firmer ground. We often encounter a tale of continuity and parity, a familiar bridging in personal areas, a quick and pragmatic regathering of broken threads. Though the dramatic leap, whether up or down, is the one that catches the eye, the next husband was more likely to be the late husband's secular or socioeconomic equal, if not his friend or associate. What was true for the great of the land was replicated, in countless instances, in village, manor, and town. The peeresses provide instances of remarriage at a slightly lower level, perhaps moving from higher to lesser aristocracy or down a gentle incline to the gentry or the prosperous bourgeoisie: shire knights, judges, and mayors of boroughs were likely choices when they descended, whatever the circumstances of each choice. But, by way of comparison, other aristocratic widows had only reached their elevated status in the first place after a previous marriage to a man of lesser rank, a commoner. They in turn became peeresses by dint of remarrying as widows, now rewidowed through the death of the aristocratic husband. Many women in these ranks just moved horizontally within the peerage, perhaps in three or four marriages, as they went from noble husband to noble husband; the logic of social structure and personal interaction suggests this as the prevailing pattern for both high and low.

For the great ladies, the widows of peers, details are at hand. Anne Holland, a duke's daughter, married two lords Neville in succession (uncle and nephew). She outlived the second, a casualty at Towton in 1461, for twenty-five years: so rests one widow's efforts at reintegration, illustrating both reengagement and withdrawal. Katherine Neville, an earl's daughter, married a duke, a knight, a viscount, and an earl, and she too proved to be the final survivor of the batch, an unmarried but oft-married widow at the last trumpet. On the other side of the coin we encounter Margaret, daughter and coheir of Lord Tibetot and widow of Roger, second lord Scrope of Bolton. After Scrope's death she married one John Niander—serious social descent on her part, given her origins and prior marital experience. Furthermore, it was not just her downward mobility that set tongues wagging. There was Niander's flight to the Continent to escape indictment for murdering a cleric who had criticized his life-style. The disparities of status, discussed in a later chapter by Charles Donahue in the context of divorce, surely ran the gossip circuit countless times before they made a formal entrance on the legal circuit.

London widows' tales present many instances of equality of status and position between marriages, even, in many cases, for the likelihood of familiarity between husbands. The *Letter Books* record the proceeding at which the widowed mother and new husband gave assurances regarding the property and custody of her minor children. They emphasize the propensity of like to remarry like:

> the guardianship of Geoffrey and Johanna, children of John Cowlyngge, late *grocer,* together with their property, committed to Robert Downe, *grocer,* who married Catherine, widow of the said John.[6]

Nor was such behavior confined to the respectable elements of society: Lollard widows were apt to remarry other Lollards.[7] Of course, we say—how better to find companionship and a basis of mutual interests, plus some element of security.

Keys to the doors of private life and emotionality are never easy to turn. When women married, and even more when they remarried, they altered their identities: surname, the mantle of coverture, kinship webs, place of residence, and then burial place, were they the survivor in the long dance. These transformations and adaptations represent, in toto, a challenge to a woman's basic ego identity. Some met the challenge with aplomb; others, among the universe of quickly remarried widows, may have been overwhelmed by an endless string of decisions and were perhaps puzzled and frustrated by their failure to find a safe port in a world of shifting identities.

Some women maintained ties with and loyalty to the family of an earlier marriage, adapting older bonds to those of subsequent marriages. Others adopted or suffered from a kind of social amnesia; the current or last husband was *the* husband, his world the one that now absorbed their full span of interest and enterprise. Widows' wills are evocative records, and they can shed some light on these matters. Some high-born ladies show us, through a policy of dividing bequests among the kin accumulated in a series of marriages and marital families, how they managed a synthesis, a measure of integration imposed upon the mosaic.

An example of this wide embrace is the elaborate will of Anne, widowed Lady Scrope of Bolton (and before that widow of Sir William Chamberlaine, K.G., and of Sir Robert Wingfield, M.P.), who died childless shortly after Scrope himself in 1498. In her vast enumeration of beneficiaries there are relatives and dependents accumulated throughout her series of marriages; could one pull a chronological string, four or five decades of domestic life would be beaded together. The panoply of beneficiaries includes:

> nevew Robert Wyngefeld . . . my son lord Scrop . . . my broder Robert Scrop . . . my broder maister Rauff . . . my sone Herry Scrop . . . my nece Wymondham . . . to my lady, wiff to my sone, now lorde Scrop . . . to my lady my lorde moder . . . my nece katerine Breuse . . . my cosyn Sir Thomas Tudenham . . . my nece Elizabeth Wyngefeld, my god doughter . . . my nevewes, my suster dame Elizabeth children . . . my suster Bygott . . . my suster Radcliff . . . my cosyne dame Elizabeth Forkewe . . . my cosyne Elizabeth Althorp . . . my nece Margaret Bardewell.[8]

Nor does this list exhaust her testamentary loquacity. Granted, one should not construct a sociology of interpersonal relationships on such impressionistic material, especially given that I have chosen an unusually rich instance for illustration. But this expansive and inclusive reach was not a rarity among the remarrying widows. Nor was affluence a sine qua non of such behavior; small estates could be divided penny by penny, small inventories doled out napkin by napkin, knife by knife, platter by platter.

The gathering of the shards of a segmentary life was not confined to the distribution of tangible items. It could be demonstrated by webs of social control and affective links, forged between the different parties and reinforced by the provisions of the will. We find children from one marriage called upon to assume responsibility for half-siblings and step-relatives. In human terms this behavior is a welcome counterweight to the theme of rivalry and competition that we so often find after the death of the patriarch or matriarch. What is striking about Lady Scrope is that, with no issue of her body, her bequests help establish a worldview that was a social construct, not a biological one. The pattern she imposed—a last comment upon nature and art—was a statement about life choices that she, a widow of affluence, imposed upon the scrambled segments of autobiography.

The impressions we draw from these quick raids upon the data, treasure houses of anecdote and incident, are but suggestions. They reinforce the view that reintegration by way of remarriage was a mainstream life course for many of the widows. It offered an opportunity to reknit the personal and socioeconomic threads of a now disjointed life, or so she hoped. From the moment of the decision to remarry, paths opened outward. She might maintain harmonious links with her earlier life and simultaneously work to fit into the textures of her next marital family. At other times she moved along a linear path, hardly looking backward. And, if she had but limited expectations about bettering herself through remarriage, we have to accept that she tried to make the best choice, as the alternatives of the moment presented themselves. Life is the road taken, read against the text of the road not taken.

Remarriage, as long as it lasted, sealed her reintegration; it was the (next) life choice for something around, or slightly above, half the widows we can trace. The *feme sole,* suddenly in command of significant resources, was about even money to return to her position as *feme covert.* This alone should caution us about the realities of her new independence. Since the widow could both remarry and ultimately die unmarried—the survivor of her last marriage—we are bracketing ultimate widows with those who made a deliberate choice, early in widowhood, against further marital adventures. Had we detailed biographical material, many whom we classify as nonremarrying actually saw themselves as on the road to another union; time just ran out on them. A large fraction of remarriages, however, were contracted within a year or two of a husband's death and only a few after much more than five years of widowhood. So we know, whether contemporaries saw the matter in this light or not, that the odds against remarriage lengthened directly with the interval. If she had remained unmarried for more than five years, there was little likelihood of a subsequent union.

For many women, as we know, the "plight" of the unmarried widow was not unattractive: a multitude of compensations and opportunities against some obvious liabilities. This is the case, with commensurate adjustments, up and down the social scale, from virgate holder to dowager duchess. The great dowager households created and presided over by such imposing, lifelong widows as Cecily Neville, duchess of York, or Alice Bryene, exemplify the empowerment of the rich and commanding matriarchal or feminist presence. Their independence came from the convergence of resources, social position, and a life-style untroubled by such mundane worries as marginalization or hunger.[9] Furthermore, before Cecily's persona became that of the quasi–mother superior depicted in the household records of her later days, she had played an active role in both family and court politics; this too may have been typical behavior for the widow of stature.[10]

Women who could support a life of prolonged widowhood, in what they deemed the style appropriate to their ambitions and status, might well have been inclined to choose in that direction. Many peeresses deliberately stayed on the marital sidelines, and many of their lesser counterparts made the same choice, scaled down to lesser horizons but still with an impressive and often a long-lived presence. The 1436 parliamentary assessment of landed incomes, accepted by the peers for taxation purposes, shows thirty-four of the realm's peerages (and their appurtenant estates) to be in male hands, thirteen shared between male heirs and (dowager) peeresses, and five under dowagers' control:[11] a lot of upper-class women, controlling a great deal of property and wealth, running independent establishments. And the tale is confirmed by regional studies, as by those of particular families, at virtually every level that can be reconstructed.

Nevertheless, we should not be too sanguine about the quality of life and the long-term prospects of widows who drew the line at partial reintegration. Opportunities open to widows of wealth may not readily translate, as we descend, into an equally enticing treasure trove of free choice. The villein- or yeoman-widow who did not remarry might try to maintain her economic level; in reality she was likely to encounter serious, if not crippling, problems. At Havering we find many who could hold their own against the worst face of adversity, but usually it was a defensive action calling for the surrender of some precious ground of socioeconomic status and resource. The future was going to be one of less land, fewer goods, and diminished revenues when compared to those of the husband-wife unit.[12] Independence and survival without male cover was a common life course but probably lived at a reduced standard. The distinction between genteel poverty and genuine want is sometimes hidden, but the winter chill could be pretty bitter for widows hugging either side of the line.

In town, if she were of some substance and opted against remarriage, she would make an effort to keep the family business going, at least for a while. The craft or shop was a vital cog in the family's definition of self, as a social as well as an economic entity, to be preserved until the shock of the husband's death had worn off and kinfolk or business associates could help shoulder the load. What we know of Coventry widows seems applicable across the national canvas: "On the death of a husband who had been a master craftsman it was clearly essential for the widow to be able to perpetuate the family business at least until her children went out to service."[13] As in the manorial setting, some withdrawal from social and economic affairs, some contraction in life-style, was her likely fate in the not-too-distant future. On the Continent as well we find that widows kept the old firm going for a while, perhaps for a year or so after his death, but then were likely to move (or be moved) toward the edges of the stage.[14]

If we draw a hard line against any sentimentality regarding her life alternatives, we must not simply jettison the widow into a refuse heap of decline and misery. One factor in her favor, for comfort and sustenance, may have been the mere fact of numbers, the ubiquitous presence of so many sisters in a comparable situation. The widow as head of household was hardly a rare bird. Urban records reveal her at almost every turn; in Coventry approximately 12 percent of households—one in every eight—was headed by a widow, the ex-wife now going it without authorized male coverage.[15]

If her future status and role were but partially under her own control, we have seen how her testamentary bequests could be woven into a defining worldview. Granted, wills are more prone to reflect affluence and integration; they are a less likely vehicle for cries of anomie or isolation. As widows reveal themselves from the deathbed, they often depict (or create) a reasonable family network. The text tells of continuity between the older domesticity and that of final or permanent widowhood. When Rose Rykhill, who remained single after her husband's death—"nuper uxor Willelmi Rykhill militis"—leaves bequests and instructions to four sons, a daughter, and the daughter's daughter, she hardly seems bereft of her near and dear ones.[16] Burial with her husband and the choice of the eldest son as executor reinforce the picture of integrated family life enduring well beyond the husband's death. But the long-lived widow was not always the wholly congenial widow, and we note occasional utterances framed in the idiom of social control: "if my sonne of Bukkyngham interrupt or sett my last will . . . thanne the biquest be voide and of noon effect."[17]

The widows who leave these records were looking back on a stewardship capably assumed and forward with a modicum of confidence. Presumably, some had deliberately rejected the option of remarriage; practical and business-minded suitors, if not lovesick swains, were now sent packing. But our widows have left few traces of their reflections concerning their choices, whether made or left unmade. They had buried a husband or two, however it had affected them, but they kept their own counsel; only by their action (or inaction) do we know them. In practice, of course, they were well able to compare their lot with those who had remarried. Comparison shopping is as old as economics, and prospective husbands were among the commodities when widows went to market.

The emphasis, either upon reintegration via remarriage or upon permanent widowhood as partial reintegration, bypasses some somber stretches of the landscape. Tragedies of mortality and demography had to be overcome, softened by time and support networks; life went on. But, as some of the widows were soon to be reyoked to the comforts and worries of domestic life and others to exercise their new franchise for independence, so still others—whether badly broken or liberated by widowhood—made a deliberate decision against secular reintegration. Some chose to leave the world for the cloister or the cell; less dramatically, but with apparent finality, others did so by a formal vow of chastity.

The encloistered widow, if not a predominant figure in late medieval nunneries, was to be found. Though the numbers are probably modest, such women might have made an impact upon their communities well beyond their numbers. Some were of exalted social status; many came with substantial dowries and corodies, and a few even rose to become abbesses. Furthermore, the vowed widow might move with an upper-class hauteur, fueled by years of command in secular households—hardly the ideal orientation for later years within the portals of sanctity.[18]

Deliberate and formal withdrawal from the world, among the widow's options, seems a reasonable alternative, at least for a few. Some who went this way chose this path in the first flush of sorrow and isolation. Others moved in this direction slowly, if logically, and via a series of decisions that leave few visible footprints but were clearly charted long before the final steps were taken. The duchess of Clarence waited seven years after the Duke's death before entering the cloister. As she aged, the childless widow looked for solace, or affluent retirement, in the healing rhythms of the regular life. Such progress, by fits and starts toward a known end, was a comfortable route from indecision to an ultimate commitment, and the duchess was hardly unique. After all, we move here in a world of genteel retirement, not of spiritual enthusiasm. Lady Grey's aristocratic husband died; three years later she remarried. After a second marriage, of eleven years, she again found herself a widow. Finally, four years after the second death she took vows of religion. It was not from the cloth of such deliberate commitment that the reform movements of the High Middle Ages had been cut.[19]

A vow of chastity was less draconic than "enclaustration." It allowed her to remain in the world, if she chose, though she could take the lesser vow and still take up residence as a monastic boarder, a permanent paying guest. The vow was just an ecclesiastically endorsed commitment to eschew marriage and domestic life, with no obligation to withdraw from worldly concerns or family affairs. As a rite de passage, it was a simple affair, taken before an ecclesiastical official, perhaps in public as one more form of medieval living theater:

> I Alice Lynne widowe a vowe to god perpeuel chastite of my body fro yis tyme fortheward in presence of you rigtworshipful fader in god.... And I behete to lyve stavely in yis avowe, and yerto withe myn owne I make yis subscripcyon.[20]

How many women, or what proportion of any group of widows, went through such a ceremony? The number was surely small, the ranks of vowesses thin. And yet the ceremony, and what it entailed for the widow and those involved in her life, was part of the common stock of life experience. In some ways the vow was an extreme statement of a theme upon which her whole life was seen, by male conductors, to be a series of variations. Its more common secular counterpart, readily found in any collection of fifteenth-century wills, was the stipulation by the dying husband that she was to live unmarried and chastely, usually as a condition surrounding the disposal of his bequests:

> Wyfe, that ye remember your promise to me, to take the ordre of wydowhood, as ye may be the better mayster of your owne, to performe my wylle and to helpe my children, as I love and trust you.[21]

By following his injunction, there would be fewer distractions regarding the children and the implementation of his last wishes. Beyond that, though not reaching the written text, was the issue of his sexual jealousy against the survivor and her new options.

With dead husband and living Church both steering the widow toward withdrawal, it is no wonder that some survivors chose this route. The new widow found herself at a crossroads—the road of quick decision making, intersecting with that of personal vulnerability. As well as the protection offered by ritualized withdrawal, the vow might enable her to come to grips, perhaps for the first time, with her own feelings about sex, childbirth, and the endless waves of marital entanglements and responsibilities. We know of the fear and articulated pain of childbed, from women's voices in the seventeenth century; had we such material for the fifteenth century, we would expect to hear a similar strain.[22] In choosing to take the vow of chastity, a woman may be letting us come as close to a view-of-life statement as we find from a gender socialized against self-expression. She may be asserting a form of control, even if only by withdrawal. It can take courage to flee as well as to stand and fight.

In talking of her options, we should also keep an eye on the calendar; within what time frame were widows operating? Sometimes we can pinpoint the date of her oath taking against that of her husband's death. She might move with some deliberate haste to register her new condition as her permanent future. Walter Calverly drew up his will on 1 October 1404; probate was dated 18 December. Also in December we find that Joan, "sometime wife of Walter Calverly, knight," appeared before the ecclesiastical authorities in York to register her vow.[23] Her decision may have been decided upon in advance, perhaps as a mutually accepted future arranged between dying husband and surviving wife.

Such a vow, made in the first flood of emotion and worry, could be repented at leisure, as grief cooled and the world looked less heartless. For widows who found themselves in such a trap there were avenues of escape:

> Mandate to commute into other works of piety the vow of chastity which Margaret, relict of William de Slengesby ... hastily made, after her said husband's death ... in as much as she fears that on account of the frailty of the flesh she will not be able to keep it and therefore desires to marry, to contract which marriage the prior (of Holy Trinity, York) is to grant her dispensation.[24]

An element of game playing here, no doubt, as in so much of the world staked out by canon law and then mediated by the Church's dispensing powers. The vow of chastity offered the widow the garb of immediate protection, often when she was most bereft, and yet this choice—as that of remarriage—might preserve the option of still further options, at some later date, when she was more in control of her future and better able to sort through her alternatives. As James Brundage tells us, society smirked and remarked that "remarriages signified shameless slavery to the voluptuous enticements of sexual passion," but a smirking society still recognized and yielded to the elemental power of these enticements.

The widow who took a vow of chastity, even if she remained in the world, removed herself from full reintegration. But at the genesis point of widowhood all our women—no matter with which group they would ultimately align and what fate regarding reintegration awaited them— had faced a definitional experience: he had died first. Whether they had been present at his death or had learned of it, sooner or later, as friends, messengers, and public tongues carried the news, it eventually came home.[25] Guild members of the sisterhood of bereavement, they had drunk from a common cup. This aloneness, with intimations of vulnerability and also new options, was an early characteristic of and response to these women's altered status. Attempts to gauge feelings, to conjecture about early moves toward reintegration, are uncertain ventures, voyages with neither charts nor rudders. We assume initial moments of grief, as of shock and disorientation; how few of these critical junctures are preserved by the sources that society cared to record.

When the husband was full of days his death was accepted with resignation, if not with cheer, and her grief was expected to be measured. In the *Goodman of Paris* the elderly (first) husband instructs the young wife so that her domestic skills, in the subsequent marriage he assumes likely, will do credit to his memory and their household economy:

> I would that you know how to give good will and honour and service in great measure and abundance more than is fit for me, either to serve another husband, if you have one, after me, or to teach greater wisdom to your daughters.[26]

Consonant with this realism regarding life probabilities, we know that many of the peers of the realm, or the knights of the shire or the well-chronicled urban burghers, had reached middle or old age by the end, even by our standards. For some of these men the widows were (still) first wives, hardy survivors of decades of domestic and marital experience. Their loss now might be considerable and deeply felt but was neither unexpected nor, in most instances, framed in a rhetoric of shock or extravagant grief.[27]

Widowhood, at some point along the life line, was a common fate.[28] We may ponder the relationship between the statistical probability of a husband's death, however comprehended, and an ability to steel oneself against what was "likely to happen." Historians have discussed the emotional crises or, alternatively, the sangfroid that supposedly was cultivated as a protection against the blow of infant mortality. It can be argued, in either direction, how she would react when she survived him. Surely, many of the wives who saw men go off to fight in France or in retinues at home after 1455 must have had some grasp of the probabilities regarding battlefield losses, along with those of desertion (of both king and family). When we include common soldiers along with their captains and the well-publicized and highly mortal peers, even minor skirmishes left dead and disabled hundreds, and, in the occasional pitched battle, totals that ran into the thousands.[29] Widow makers in profusion, coming with a suddenness and drama only matched by the plague.

We have all read our Huizinga; the morbidity of medieval public and private life, as we can gauge it, is a phenomenon we should bring into our systemic explanations. A world replete with chantries and ubiquitous masses for the dead was not one inclined to bury its departed in order to forget or ignore them. The liturgy of daily prayer, the innumerable family rituals and ceremonies, and the physical profile of towns and cities—with their heady quota of churches and graveyards and funeral processions of pomp and splendor—all served to remind the living of the high roads of time and mortality. If it is easy to exaggerate the dark hues that supposedly determined the timbre of public culture, there is no gainsaying that reminders of life lived in the midst of death were regular components of the body politic and the body social. Easy mortality, familiar and regularly incorporated into spectacle, helped set the tone for much of the personalized self-expression we can recover. Death as a set scene with foreground and background, and the survivors' need to respond to its aggressive challenge, takes us back to the rituals of mourning and reintegration with which we began.[30]

When widows turned their thoughts to their own burial sites and ceremonies they were offering final reflections on husbands and marriages. Some asked to be buried with a first or earlier mate—voting with their bodies, we might say. Others, in keeping with the variety that marks social life, decided that the last husband was good enough for the purpose. Her request that "My body aftir my dethe in all the goodely hast that hit may be caried to Jervaux and ther to bee biryed afore the hegh auter besides my lords body" is in support of the most traditional course of husband-wife relations.[31] But when such pieties are tempered by the qualifying clause "or ells where by the discrecon of myn executors," the tie is not quite as firmly tied.[32] Other widows went their ways, perhaps with the first of their three husbands or with the second, sometimes even with their own family of birth, completely bypassing the encumbrances and memories of marriage and widowhood.[33] Though we do not know her motives, we know that, despite her many years as *the* Paston, Margaret went home at the end: "my body to be beried in the ele of the cherch of Mauteby, byfore the ymage of Our Lady there. In which ele reste the bodies of divers of myn auncesteres, whos sowles God assoile."[34]

There are several instances in which women, widows but for a year or so, were moving toward their own final statements on life, family, and property. In these cases the ties with the husband were strong, the will a document of completion or reunification. Jane Nevill started with the customary "to be buried... wher the body of Sir Herry Nevill, knyght, late my housband, liettht buried." By the time she added prayers for him in three churches and distributed gowns, "on of whiche belongeth unto the body of my late housband," one can see, his death—killed at Edgecot not much more than a year before—still shaped her identity. Would she have remarried had she lived? One year-plus leaves the question moot. Sometimes the final choices of wife-mother need little gloss: "My body to be buryd at the Gray Freeres... in that same place that my sone Henry Sotehill is buryed, and my hert to be take out of my body and buryed at Stokfaston by my housbande."[35]

These comments about choices are polished by the wisdom of hindsight, the historian's ultimate trick in hand. We can pin down little hinting of any heightened sensitivity from her moments of green bereavement. Where are the signs of the burdens and pain of the young mother, now without anchor and rudder in the troubled seas of parenthood and responsibility? Her sanguine thoughts about burial and final resting place, thoughts removed by some interval from the moment of widowhood, may argue for memories of sufficient strength to counter the inevitable erosion of time and separation. Alternatively, her summation, as expressed by burial preference, may be a weak reed by which to gauge her marriage in its days of give-and-take. A widow's memory may owe more to the pieties than to the daily ledger. Final statements are a guide to the way she chose to depict herself at the end, a last opportunity for "contextualization." Like testamentary bequests, burial instructions were to fix a retrospective order upon the segments of her life.

Memories of the lost husband, however expressed, were not the only burden a widow might be called upon to assume on short notice. We have not dwelt here upon problems of dower recovery, nor have we delved into the possibility of legal and economic obstacles that lay ahead. The essays by Janet Senderowitz Loengard and Sue Sheridan Walker in this volume take us into a world of complex problems not even hinted at in this chapter. Raising young children or, alternatively, shucking them off, or some combination of alternatives, was an item high on the agenda she had suddenly inherited. There were endless worries and countless details, no doubt, before even the most affluent and least scarred could settle into the life of independence and women's choices that might ultimately await them. At the beginning of it all, as Maitland said, he had died. For a while it might not be an easy time.

Some widows had to face woes that included problems relating directly to the dear departed, not (yet) resting in peace. After Hotspur was killed at Shrewsbury in 1403 and properly buried, he was disinterred and dismembered so that his distributed sections would dispel rumors of his escape. It fell to his widow to petition the king so that she could literally pick up the pieces:

> Mayor and sheriffs of York: Order to deliver to Elizabeth, who was wife of Henry de Percy, knight, for burial, the head of said Henry, which by command of the king was set up over the gate of the city: as the king has granted her his head and quarters for burial.

As lord Bardolf's widow was permitted in 1408, so Lady Percy was allowed to have the five portions (consisting of the head and the four quarters) reassembled: Hotspur had been on show in York, Newcastle, London, Bristol, and Chester, whereas Bardolf was to be found at London, Lincoln, Bishop's Lynne, York, and Shrewsbury.[36] If such devoirs did not bring the wives with sorrow to their grave, they were hardly soothing auspices for the beginning of a lonely journey.

Happily, few widows had to confront such dramatic challenges. More common, no doubt, were the obvious practical problems of a world in which death came routinely to young and old. In the administrative proceedings that produced Inquisitions Post Mortem we often run across the likes of such prosaic, if chilling, statements regarding a widow's future and its burdens, as, "Joan, his wife, is pregnant," or "Beatrice, late his wife, was pregnant at the time of his death and still is."[37] If the widow of Richard Gambon was more fortunate, it is only by the smallest of margins: "He died on 25 September last; by Margaret, his wife, who survives him, he had issue Richard, aged one-quarter year, his next heir."[38] We know the response to disaster: one says he or she can cope, but *not yet*. It seems an apt thought when looking at these laconic summations of life situations, transmitted in the unreflective voice of the administrative record.

Nor was motherhood her only vulnerable side. Widowhood, as a life condition—even if not a permanent one—could leave her cruelly exposed. There was the Humberside widow who told of how she had been attacked:

> With force of arms, to wit, swords, bows, and arrows, [by local bullies who] broke the close and buildings . . . and there made an assault upon her . . . and beat, wounded, and ill-treated her, and took and carried off her goods and chattels.[39]

We get an inkling of why so many women remarried before his first anniversary mass had been sung. A widow in Cornwall had expected an escheator's inquiry to provide her with her property, on which her well-being clearly depended. Instead, a local gang showed up, "arrayed for war, [and] insulted and threatened Eurnus (the clerk) who was unable to hold the court . . . [and they] levied £8 in rent from the tenants and carried it off."[40] In each of these instances the widow at least had redress to law—and so we hear her story—but her ultimate fate is beyond our ken.

This patchwork quilt is offered at the end, not because its scraps are necessarily more typical than the tales of reintegrated and independent widows who dominated the worlds of brewing, silk weaving, and small credit finance. Rather, it is because these scraps are a counterweight to the success stories, with their soothing moral lessons. The idea that the fifteenth-century was a golden age for widows is an attractive one, today well buttressed by a weighty edifice of scholarly research.[41] But it is equally possible that the brightest portraits in the gallery—the ones before which we are inclined to linger—only show the privileged few, the attractive "others" who stand out in the crowd. Only the luckiest, the richest, and the hardiest, stepping forward from the ranks of a population of widows who were severely controlled by mutable life circumstances and callous and unreflecting sexism, sat for their picture.

Widows, in aggregate, came in legions, of whom only a few were called, and widowhood, even for the high and mighty, was not a guarantee against the sooner-or-later turn of fortune's wheel. Note the final plaint of the twice-widowed queen mother, Elizabeth Wydeville, a pathetic and badly abused old woman: "I have no worldly goods to do the queen's grace."[42] That some widows got back into stride, and even moved forward, as judged by the criteria of personal as of social and economic mobility, should not turn us away from a moment of sympathy for all widows—a reserve army of women suddenly on their own—who had to deal with what must have been a serious, if not always an irreparable break, in their life line.[43]

NOTES

My thanks to Caroline M. Barron, Anne Sutton, and the participants of the "London Widows Workshop," held at the Institute of Historical Research, Oct. 1990. I have been encouraged and advised, step by step, by Sue Sheridan Walker, and I owe a debt to the anonymous readers of the University of Michigan Press. To the comments my colleagues in this volume make about the leadership and support we have received from Michael Sheehan, over the years, I can only add my wholehearted endorsement.

1. Frederick Pollock and Frederic W. Maitland, *The History of English Law*, 2d ed., intro., S. F. C. Milsom (Cambridge, 1968), 2:428.

2. Louise Mirrer, ed., *Widows in the Literature and Histories of Medieval Europe* (Ann Arbor, 1992), for a recent gathering of materials on this subject, with references and introductory material to steer the reader. Also see B. A. Holderness, "Widows in Pre-Industrial Society: An Essay upon their Economic Functions," in *Land, Kinship and the Life Cycle*, ed. R. M. Smith (Cambridge, 1984), 428; Peter Franklen, "Peasant Widows, 'Liberation' and Remarriage after the Black Death," *Economic History Review*, 2d ser., 39 (1986): 186–204; Barbara J. Todd, "The Remarrying Widow: A Stereotype Reconsidered," in *Women in English Society, 1500–1800*, ed. Mary Prior (London, 1985), 54–92; Rowena E. Archer, "Rich Old Ladies: The Problem of Late Medieval Dowagers," in *Property and Politics: Essays in Later Medieval English History*, ed. Tony Pollard (Gloucester, 1984), 15–35.

3. Although my approach is not that of law and legal history, such an approach should be part of the foundations of any such essay. A thorough survey of work on women, wives, and widows that moves outward from legal history is Janet Senderowitz Loengard, " 'Legal History and the Medieval Englishwoman' Revisited: Some New Directions," in *Medieval Women and the Sources of Medieval History*, ed. Joel T. Rosenthal (Athens, Ga., and London, 1990), 210–36.

4. Where I refer to aristocratic widows but give no specific citation, the material has been lifted from some previous studies that I have published: "Aristocratic Widows in Fifteenth-Century England," in *Women and the Structure of Society*, ed. Barbara J. Harris and Joann K. McNamara (Durham, N.C., 1984), 36–47, 259–60; "Other Victims: Peeresses as War Widows, 1450–1500," *History* 72 (1987): 213–30; *Patriarchy and Families of Privilege in Fifteenth-Century England* (Philadelphia, 1991), 175–256. Biographical material on the peeresses is extracted from *The Complete Peerage*, ed. Vicary Gibbs et al., 12 vols. (London, 1910–59).

5. Eileen Power, *Medieval English Nunneries* (Cambridge, 1922), 38. The essay by Barbara Hanawalt published in the present volume gives a valuable, detailed analysis of a particular group of women, and the material cited in n. 2 offers further details.

6. Reginald R. Sharpe, ed., *Calendar of the Letter-Books of the City of London* (London, 1909), 1:24. Such examples run throughout the *Letter-Books:* I:39, "John Yonge, fishmonger, who married the widow of Edmund Olyver, 'stokefisshmonger'"; or I:49, "guardianship . . . [of] William, son of Thomas Reygate, late chandler, together with his patrimony, committed . . . to John atte Lee, chandler, who married Matilda, the orphan's mother."

7. Richard G. Davies, "Lollardy and Locality," *Transactions of the Royal Historical Society,* 6th ser., 1 (1991): 196. Such behavior is found "only amongst the core members," which reflects on both in-group purity and the common sense of the members. Davies also cites arranged marriages, between adults who had never met, among Lollards. This is probably common behavior within cults and sects, especially those under the threat of persecution.

8. James Raine and James Raine, Jr., eds., *Testamenta Eboracensia,* i–iv (Surtees Society, vols. 4, 30, 45, 53 [1836–69]) 4:149–54 (hereafter TE).

9. For Cicely, see *A Collection of Ordinances and Regulations for the Governing of the Royal Household,* Society of Antiquaries (London, 1790); and C. A. J. Armstrong, "The Piety of Cicely, Duchess of York: A Study in Late Mediaeval Culture," in *For Hilaire Belloc: Essays in Honour of his 72nd Birthday,* ed. Douglass Woodruff (London, 1942), 73–94; for Alice, see Vincent B. Redstone and Marian K. Dale, *The Household Book of Alice de Bryene,* Suffolk Institute of Archaeology and Natural History (1931). The two dowagers, and their households, are discussed in Rosenthal, *Patriarchy,* 232–46.

10. E. A. Goodman tells me that in the *All Souls Formulary* there are numerous references to Henry IV coming under pressure from his Bohun in-laws.

11. Howard L. Gray, "Incomes from Land in England in 1436," *English Historical Review* 49 (1934): 607–39. Virtually any detailed study of a family of property reinforces these points about the ubiquity and longevity of widows holding a dowager's share: see, e.g., Carole Rawcliffe, *The Staffords, Earls of Stafford and Dukes of Buckingham, 1395–1521* (Cambridge, 1978).

12. Margery K. McIntosh, *Autonomy and Community: The Royal Manor of Havering, 1200–1500* (Cambridge, 1986), 170–76; for a sober assessment of widows in rural society, mostly in the late thirteenth and early fourteenth centuries, see Judith M. Bennett, *Women in the Medieval English Countryside: Gender and Household in Brigstock before the Plague* (Oxford, 1987), esp. 142–76.

13. Charles Phythian-Adams, *Desolation of a City: Coventry and the Urban Crisis of the Late Middle Ages* (Cambridge, 1979), 91; see 155 for a discussion of residential patterns that seem to uncover "elderly mothers . . . residing close to their offspring." There is a useful summary of some recent literature on families, women, and town life in Maryanne Kowaleski, "The History of Urban Families in Medieval England," *Journal of Medieval History* 14 (1988): 47–63.

14. William C. Jordan, "Women and Credit in the Middle Ages: Problems and Directions," *Journal of European Economic History* 17 (1988): 33–62; the

essays by Kay Ryerson, Maryanne Kowaleski, and Martha Howell, in *Women and Work in Pre-Industrial Europe,* ed. Barbara A. Hanawalt (Bloomington, 1986), fill in many gaps in the puzzle; Martha C. Howell, *Women, Production, and Patriarchy in Late Medieval Cities* (Chicago, 1986), with much material on German cities.

15. Phythian-Adams, *Desolation of a City,* 202; David Herlihy, *Opus Muliebria* (New York, 1990), 171: Saint Lidwina responded to a widow's questions about withdrawing from society by saying "I do not recommend idleness, for you know the art of making wool." For women in the silk industry in London—a small but high visibility industry, staffed and run almost totally by women—see Marian K. Dale, "London Silkwomen of the Fifteenth-Century," *Signs* 14 (1989): 489–503 (reprinted from the *Economic History Review* [1933]).

16. E. F. Jacob, ed., *The Register of Henry Chichele, Archbishop of Canterbury, 1414–1443* (Oxford, 1938), 2:161.

17. Public Record Office, Wills of the Prerogative Court of Canterbury (hereafter PCC), 2 Logge.

18. Eileen Power, *Nunneries,* 39: "Was she [Lady Clinton] to submit to the rule of Prioress Agnes of Alesbury, she without whose goodwill Prioress Agnes had never been appointed? Was she to listen meekly to chiding in the dorter, and in the frater to bear with sulks? Impossible." See Ann K. Warren, *Anchorites and Their Patrons in Medieval England* (Berkeley and Los Angeles, 1985), 27–29, for a description of the process whereby a woman took these vows.

19. Warren, *Anchorites,* 169, for an account of a widow in the world for thirteen years after his death who then became a recluse when her children were grown and on their own.

20. Jacob, *Chichele's Register,* 4:221. Robin L. Storey, ed., *The Register of Thomas Langley, Bishop of Durham, 1406–37,* 6 vols., Surtees Society, vol.1 (1956–70), 190, "promytte to lyve in chastite sool with oute compaygne of man terme of my life." Mary Erler of Fordham University is making a full study of widows and vows of chastity in late medieval England, though she is starting with early Church examples and injunctions that proved influential and moving to the incidence of such women, or such behavior, in the fifteenth century.

21. PCC, 28 Godyn. This was a common injunction, sometimes with the corollary or harsh other side: "if that she kepe soole unemarreid, and if she marrye and taike any man to husband after my disceace, that then she to have bot only the theirde parte of the forsaid landes and tennements" (J. W. Clay, ed. *North Country Wills,* Surtees Society, vol. 116 [1908], 4). These injunctions are discussed, as a generic set of conditions, by Ann J. Kettle, " 'My Wife Shall Have It': Marriage and Property in the Wills and Testaments of Later Mediaeval England," in *Marriage and Property,* ed. Elizabeth M. Craik (Aberdeen, 1984), 89–103.

22. Charlotte F. Otten, ed., *English Women's Voices, 1540–1700* (Miami,

1992), 173–273, which covers "Women Taking Charge of Health Care" and "Women Describing Childbirth, Sickness, and Death."

23. R. N. Swanson, *A Calendar of the Register of Richard Scrope, Archbishop of York, 1398–1405,* 2 vols., University of York, Borthwick Institute of Historical Research, Texts and Calendars: Records of the Northern Province, 8 and 11 (1981–85), 1:42 and 2:32; see 2:31, for John Jankyn's will, probated 29 April 1404; and 1:93, for his widow Alice's vow of chastity, April 1404 (printed, *TE,* 3:318).

24. *Calendar of the Papal Letters, 1396–1404,* 536; see Warren, *Anchoresses,* 182, citing another such instance: she took the vow, "in her first fervour of sorrow, which soon wore off, so that the widow grew weary of confinement." Mary Erler has found some interesting variations of vowed behavior, including instances of husband-wife vows that involved remaining together as well as separating.

25. Norman Davis, ed., *The Paston Letters and Papers of the Fifteenth Century,* 2 vols. (Oxford, 1971–76), 2:676: John Russe tells John Paston of a fight in the Channel, and he reports that "there is slayn of thys partyez the Lordys Clynton and Dakyr and many jentilmen, Ince, and othyr, the noumbre of iiij m." However, neither Clinton nor Dacre were killed. William, fifth Lord Clinton (1410–64) was married to Margaret St. Leger, who survived him, married twice again, and died in 1496. Richard Fiennes, summoned as Lord Dacre by virtue of his marriage to the Dacre heiress, lived until 1483. His wife had been born ca. 1430, and he presumably was not younger than she. She outlived him and died in 1486. We do not know if Clinton's wife was an ultimate widow.

26. Eileen Power, trans., *The Goodman of Paris* (London, 1928), 42. By way of comparison, Owst cites Bromyard's tale of a "certain noble widow [who] . . . is said to have repulsed all the suitors who begged her to marry them with the words, 'I want no more husbands, for, if I had a good one, as the other was, I should be afraid of losing him as I lost the other; and if he were bad, it would be an annoyance for me to live with him'" (G. R. Owst, *Literature and Pulpit in Medieval England* [Oxford, 1966], 379).

27. Kings who lost their wives provide us with some examples of extravagant grief, acted out before the usual vast audience. For Edward I, on the death of Eleanor of Castile, see Joan Evans, *English Art, 1307–1461* (Oxford, 1949), 1–5: "my harp is tuned to mourning," as the king supposedly said. For Richard II and the death of Anne of Bohemia, see Anthony Steel, *Richard II* (Cambridge, 1941), 203–4, 213–14.

28. Along with the data provided in Barbara Hanawalt's chapter, in this collection, see S. J. Payling, *Political Society in Lancastrian England: The Greater Gentry of Nottinghamshire* (Oxford, 1991), 56: "the frequency with which wives survived their husbands: of the twenty-one heads of families of the Nottinghamshire elite who died during the Lancastrian period, as many as fourteen

definitely left a widow . . . the second [factor against the male heir] was the long life expectancy of these widows."

29. On the casualties of the wars, see Anthony Goodman, *The Wars of the Roses: Military Activity and English Society* (London, 1981), 208–10. The Paston letter, quoted in n. 25, was quite willing to pass along a death toll of four thousand, presumably as another aspect of the false or exaggerated news it was transmitting.

30. For weltenschauung literature, see Johan Huizinga, *The Waning of the Middle Ages* (Harmondsworth, 1955); Philippe Aries, *The Hour of Our Death,* trans. Helen Weaver (New York, 1981); T. S. R. Boase, *Death in the Middle Ages: Mortality, Judgment, and Remembrance* (London, 1972); Joachim Wheley, ed., *Mirrors of Mortality: Studies in the Social History of Death* (New York, 1981).

31. Storey, *Langley's Register,* 3:691.

32. J. W. Clay, ed., *North Country Wills,* Surtees Society, vol. 116 (1908), 54.

33. Lady Wenlock asked for burial by "my last husband," Sir John Frey, rather than with the most distinguished member of the group: a priest was instructed to pray for all three of "my husbands" (PCC, 34 Wattys). See Warren, *Anchoresses,* 254, for the tale of Jane, Viscountess Lisle, a peeress only by virtue of her third marriage and choosing instead to lie beside her second husband.

34. Davis, *Paston Letters,* 2:281: the will is dated 4 Feb. 1482. She left elaborate instructions for the stone; though both Paston and Mautby arms were to be engraved, "in the myddys of the seid stoon I wull have a scochen sett of Mawtebysamres allone."

35. Clay, *North Country Wills,* 55–56; see 54–55 (for the will of Elizabeth, Lady Welles, whose husband also had predeceased her by a year or two); see 65 for the Sotehill will.

36. For Hotspur, see *Calendar of the Close Rolls, 1402–5,* 202. On his first burial, see Charles L. Kingsford, *English Historical Literature in the Fifteenth Century* (Oxford, 1913), quoting from "A Northern Chronicle:" "et prefatum Henricum de Percy postquam sepultus fuerat apud Whitchurche, Rex fecit extrahi de sepulchro, et quatuor corporis sui quarteria misit ad diversa loca, et capud eius fecit suspendi super portam borealem apud Ebor." The widow, hardly the flirtatious young thing of Shakespeare's *Henry IV,* pt. 1, had been married to Percy for at least twenty-four years, and she overcame her grief to remarry Lord Camoys before her own death in 1417. On Bardolf, see *Calendar of the Close Rolls, 1405–9,* 323: "to deliver to her [the widow] for burial, or for her attorney . . . one quarter of her husband's body, lately set up over the city gate."

37. *Calendar of Inquisitions Post Mortem,* 18 (1–6 Henry IV) (hereafter *CIPM*), 128; *CIPM,* 15 (1–7 Richard II), 766. Such instances are not hard to come by: *CIPM,* 17, 96: "The said Margaret, his wife, is pregnant by him";

428: When he died, "the said Joan was pregnant at the time of her husband's death and near to the birth of a daughter"; 491: "Elizabeth his wife is pregnant, and if the child is born it is his heir"; *CIPM,* 18, 408: "Joan his wife is pregnant. Failing Joan's child, Isabel, daughter of Maurice Berkeley, aunt of Maurice, would be heir, aged 50 years and more."

38. *CIPM,* 18, 117. Also, *CIPM,* 17, 25, "aged one-half years"; no. 1079, "Aged a quarter of a year and more . . . [and] his heir"; no. 1283, the heir was either 43 weeks or 47 weeks or one year; *CIPM,* 18, 104: 32 weeks, or 33, or 34, or 35, or 27 weeks.

39. Isobel D. Thornley and T. F. T. Plucknett, eds., *Year Books of Richard II: 11 Richard II, 1387–88,* Ames Foundation (1937), 218–19.

40. *CIPM,* 18, 13–14.

41. Caroline M. Barron, "The 'Golden Age' of Women in Medieval England," *Reading Medieval Studies* 15 (1989): 35–58; this is an excellent study, only singled out here to illustrate the dangers of leaping while we are looking. In Mary Erler and Maryanne Kowaleski, eds., *Women and Power in the Middle Ages* (Athens, Ga., 1988), 276, the index entry for widows reads, "Widowhood: power enhanced due to." For the other side of the coin, the life of Christine de Pisan offers a cautionary tale, whatever her eventual triumphs. It is recounted, with balance, in Charity Cannon Willard, "A Fifteenth-Century View of Women's Role in Medieval Society: Christine de Pisan's *Livre des Trois Vertus,*" in *The Role of Women in the Middle Ages,* ed. Rosemarie Thee Morewedge (Albany, 1975), 90–120.

42. Agnes Strickland, *Lives of the Queens of England* (London, 1905), 3:377.

43. Once we get to the early modern period our ability to identify and analyze the voice of women improves dramatically. See Ralph Houlbrooke, ed., *English Family Life, 1576–1716: An Anthology from Diaries* (Oxford, 1988); and Miriam Slater, *Family Life in the Seventeenth Century: The Verneys of Clayden House* (London, 1984), 78–107. For a recent study of a fifteenth-century widow who was a successful integrator of a family life that ultimately included three husbands and children from different marriages, see Kristine G. Bradberry, "The World of Etheldreda Gardener," *Ricardian* 9, no. 115 (Dec., 1991): 146–53.

Chapter 3

Rationabilis Dos: Magna Carta and the Widow's "Fair Share" in the Earlier Thirteenth Century

Janet Senderowitz Loengard

If a thirteenth-century Englishwoman found herself in court just once in her life, it was very likely because she had been widowed and was asking her late husband's heir or his lord, or even a third party to whom her husband had conveyed property, for what she considered her rightful dower. In principle, of course, the lawsuits should not have been necessary. Taking possession of one's dower theoretically required no legal action; a woman could simply enter into specifically nominated lands if they were vacant, remaining on them with the consent of the heir. When dower was to be a third of the late husband's holdings, the heir was to assign the widow property to the appropriate value. There were doubtless many widows who entered peaceably into their acres and many heirs who yielded widows their thirds quickly and willingly. They have left no records. Others seem to have been party to actions that look as if they were brought simply to protect against future claims by recording the nonheritable nature of the widow's interest; they often ended in fines. But hundreds—thousands—of women were not so fortunate. When they appeared to demand their dower, in their warrantor's court or in the county or before the justices itinerant or at Westminster, they could expect a vigorous attempt to delay or pare down their claims or deny them altogether. The results are spread across the records of the king's courts, with which this chapter is concerned.[1]

It is not surprising that the action should have been so common. For one thing, it was being used for purposes that the creators of the writ of right of dower probably did not envisage. Establishing—or disproving— a dower right was one means of testing conflicting claims to land among litigants not primarily concerned with the widow's life interest, a method of challenging the legitimacy of one who claimed to be an heir, or simply a way of making an indisputable record of rights in land that could be relied on at some future time.[2] But beyond that it was a theoretical anomaly in a system of landholding based on primogeniture and preference of the male for collateral inheritance, as much of England's was by the end of the twelfth century.[3] It meant that holdings carefully concentrated in one man would be divided at least for the life of his mother—or stepmother or sister-in-law or even more distant relative—and it meant that a woman's claim would take precedence over a man's rights as purchaser or heir. In short, dower turned the accepted conventions and the rules based on them inside out. Moreover, the institution did not only contravene theoretical principles; in practice, its economic consequences were significant. Land could leave a family's control for half a century or more, if a teenage widow carried her dower into a second marriage, and there was always the possibility that it would not be recovered.

Balanced against all that—and balanced rather precariously—were the interests of the bride and her family. Dower was the medieval woman's insurance policy; what father would permit his daughter to marry without providing her with some security in the event of widowhood? Fathers bargained, drafted charters, and caused witnesses to be present at weddings in an attempt to protect their daughters' futures. Their prudence was justified. Later in this volume Sue Sheridan Walker discusses stakes and strategies involved in the numerous dower cases in the royal courts in the later thirteenth and early fourteenth centuries, while Barbara Hanawalt shows how dower affected the position of urban wives and widows. At the beginning of the thirteenth century the right to dower depended on so many variables. It required, of course, both a valid marriage and the subsequent death of the husband, the first always capable of being litigated and the second particularly so in an age of crusades and overseas wars. It was available only to free women whose free husbands had been "seised" in demesne of a free tenement at the time of marriage, all points open to exception.[4] A bridegroom could announce what his bride and prospective widow's holdings were to be rather than granting a percentage of his property, but, if the land so nominated turned out to be more than the permissible fraction of his holdings, his heir could sue for admeasurement to bring the widow's share down to that fraction—a third when lands were held in military tenure, a half in socage.[5] A woman indisputably entitled to dower might find herself obliged to pay a crippling sum to her late husband's lord in order to be allowed to enter onto it. Being a doweress also could seriously circumscribe her freedom of action: if she married without the permission of her warrantor, she lost the dower.[6] And, worst of all, threat of forfeiture was used by lords, from the king down, to compel remarriage of unwilling widows.[7] A woman who lost her husband might well feel discouraged. The provisions for her protection must sometimes have seemed insubstantial, insufficient, and ineffective as they stood.

But they did not stand still. Some important changes came only in the second half of the thirteenth century and cannot be discussed here, among them expansion of the widow's ability to use the writ of dower *unde nihil habet* (in the Statute of Westminster I, c. 49); her protection (in the Statute of Westminster II, c. 4), against collusive suits designed to foreclose her dower rights; and—a reminder that all widows were not blameless—the protection of the heir (in the Statute of Gloucester, c. 7), by a grant to him of a writ of entry if a doweress attempted to convey more than her life interest. But other changes, or the beginnings of others, are found in an earlier period, the years between the late twelfth century, when *Glanvill* was written, and 1236, when the Statute of Merton included the first legislated remedy for widows wrongfully deforced of dower or quarantine. Some of these innovations seem to have come about through usage ratified by court decisions or, indeed, primarily through judicial decisions; they are reflected in the rolls without comment, and when Bracton speaks of them they are already settled law. Other alterations have less to do with legal theory than with the political events that crowded the first third of the century; they are a reaction to the behavior of King John, to the unrest that followed John's death, and to the minority of Henry III. In fact, as the pipe rolls make clear, their roots can be traced beyond that, back to the reigns of John's brother and father, back through the second half of the twelfth century. Magna Carta itself was such a reaction to all three Angevin kings, and Magna Carta touched repeatedly on dower, even if not always clearly and unambiguously, in provisions that varied through the Charter's several reissues.

Two developments concerning dower will be examined here. There has been debate about the Charter's influence on the first, which lay in attempts to alter the widow's claim by ending the role of the wedding day as sole determinant of what property would be subject to her share. The second, mandated by Magna Carta chapters 7 and 8, both relieved widows of payments for dower and secured for them freedom from unwanted marriages, thereby giving them, at least in theory, a control of their own lives unknown to other women. It is worth looking at each point in some detail, to gain some sense of thought about widows in the earlier thirteenth century and to understand the course that dower took during that period.

A wide-reaching alteration of common law dower in the thirteenth century lay in the amendment of the class of property subject to the widow's share. Eventually, of course, lands and tenements acquired by the husband at any time during the marriage were included for the computation of dower. But before that was settled there seem to have been sporadic, rather isolated, and ultimately unsuccessful moves to base the widow's "third" on only that property held by her husband on the day he died, rather than on that of which he had been seised on the day of his marriage—the rule at common law at least as far back as *Glanvill*.[8] Such efforts could have had both theoretical and practical bases. Since, again at least from the time of *Glanvill*, husbands had been able to specify that future acquisitions should be included for computation of the third,[9] it may have seemed only logical for heirs and courts to use the day of a husband's death, the final date when acquisition was possible, as the date for computing his widow's share in all cases. Even more logically, dower may have mimicked the *legitim* that a widow could claim, the right to one-third of a deceased husband's movable goods. Since the *legitim* referred to chattels held at the time of the husband's death, would that not provide an impetus for using the same date to measure the same widow's dower rights?[10] And would not the rationale be even stronger, in the eyes of many heirs and perhaps some judges, if the widow's dower third was not ordinarily subject to her husband's debts?[11] Nor would judges or heirs have to look far to find precedents supporting such a position: various borough customs both in the thirteenth and later centuries allowed dower only on land of which the husband had been seised when he died.[12] Finally, and very practically, a fractional share based only on holdings at death would end or at least greatly reduce dower's effect as a clog on alienation. There need be no more concern over a wife's consent to a grant, no more awkward arrangements needed to rearrange holdings for a generation when it had not been obtained.

Magna Carta was involved in the efforts to alter dower rights, possibly as the product of such thinking and less possibly even as a reaction to it. Chapter 7, as the Charter was issued in 1215, says simply that a widow shall pay nothing for her dower, which is to be assigned to her within forty days of her husband's death. But the reissues of 1217 and 1225 expand the chapter to deal with other aspects of a widow's welfare: if her husband's house is in fact a castle, a suitable home is to be found for her; she is to have "estovers," and so on. There is a further provision about dower: "Let there be assigned to her [the widow] for her dower a third part of all the land of her husband which was his in his life, unless she was endowed of less at the church door."[13] That language, clear as it appears on first reading, is susceptible to more than one interpretation. Apparently, no one ever argued for the most literal meaning: that any land ever held by the husband was subject to dower even if it had been alienated before his marriage. But there are still two alternatives: Did the section mean "the land which was the husband's at any time during his marriage" or "the land which was his on the day he was last alive"?

Early in this century William McKechnie declared flatly that the latter was the true construction, that the intent was indeed that the widow should take only a third of the property of which the husband "died seised." Late medieval lawyers, he said, had distorted the provision: "Lawyers of a later age have, by a strained construction of the words *in vita sua,* made them an absolute protection to a widow against all attempts to lessen her dower by alienations granted without her consent during the marriage. Magna Carta contains no warrant for such a proposition."[14] In other words, a "day of death" measuring date was to be substituted for one based on the "day of marriage." The change could produce dramatic results. It could favor the widow if the day of marriage standard meant dower only in lands the bridegroom then held, because many young men held less when they married than they would later in life. But it also opened the possibility of loss of all dower. There is no evidence that using the day of death as a measuring date was intended to limit dower to property held continuously by a husband from his wedding day until he died, but, even granted that the "died seised" test took into account after-acquired property, what was to keep a husband from alienating his land in his old age—perhaps to his heir, perhaps for his soul's health—and thereby leaving little or nothing of which his widow could claim a third? And how much greater the risk to a second wife who married an already mature landowner and who was not the mother of his heir!

Can Magna Carta have contemplated and tacitly endorsed that possibility? Did its drafters thereby mean to widen the already existing gap between the certainty and protection afforded by nominated dower, which by the terms of chapter 7 would not be affected, and that of the third, offering widows the choice of modest security or a grand gamble?[15] It seems unlikely, if only because chapter 7 was clearly intended for the protection of widows; it was not designed to benefit heirs—as were the provisions on relief in chapters 1 and 2, for example— or even purchasers. Moreover, McKechnie's interpretation means that the men who drafted the Charter chose remarkably ambiguous terminology for an alteration of rights that would sooner or later affect almost every family in England.

Frederic Maitland, writing not long before McKechnie, saw a different impetus for the new wording. He wrote that the Charter's language might be a layman's reaction to royal justices who, at least partially in the interest of making land more alienable, favored giving a widow no more than a right to a third of what actually descended to the heir; as Maitland put it, why should a wife be better treated than a son?[16] In his view chapter 7 could have been aimed at such thinking; not only was the wife to be better treated than the judges would have proposed; she was also to be better treated than past custom had provided. Both the day of marriage and the day of a husband's death were to lose their determinative function, and a husband's seisin at any time during a marriage was to be enough to support dower. The problem is that there is little evidence of pre-1217 efforts by royal justices to put their theory, if they held it, into practice. There is a case from 1204 in which one Ida, widow of Osbert, asked dower of "that of which he was seised on the day he married her and the day he died," but there was no discussion of her choice of wording. She may, of course, have been responding to a requirement that property be held on both dates to be subject to dower, but that is unlikely, since such a test is not mentioned in *Glanvill* or found in any other case at the turn of the century. It is more likely that she was simply emphasizing the strength of her position.[17] Even earlier than that there is a Pipe Roll entry that Beatrix Fossard owed the king ten marks for her rightful dower of the land that her husband held on the day he died; the entry is identified as coming from Yorkshire, and there is no further explanation.[18] Granted that there may be other cases, there still do not seem to have been enough instances to cause widespread alarm on the part of England's greater landholders.

There is another possible explanation for the provision. It is not necessary to set up sharp alternative meanings based on theories about alien-ability and inheritance, in order to understand what was being said in chapter 7. The men who put together Magna Carta may not have intended drastic alterations to existing arrangements so much as their safeguarding. Given then current endowment practices, they may well have meant only to institutionalize what they regarded as the behavior already followed by decent men: the explicit inclusion in the church door endowment of one-third of all lands and tenements that might be acquired after marriage. Even less dramatically, they may simply have been restating that practice, well enough known that it did not need to be spelled out in detail.

All that said, there is evidence that, for whatever reason, at least some lay people—and maybe some justices—did think in terms of the day of death as an appropriate measuring standard *after* Magna Carta, perhaps interpreting the language of chapter 7 to justify it. The evidence is very slight; there are not many examples, fact situations are usually not clear, and language is cryptic. But a number of entries mention a husband's seisin at his death, sometimes as a point of litigation, even more often as the basis for agreement—suggesting that its use represents not a widow's legal rights so much as her bargaining position and/or her relationship with her warrantor. There is a concord between a mother and her son or stepson in 1225,[19] another in 1230,[20] a third in 1234,[21] and a fourth in 1235.[22] There is a jurors' cryptic finding in the Yorkshire eyre of 1219,[23] a 1233 case in which the parties agreed that the late husband died seised of land from which dower was claimed but differed about whether he held it in fee,[24] a 1234 suit in which the defendant agreed that the husband had died seised of land underlying a dower claim but asserted that his widow had already received her dower,[25] and an instruction to a sheriff in 1225.[26] There are three entries in point in Easter term of 1227, two of them recording settlements. In each of those a defendant acknowledged the widow's right to dower and granted her a third part of the lands and tenements of which her husband "died seised" or "of which he was seised on the day he died."[27] In the third case from the same roll the record showed that a husband had recovered land held in socage shortly before his death, and the justices ordered the sheriff to give the widow seisin of "half the land of which Richard her husband had died seised as of fee"; the problem is, of course, that the justices may simply have been thinking in terms of the rule that there could be no dower in land lost by judgment rather than refusing to use

the wedding day as a measuring date.[28] The most interesting case comes
from the rolls of the Justices Itinerant in 1228. Isabella, widow of Robert
de Vere, asked William and Cecilia Blund for two carucates and a messuage, except for thirteen acres, as dower with which she had been
endowed on her wedding day. They replied that she already had dower
of all the land of which her husband had died seised and the other two
parts of that land by a fine, which she made with the king for custody
of her son. Isabella explained that she held *all* the land in custody and
nothing in dower and that she had been specifically endowed of the
carucates and messuage as *dos nominata*. By law, as she and the Blunds
well knew, a husband's later alienation of land that had been specifically
nominated as dower did not foreclose the widow's claim to it. They
responded that she had not been so endowed; her dower was a third of
the land her husband held. Essentially, they were saying that Isabella's
share was indeed a third of the lands for which she had made a fine with
the king—that is, one-third of those of which her late husband had been
seised at his death.[29] William and Cecilia Blund may or may not have
believed that Magna Carta supported their position—it is not mentioned—but they no doubt would have welcomed the reading of the
Charter for which McKechnie argued.

Even assuming that there were many times more than the number of
cases here cited, they are a tiny minority. The fact is that, whatever the
intent of the drafters of Magna Carta, on one hand, whatever the theore-
ticians—or heirs or purchasers or judges or sometimes even widows—
might have preferred, on the other, there was no decisive change in
dower either in 1217 or in 1225. As Maitland concluded, even from the
few cases on the point in *Bracton's Note Book,* the Charter did not in
the short run change the rule that, without a specific provision to the
contrary, it was the lands held by a husband on the day of his marriage
that were subject to dower, whether or not they were later alienated.[30]
In the 1220s and 1230s doweresses and their opponents by the score
continued to assert or deny husbands' wedding-day seisin, irrelevant if
the only significant date were that of death. They did not mention the
husband's death. Over and over again widows produced witnesses, or
jurors were called, and over and over they spoke of the situation at the
beginning of a marriage or over the years of its duration, not at its end.[31]

As for judicial attempts to change the common law rule, the one clear
attempt I have seen by a doweress to use seisin of land at her husband's
death as the sole determinant of dower rights was firmly squelched by a

court itself. In 1222 Isabella and Roger de Cressy had asked for a third of the vill of Hanton as Isabella's dower "whereof Geoffrey de Chester, her former husband, was seised after he married her and died seised, and that land ought to fall to [descendere] Isabella in dower after Geoffrey her husband's death." The tenant, Matilda de Lacy, pointed out that Isabella and Roger did not say that Geoffrey had endowed Isabella with the vill on the day he married her nor produce suit to that effect; that is, they had not effectively claimed nominated dower. The court ruled that, because they did not say so, Matilda went *sine die,* excused from further appearance in court, with the matter dismissed. Roger, on the other hand, was fined, presumably for bringing a groundless claim on behalf of himself and his wife.[32] It is hard to imagine a clearer rejection of the literal language of the 1217 version of Magna Carta chapter 7, however that is interpreted. The attempt was apparently not repeated—at least, I have seen no other such case in the plea rolls for the period here discussed—and the court's position seems to have reflected common understanding. Clearly, the older test was in a tenant's mind when in 1225 a widow asked for a messuage and he responded that he had bought half of it from her husband before her husband married her and the other half afterward, and "of that half which he bought afterwards he concedes her a third part."[33]

It is accurate, if not very helpful, to characterize the period immediately following Magna Carta as one of transition. Perhaps it is also accurate to characterize as in transition the idea that the end of a marriage was a significant date for dower. Whether or not based on an unarticulated interpretation of Magna Carta, the idea hovered in men's minds, as its appearance in fines bears witness. At the least, a husband's seisin of lands when he died conferred additional certainty, strengthening his wife's claim. That attitude may lie behind the Statute of Merton provision concerning damages for widows deforced of dower under certain circumstances. Chapter 1 of the statute is aimed at those who deforce widows of their dowers "of the lands whereof their husbands died seised, which the same widows shall recover by plea," and it assesses damages equal to the value of the dower for the period from the husband's death to the recovery of seisin as well as making the deforcer liable to amercement at the king's pleasure.[34] The statute does not, however, inhibit or prevent recovery of dower in lands held by a husband on his wedding day but later alienated; it can be argued that the provision is simply concerned with worst-case scenarios, those in which the husband's seisin after his marriage could not be disputed and in which the withholder of dower was seen to have had no colorable reason for his refusal to render it.

Certainly, that seems to have been the way the chapter was interpreted. Bracton, writing on dower sometime after the Statute of Merton—its provisions on the subject are cited several times—begins by explaining that rightful dower is the third part of all the lands and tenements a woman's husband held in demesne and in fee so that he could endow her on the day he married her. Returning to the subject some two hundred folios later, the treatise discusses the many exceptions to a dower claim. One such is that a husband never held seisin of the land or tenement at any time during his marriage, whether on the wedding day or thereafter. But there is no mention of an exception based on a husband's failure to continue in seisin until his death, except if he had lost the holding by judgment or in some instances by court-approved concord.[35]

Tracing the progress of dower during the second half of the thirteenth century is beyond the scope of this chapter, but the wider protection suggested by the literal language of Magna Carta had come into being by the time of *Britton,* if that treatise reflects practice: a widow who "complains by the common writ of dower close and demands her reasonable dower . . . shall recover the third part of all the tenements which her husband held in demesne and in fee as his own right on the day of his marriage with her, and also of all such tenements as were his after he married her."[36] Moreover, the actual wording of the Statute of Merton seems to have been ignored; if a widow proved that she had been wrongfully delayed in obtaining that dower, she was to recover damages—presumably based on the value of all of it, since no qualifying language is added. And by 1311 it was simply assumed even in the courts that Magna Carta had meant to convey the wider protection that then in fact existed: a *Year Book* report for that year remarks, in another context, that "on the other hand, the Great Charter wills that everyone have dower of the things of which the husband had the fee during the marriage . . . the Great Charter wills that a woman have dower of the things which her husband had in fee, and the common law likewise."[37] That issue was settled. There was one less hurdle for the doweress in her quest for her *rationabilis dos,* her fair share.

On another dower-related issue Magna Carta spoke unambiguously. Chapter 7 of the 1215 Charter laid down that a widow was to pay nothing for her dower: "A widow after the death of her husband shall at once and without difficulty have her marriage portion and inheritance, nor shall she give anything for her dower." Taken with the additional provision, in chapter 8, that a widow could not be compelled to re-marry—and so need not fine for freedom not to do so—the result would have been to lift a potentially crippling financial liability from women who thereafter lost their husbands.[38] Dower and the obligation to re-marry had very frequently been entwined; the Pipe Rolls of Henry II, Richard I, and John make clear the financial difficulties a new widow in the king's gift could face if she wished both to claim her *dos* and to remain without a husband.[39] One mark to be paid by a woman of modest means could have as significant an impact on her financial situation as the hundred pounds offered by the Countess Gundreda—wife succes-sively to Hugh Bigod, first Earl of Norfolk, and Roger de Glanvill, the justiciar's brother, and one of the richest women in England—had on hers.[40] Indeed, the result could be to leave a widow no satisfactory option: she could either accept an unwanted husband, lose her dower for refusal to remarry, or be obliged to give it up to obtain funds for the purchase of freedom from doing so.[41]

Judging from the pipe and plea rolls, Henry III's government honored the rules for women widowed after 1215. There may, of course, have been lapses. An incomplete 1221 plea roll entry from Cambridgeshire notes that in May of that year—described as "the fifth year of the earl Marshall," who was then *rector* of the realm—Nicholaa, widow of Wal-ter Daubernun, paid ten marks that she owed of the thirty "whereof she had made a fine with him [the earl Marshall] to have her dower."[42] If the earl Marshall was indeed acting as *rector,* he would appear to be in direct violation of Magna Carta, since he could not have made the fine in that capacity before the end of October 1216, a few days before the first reissue of the Charter.

One might also assume that after 1215 widows of an earlier vintage, or their heirs, would be relieved from the fines they had already made to secure dower or celibacy. Chapter 55 of the 1215 Magna Carta prom-ises that "all fines which were made with us unjustly and contrary to the law of the land, and all amercements imposed unjustly . . . shall be com-pletely remitted or else they shall be settled by the judgement of the twenty-five barons mentioned below." It is likely that the men who drafted the provision intended to include most, if not all, fines already made for dower, since chapter 37 of the Articles of the Barons mentions them specifically: "That fines which were made unjustly and against the law of the land for dower, maritagiums, inheritances, and amercements shall be altogether remitted."[43]

Certainly, chapter 7 supports the interpretation that not only outrageously large but *all* fines paid simply for possession of rightful dower were unjust and against the law of the land. But the provision on remission of fines disappeared from later reissues of the Charter, and, in fact, neither its presence nor its absence seems to have altered the pursuit of such fines already owed the king. The pipe rolls for the early years of Henry III include a number of those debts; none is under "New Oblations," and many appear to be payment by a son of an amount possibly long overdue for the dower of his dead mother—in other words, payment owed for a terminated dower interest in lands that would presumably now pass to the individual making the payment. Several entries refer explicitly to rolls of the reign of King John that set the original proffer.[44] Other listings simply set out the debt; possibly, some of them were not being paid, but they were not forgotten during the young king's minority. There is no attempt to hide or dissemble the effort at collection—there was, after all, no chapter 55 in any reissue of the Charter—and the attempts persisted, although rarely, until after the last issuance of Magna Carta during the reign, in 1225. The roll for 10 Henry III notes, for example, that the heirs of Amabilia de Limesey still owed £244.14s.10d and 3 palfreys, left over from Amabilia's fine made in the sixth year of King John that she not be distrained to marry. Alice Sorel owed 15 marks and a palfrey to have her dower. Robert de Tateshall owed 15 marks and a palfrey "for Ysand' de Baskervill, pro habend' dotem." Again, the entries are not shown under "New Oblations"; they are efforts at the collection of old debts.[45]

Magna Carta was, of course, intended to apply not only to the king but also to his barons. The provisions for assignment of dower free of payment and without respect of remarriage were badly needed,[46] but it is difficult to know how closely they were followed. Possibly, William the Marshall in his 1221 dealing with Nicholaa Daubernun was himself acting privately, as a great feudal lord. As such, he could have been simply collecting on an old debt from the reign of John, much as his own lord's government did. But, conceivably, the plea roll entry refers to a post-1215 fine—in violation of Magna Carta. It would have been a particularly brazen violation, but he would not have been alone: a few years earlier Alice, widow of Roger de Laston, had asked Philippa,

widow of Hugh de Laston, for her dower, and Philippa answered that
Alice had already gone to Roger's son, William, to ask her dower and
that "she gave the said William three marks so that he would assign her
reasonable dower to her without impediment and he by that fine assigned
her reasonable dower."[47] There were less direct ways of circumventing
chapter 7. Particularly before the sanctions imposed by the Statute of
Merton, what was to stop a lord from raising even the most nonsustain-
able objections to a dower claim by the widow of a former tenant, or
perhaps from simply dragging his feet in the matter? A widow in that
position might willingly agree to make a payment in return for assignment of the appropriate share. Enough feet of fines exist in dower matters at least to raise the possibility of such behavior—no more than the
possibility, because generally neither the relationship of the parties nor
the grounds for their dispute are specified.

One other protection for dower was granted in Magna Carta of 1215
and omitted in later drafts. Chapter 11 declared that a widow should
have her dower free of any share of repayment on debts owed to Jews
or others by the deceased. The provision specifying Jews was presumably
because the king himself received debts owed to dead Jews, so that the
creditor faced by a new widow might be the monarch himself. But in
either that instance or one in which the debt was owed to Christians, the
language of the 1215 provision meant that the burden of repayment
would fall in its entirety on the heir. It may have been from angry sons
and brothers who found themselves with a fraction of their inheritance
but burdened with the entirety of its debt that caused the language to be
omitted when the Charter was reissued.[48] Nonetheless, the provision
appears to have reflected widespread practice, and the thinking behind
it persisted.

Bracton declares that dower, once assigned, should be free; it should
not go to pay the debts of the late husband, which are the concern of the
heir.[49] A particularly complex case from 1230 both confirms that such
was accepted custom and shows the nature of heirs' objections. Matilda
de Colevill and her stepson, Roger, litigated about dower that she
claimed in three counties from no fewer than nine tenants, most of whom
called him to warranty. At the same time they may have been struggling,
in or out of court, over Matilda's share of her husband's movable goods;
in 1230 the custom of *legitim* was still strong, and the common law
courts had not yet entirely yielded to the Church control over succession
to chattels.[50] In Michaelmas term of 1230 the justices gave Roger and

Matilda a day later in the term to "take a chirograph [finalize a document of agreement] about a plea of dower," and the entry noting that also sets out the compromise reached on chattels. Roger conceded that all his father's debts were to be paid from his pooled chattels with the residue divided so that Matilda had a third part of them, the *legitim*. But Matilda found named pledges that she would "respond from her third part" to Christian creditors and those to whom debts were owed in cases in which the debts were clear, because she had a third of the chattels.[51] Roger was in effect saying that she would get her dower, free of her late husband's debts, but that she could not have both dower and a share of the chattels equal to his own. Apparently, certain debts, set aside from those paid out of the pooled chattels, were to be satisfied solely out of Matilda's share of the residue, and Roger needed her agreement to the arrangement because she was giving up a recognized right.[52]

Omission of the clause from later reissues of Magna Carta meant, however, that the widow's protection had a less certain foundation and could, if necessary, be limited. An entry in the Memoranda Roll for Trinity term 1230 suggests that a widow's dower was not to be distrained for the debts of her late husband when his heirs did have other lands against which the king could move: William de Munceaus, second husband of Matilda de Hastings, complained that a distraint had been made on lands that he held as the dower of his wife for debts of her first husband. The sheriff was ordered that, if so, William de Munceaus should be allowed to hold in peace and that the heirs of the late husband should be distrained by other lands.[53] I have not traced the point beyond 1236, but *Britton,* later in the century, remarks that in cases in which the heir could not pay a debt to the Crown or to another when the debt was acknowledged in the king's court, "then the hand must be extended to reach the dower."[54] An heir might suffer; the Crown, and those it protected, should not.[55]

In sum, Magna Carta's miscellaneous array of alterations and amendments to the rules on dower meant, for the most part, improvement of widows' legal position during the first third of the thirteenth century. And at the same time disgruntled sons and stepsons, brothers-in-law, and lords continued to devise ways to redress the balance: by simple inaction, by negotiation, by collusive suit, by violence, if necessary. When they did, another recruit would be added to the army of doweresses whose complaints march across the plea rolls.

NOTES

1. There are, e.g., more than 250 entries related to dower in the curia regis rolls covering Hilary term 11–Trinity term 14 John (1209/10–12), almost 500 in those for Easter term 11–Hilary term 14 Henry III (1227–30): *Curia Regis Rolls of the Reigns of Richard I and John,* vol. VI (London, 1932) (hereafter CRR VI); *Curia Regis Rolls of the Reign of Henry III,* vol. XIII (London, 1959) (hereafter CRR XIII).

2. A sizable number of assizes of *mort d'ancestor,* e.g., seem to have been brought against the widow of the decedent claimed by plaintiff as his ancestor. The widow's response was usually to allege a dower interest and vouch her warrantor who, in asserting his right to assign dower, was also asserting his heirship.

3. With few exceptions, primogeniture—the system whereby the eldest son inherited all his ancestor's real property to the exclusion of his siblings—was the rule in military tenure by 1200 and became the rule in socage tenure over the course of the thirteenth century; this chapter is concerned only with those tenures.

4. Villein widows had customary rights, but they were not heard in the king's courts. Moreover, a successful defense that a free husband had held the relevant land in villein tenure would defeat a dower claim made there.

5. The proportion could vary according to type of tenure or local custom. In the period here discussed a widow was entitled to one-half of land held in socage; Kentish gavelkind yielded dower of a half so long as the widow lived chaste and unmarried. Without proof of the nonchivalric nature of the tenure or of local custom, the common law courts recognized maximum dower of one-third.

6. *Tractatus de legibus et consuetudinibus regni Anglie qui Glanvilla vocatur,* ed. and trans. G. D. G. Hall (London, 1965), 7:12 (hereafter *Glanvill*); and see n. 38.

7. See n. 39.

8. *Glanvill,* 6:1.

9. *Glanvill,* 6:2.

10. *Glanvill* takes up the right to *legitim* without using the word: one seriously ill and wishing to make a testament will have his chattels divided into three parts, one due the heir and the second his wife; he may dispose of the third as he sees fit. If he is unmarried at the time of death, he may dispose of half; presumably, the other half is for the heir. The wording of the paragraph suggests that, if there are debts, they are to be paid before there is any attempt at testation (7:5). Magna Carta confirms this indirectly in chapter 26 of the 1215 draft (chap. 18 of the 1225 redaction), which recognizes the right of wife and children to a

share of the chattels of a dead tenant-in-chief if there are no debts outstanding to the king. Bracton says that debts are to be paid and then the residue divided equally among wife, children (not "heir"), and the "dead man," the last being the part subject to his testament: (Henry de Bracton, *Bracton on the Laws and Customs of England,* ed. G. E. Woodbine, trans. and rev. Samuel E. Thorne, 4 vols. [Cambridge, Mass., 1968–77; hereafter *Bracton*] ff. 60b, 61 [2:180]). In the early thirteenth century *legitim* was apparently enforceable in the common law courts as the custom of England, despite its roots in Roman and canon law; later it was sometimes said to be based on the reference in Magna Carta. For a discussion of *legitim* as it affected wives, see Sir Frederick Pollock and Frederic William Maitland, *The History of English Law before the Time of Edward I,* 2d ed., with intro. and biblio. by S. F. C. Milsom, 2 vols. (Cambridge, 1968), 2:349–56. For a discussion of its Romano-canonical background, see R. H. Helmholz, "Legitim in English Legal History," in *University of Illinois Law Review,* no. 3, (1984): 659–74.

11. Bracton suggests this kind of thinking in explaining why there was sometimes a custom against *legitim* (*Bracton,* f. 61 [2:180]).

12. According to Bracton, at Lincoln in the 1220s a woman could claim dower only from tenements of which her husband had been seised on the day he died; the rule apparently held only for tenements within the city (*Bracton,* f. 309 [3:389]). Later reported customs are similar. Scarborough's 1348 statement of its liberties spoke of wives' dower in land "whereof the husbands died seised" (*Borough Customs,* ed. Mary Bateson, Selden Society, vols. 18 and 21 [London, 1904, 1906], 1:1, 2:128). Sandwich had a similar rule, reported in a late fifteenth-century collection purportedly based on one originally written down in 1301, as did Romney, which also had custumals from both the fourteenth and fifteenth centuries (*Borough Customs,* 1:xlvii–l, 2:128). At Ipswich, at the end of the thirteenth century, a woman held as freebench the chief messuage of which her husband had died "seised," in addition to dower of half her husband's other property in the town "as she may rightly have dower of" (*Borough Customs,* 1:xxxiv, 2:123).

13. "A widow after the death of her husband shall at once and without difficulty have her maritagium and inheritance, neither shall she give anything for her dower, or for her maritagium, or for her inheritance which inheritance her husband and she shall have held on the day of death of that husband, and let her remain in her husband's house for forty days after his death, within which let her dower be assigned to her" (Magna Carta 1215, chap. 7). Magna Carta 1225, chapter 7, changes "house of that husband" to "capital mesuage of that husband" and adds: "unless [the dower] shall have been first assigned to her or unless that house is a castle; and if she leaves the castle let there be provided for her at once a competent house in which she can live decently, until her dower is assigned to her according as has been said, and let her have reasonable estovers

of the common in the meantime. Moreover, let there be assigned to her for her dower a third part of all the land of her husband which was his in his life, unless she was endowed of less at the church door."

14. William Sharp McKechnie, *Magna Carta*, 2d ed. (1914; reprint, New York, n.d.), 216. See also on this point Joseph Biancalana, "Widows at Common Law: The Development of Common Law Dower," *Irish Jurist*, n.s., 23 (1988): 255–329.

15. A widow suing for a specific holding and proving nominated dower received the land in question even if it had later been alienated; if the dower were simply of a third, she got other land to the value thereof. The widow's rights in nominated dower have sometimes seemed to modern writers to verge on the truly proprietary; see on this, Pollock and Maitland, *History*, 2:422–24. F. Joüon des Longrais believed that the constitution of named dower conveyed seisin in it to the wife (*La Conception Anglaise de la Saisine* [Paris, 1924], 331; "Le Statut de la Femme en Angleterre dans le Droit commun médiéval," *La Femme*, Receuils de la Société Jean Bodin, vol. 12 [Brussels, 1962], pt. 2, 135–241, at 214–15). I think he is mistaken, even for the period here considered. For further discussion, see my article " 'Of the Gift of Her Husband': English Dower and Its Consequences in the Year 1200," in *Women of the Medieval World*, ed. Julius Kirshner and Suzanne F. Wemple (London and New York, 1985), 215–55, at 221–24 (hereafter "English Dower").

16. Pollock and Maitland, *History*, 2:424.

17. *Curia Regis Rolls of the Reigns of Richard I and John*, vol. II (London, 1925), 258.

18. *Pipe Roll 7 Richard I* (1195), ed. Doris M. Stenton, Pipe Roll Society, n.s., 6 (1929): 91.

19. *Curia Regis Rolls of the Reign of Henry III*, vol. XII (London, 1957), no. 653 (hereafter CRR XII). He gave her "one-third, namely of all the lands which Richard, her husband, held on the day he died." See also no. 166 in the same volume, where the day of death seems to be used as a measure of part of the dower.

20. CRR XIII, no. 724: "afterwards Roger came and conceded to her one-third part of all the lands and tenements whereof his father died seised as of fee . . . namely."

21. *Curia Regis Rolls of the Reign of Henry III*, vol. XV (London, 1972), no. 921 (hereafter CRR XV): "By leave of court, he gives her one-third of all lands of which his father, Walter, died seised. She concedes that she will make services pertaining to her third."

22. CRR XV, no. 1372: "Peter says they are all agreed that all the lands [of the dead husband] will be valued. If those which he held in Cornwall . . . make up one-third of all lands and tenements which he held on the day he died, then they will go to Peter and Amie as her dower . . . . If they do not suffice for

one-third of all he held on the day he died, then they [defendants] will pay what is lacking in the manor of Babington."

23. *Rolls of the Justices in Eyre for Yorkshire 3 Henry III (1218–1219)*, ed. Doris Mary Stenton, Selden Society, vol. 56 (1937), no. 219: "It is found by 12 jurors that Adam ... did not die seised of one bovate of land ... and Maud his widow has brought a writ of dower ... about the bovate. Let her take nothing by her writ." The issue is unclear; if Adam had lost the land by court decision, then there would, of course, be no dower in it, no matter what measuring date was used.

24. CRR XV, no. 761: "John acknowledged that the said Robert died seised of the land but not as of fee and Juliana showed by charters that he died seised as of fee."

25. Public Record Office (PRO) JUST 1/80, m 6: Widow asks for one-third of land, waste, and meadow and defendant acknowledges that the late husband died seised of them but says that she elsewhere demanded her dower of him and he made satisfaction to her with eighteen acres; she denies it and wins what she asked for.

26. PRO JUST 1/755, m 9; and *Somerset Pleas, Civil and Criminal, from the Rolls of the Itinerant Justices ...* , ed. Charles E. H. Chadwyck-Healey, Somerset Record Society, vol. 11 (1897), 87: a sheriff is ordered to value "all the lands which were Thomas de Campo Florido's," divide them into three parts, assign one-third to Thomas's widow (and her new husband), and assign the other two-thirds to Thomas's daughters as their inheritance. Since the daughters could take only such land as Thomas held at his death, his widow's third had to be based on the same standard.

27. CRR XIII, nos. 21, 110.

28. CRR XIII, no. 178. For a statement of that rule, see *Bracton* ff. 94b, 309b (2:272, 3:390).

29. See *Bracton's Note Book*, ed. F. W. Maitland, 3 vols. (1887; reprint, Littleton, Colo., 1983), no. 1919 (hereafter *BNB*); also see PRO JUST 1/819, m 22. The dower litigation between Isabella, countess of Oxford by marriage and an heiress in her own right, and the Blunds went on from at least as early as 1223 until William's death in 1228 (CRR XIII, no. 1066). Because first her niece (also named Isabella and also married to a de Vere) then her sister died leaving no issue, Isabella, the sister of Walter de Bolebec, inherited first half a barony and then the other half. Robert de Vere, earl of Oxford, was her second husband (I. J. Sanders, *English Baronies: A Study of their Origins and Descent, 1086–1327* [Oxford, 1960], 98).

30. *BNB*, nos. 970 (1224) and 1531 (1221); Pollock and Maitland, *History*, 2:421. I do not here address the issue of whether, as Maitland believed, after-acquired lands were not included in the computation of dower without a specific wedding-day provision to that effect.

31. Almost every roll has examples; see, e.g., PRO JUST 1/80, mm 6, 11d, 12d. The roll dates from 1234–36.

32. *Curia Regis Rolls of the Reign of Henry III*, vol. X (London, 1949), 315 (hereafter CRR X). It is unlikely that Isabella intended to ask the one-third vill as nominated dower; the entry reports no use of the word *nominatim*, and, as the tenant pointed out, there was no offer to produce the suit required in support of such a claim. Matilda seems, in fact, to have been making the point that Isabella had claimed a "third" and that she could succeed only in the case of nominated dower. The entry does not explain why the vill was not recoverable as part of a third, as land that accrued to Geoffrey during his marriage, but the most probable answer is that Geoffrey's constitution of dower, made at the end of the twelfth century (Sanders, *English Baronies*, 53), did not include accretions. That, in turn, raises the issue of when and under what circumstances after-acquired property became subject to dower without specific provisions to that effect. The determinative fact in this case may be that Geoffrey died in 1206, well before Magna Carta's provisions on the subject.

33. CRR XI, no. 633; see also the fragmentary entry at CRR XV, no. 1193.

34. *Statute of Merton* (20 Henry III), c. 1, in *The Statutes at Large* (London, 1786), 1:16.

35. *Bracton*, f. 92 (2:265), ff. 301b–311b (3:370–97). Entries in plea rolls after Merton support the interpretation of the statute here suggested: women continue to recover dower in lands alienated during the marriage, but in instances in which a husband held land until his death there is a note at the end of the entry that, because the husband died seised, the sheriff is to inquire about damages for the detention. Eventually, it was shortened to read: "Et preceptum est vicecomiti quod inquirat de dampnis etc."

36. *Britton*, ed. Francis Morgan Nichols, 2 vols. (1865; reprint, Holmes Beach, Fla., 1983), V, III, 2.

37. *Year Book Michaelmas 5 Edward II*, pl. 1. The case did not involve the date on which a husband acquired property but, rather, whether dower in common of pasture could be demanded by a writ that spoke only of reasonable dower from the free tenement of a former husband.

38. The Pipe Rolls of Henry II, Richard I, and John make clear the financial difficulties a new widow could face; for examples during a single year of the reign of Henry II, see *Pipe Roll 31 Henry II* [1184–85], Pipe Roll Society, vol. 34 (1913), 15, 65, 76, 84, 111, 115, 145, 175. Other examples may be found in "English Dower" at 234–37 and nn. 37–44. Magna Carta's provisions did not, of course, mean that a widow was free to remarry without her lord's consent, whether her lord was the king or another; she could still lose her dower for doing so. See, e.g., CRR XII, no. 2374, and *Rolls of the Justices in Eyre at Bedford, 1227*, ed. G. Herbert Fowler, Publications of the Bedfordshire Historical Record Society, vol. 3 (1916), 82. But Bracton says the rule had changed when he was

writing; he speaks of usage in his own time ("hodie") as being otherwise: *Bracton,* f. 88 (2:255). Unfortunately, "hodie" is made less exact by uncertainty about the date of the treatise. Current scholarship suggests a date in the 1230s or even earlier, with subsequent interpolations at mid-century. See J. H. Baker, *An Introduction to English Legal History,* 3d ed. (London, 1990), 201.

39. Both Doris Stenton and J. C. Holt have written of the Angevin kings' efforts to marry off the widows of tenants-in-chief and the efforts of those widows to avoid remarriage. Lady Stenton commented on the "crying need" for Magna Carta's protection, in her introduction to *Pipe Roll 6 Richard I* (1194), Pipe Roll Society, n.s., vol. 5 (1928), xxxiv; she returned to the subject in *The English Woman in History* (London, 1957), 49–51. Holt, on the other hand, saw Magna Carta's provisions in chaps. 7–8 as the confirmation of an existing trend (*Magna Carta* [Cambridge, 1965], 44–47, 113–15) and suggested that in fact the widows' proffer that they not be distrained to remarry marked "one of the first great stages in the emancipation of women" (46).

40. *Pipe Roll 10 Richard I* (1198), ed. Doris M. Stenton, Pipe Roll Society, n.s., vol. 9 (1932), 146, 94.

41. Matilda de Bussey faced such a choice; in 1200 she came before the justices to concede her dower to Hugh de Nevill so long as he should have custody of her minor son, in return for Hugh's payment of forty of the eighty marks that she owed the king for permission not to remarry. When the son came of age he would receive the same dower as part of his inheritance; Maud would recover none of it (*Curia Regis Rolls of the Reigns of Richard I and John,* vol. I [London, 1922], 265).

42. CRR X, 84.

43. The articles are printed in Latin by McKechnie, *Magna Carta,* 487–93.

44. See, e.g., *Pipe Roll 3 Henry III* (1219), Pipe Roll Society, n.s., vol. 42 (1976), 9, "Robertus f. Willelmi de Berkelay [blank] xxii li pro Dionisia matre sua pro habenda dote sua"; 40, "Willelmus de Warenn' debet clj li et dim m pro habenda rationabili dote uxoris sue sicut continetur in rotulo xiii"; 97, "Alina que fuit uxor Willelmi f. Walkelini debet xxx m et j palefridum pro habenda rationabili dote sicut continetur in rotulo xvj R.J." It is not clear whether the entry recording twenty-two pounds owed or paid by Robert, son of William de Berkelay, for his mother to have her dower means that he was acting on her behalf or that she had died and the land that she held in dower had reverted to him.

45. PRO E372/70, rot. 6d (A.D. 1225–26) for all three entries. They may represent an aberrational practice; all the entries are from a single account, Warwickshire and Leicestershire. But, if so, it was not a temporary aberration. A further stage in each matter is recorded in the roll for 13 Henry III; there is no mention of Alice Sorel, and the debt for Isanda de Baskerville has been paid and has disappeared from the rolls, but the debt for Amabilia de Limesey is

reported (*Pipe Roll 14 Henry III* [1230], ed. Chalfont Robinson, Pipe Roll Society, n.s., vol. 4 [1927], 214). More startling, what is one to make of the entry in the same roll under "Nova Oblata": "Philippa Comitessa de Warewyc debet c m. ut non distringatur ad se maritandam quamdiu voluerit vivere sine marito et quod possit se maritare cui voluerit" (214), followed by an entry "Ric Suward c m. qui requiretur de Philippa Comitissa Warewyck qui requiretur ibidem" (259)?

46. For discussion of the point, see "English Dower," 236–37.

47. "Et dedit predicto Willelmo iii marcas per sic quod rationabilem dotem suum sine impedimento ei assignaret" (PRO JUST 1/180, m 2); the roll dates from 1218–19.

48. Maitland's point, already quoted in another context, is again relevant: there may have been some feeling that a widow should not be treated better than a son and heir, and some judges were perhaps willing to let the widow have one-third of what eventually descended to the heir, with no more protection than he had (Pollock and Maitland, *History*, 2:424).

49. *Bracton*, f. 98 (2:281). Since under Magna Carta chapter 7 dower was to be assigned within forty days of a husband's death, the extent of debts might not be known until well after the assignment. Moreover, since the widow's right in nominated dower did not have to await an assignment, it should have been even more secure against claims for repayment of a husband's debts.

50. Helmholz has suggested the reign of Edward I as the period when the common law courts withdrew from handling succession to movables ("Legitim in English Legal History," 665).

51. *Curia Regis Rolls of the Reign of Henry III,* vol. XIV (London, 1961), no. 773. The distinction among debts may be between those due to Jews and those to Christians, but the original reference to "all debts" of the dead man makes the meaning unclear. Other entries concerning Matilda's dower litigation are to be found in the same volume: the last, no. 1489, is from Easter term 15 Henry III (1231), after the day given Roger and Matilda to take their chirograph, and reports an inquiry held to decide her dower right in land she claimed earlier from him.

52. Matilda was not simply giving up rights; she was also using them as an instrument of family planning. The arrangement with Roger provided for the future of her two daughters by her late husband; Roger was to take his half-sisters into his household, find them their necessaries, and marry them off.

53. *Memoranda Roll 14 Henry III,* ed. Chalfont Robinson, Pipe Roll Society, n.s., vol. 11 (1933), 89.

54. *Britton,* V, III, 8.

55. There is no writ prohibiting distraint in dower lands for a late husband's debts in the pre-Merton registers printed in *Early Registers of Writs,* ed. Elsa de Haas and G. D. G. Hall, Selden Society, vol. 87 (1970). The volume includes

only two such registers, but very few others exist (xxiii–xxvii). Moreover, none of the later registers included in the volume—from the later thirteenth and early fourteenth centuries—includes the writ. But the last printed edition of the register has several writs ordering that widows not be distrained for debts of their late husbands in the lands that they hold in dower because that is "contrary to the law and custom" of the realm (*Registrum Brevium* [London, 1687], ff. 142b–143b). I do not know when they first appeared in registers nor their application.

Chapter 4

Litigation as Personal Quest: Suing for Dower in the Royal Courts, circa 1272–1350

Sue Sheridan Walker

The death of a husband continued to drive a great many widows to the royal courts to claim their share of the late husband's free tenures and to become a doweress. While the tide of dower pleas described by Janet Loengard in this volume constituted a smaller percentage of the total number of cases in the early fourteenth century, a great many suits for dower continued to be brought before the king's courts. Dower of one-third or one-half, depending upon the tenurial arrangements, was still an essential element in the reconstitution of the family—to provide for children who did not inherit or, at least, to maintain the widow—after the death of the landholder. The remaining portion of the estate, assuming it was unencumbered by the life interest of any doweresses of previous generations, went to her late husband's heir or heirs. To endow the widow was inevitably to deprive the heir during her lifetime. While medieval English widows claimed dower in a variety of legal jurisdictions, a great number of dower pleas appeared on plea rolls of the royal courts. The argument here is that the common practice of going to law was a compelling personal experience that often called forth an active and competent response by the women. The widow's litigation in quest of her dower will be discussed on the basis of extensive new evidence from the Court of Common Pleas, circa 1272–1350.

These widow plaintiffs are part of a notably litigious society in which involvement in lawsuits was much more routine than for their modern counterparts.[1] As Palmer argued: "a discussion of the common law is not confined to abstruse matters irrelevant to all but a handful of the wealthy. Rather, such a discussion can yield valid conclusions about normal social structure and behavior."[2] Naturally, property litigation tells us about property holders, but landholding was widespread in medieval England. The royal court records offer evidence of a large number of free tenants involved in property disputes. Medieval women also were frequent litigants, and dower, alone of all the major civil pleas, required a woman to be the plaintiff. While it is true that, if the widow remarried, her new husband was joined in the demand for dower and that any plaintiff might use a legál advisor, dower litigation was, in a real sense, "women's business."

In the search for women's "space," we must think of Westminster Hall and the buildings that housed the sessions of the royal justices itinerant in the countryside. To hear women's "voices" we must listen to their demands in the texts of the royal court plea rolls. The control of property—as heiresses, landholders by their own acquisition, joint tenants, and doweresses—gave medieval women power, status, and a need to be familiar with the land law. Property law was part of the general culture of landholders, and most freeholders, great and small, became familiar with the royal courts as plaintiffs, defendants, warrantors, or guardians of minor heirs. Litigation about real property and appurtenant rights required that women, especially widows, be an active part of that pervasive legal culture.

The widows whose dower cases appear on the records of the royal Court of Common Pleas are seen here as part of a cohort group participating in a shared experience in following their plea to its conclusion. It is important to recognize the social and economic diversity of the parties. The most tenable generalization is that the plaintiffs' late husbands held land by one of the three types of free tenures: feudal military tenure, otherwise known as knight tenure; socage tenure; and serjeanty tenure. From the earls downward land was held by a variety of tenures. Feudal military tenure provided the widow with a cumulative life interest of a third of the property. Socage was a free tenure in which the service was rent. Socage tenure, which included burgage, or town land, and gavelkind, the customary free tenure of Kent, was subject to local variations. Often it provided the widow with half the property of her late husband, but some socage dowers were for one-third. Socage dower of both one-half and one-third continued to be claimed in the fourteenth-century Court of Common Pleas. Unlike feudal dower, control of certain socage dowers may have been ended by remarriage, but the evidence is unclear. A number of pleas for dower of one-half were, however, brought by the

widow and her new spouse. Serjeanty tenure was divided into grand
serjeanty, which followed feudal rules regarding both dower and wardship, and petty serjeanty, which conformed to the rules governing socage
tenure.[3] Many dower pleas demand named properties and thus give no
percentage. The type of tenure is only infrequently mentioned in dower
pleadings in the late thirteenth and early fourteenth centuries.

On the basis of evidence from the medieval royal courts tenure and
social status cannot be rigidly equated. The dower claimants in the Court
of Common Pleas were a broad, diverse group, including those who
were the widows of tenants-in-chief of the Crown; far more had spouses
who were mesne tenants, who often held both feudal and socage land
of tenants of the Crown. A surprising number sought dower from very
small holdings. Many of the litigious lesser widows seeking socage dower
had husbands who had served the royal government in a variety of
administrative capacities, such as tax collectors, and had become ac-
quainted with the advantages of the royal courts. Small claims were not
excluded. The initial dower claim was for a third or a half of so much
property and was not expressed in monetary terms unless a rent was
sought.[4] Because only through the royal courts could litigants vouch to
warranty on a national basis or request an ecclesiastical court to certify
the validity of a marriage, dower cases from the London Court of
Husting and other urban jurisdictions also appear on the rolls of the
Court of Common Pleas. Such evidence broadens the socioeconomic
basis of this study.[5]

Widows of great, middling, and small holders of feudal and socage
land often had recourse to the courts when refused part or all of their
dower or shortchanged in the apportionment of the property. Those
widows whose late husbands held any land of the king in-chief received
that dower from the Crown by administrative process. If that land were
held by feudal military tenure, the widow was endowed of the land,
subject to her promise not to marry without royal license.[6] Mesne lords
might have been reluctant to grant dower, but they probably could not
profit from the remarriage of the widows of their feudal tenants. With
Crown-granted dower in hand some widows sued those lesser lords who
had withheld their dower. There is no way of knowing what proportion
of freeholders' widows were put to litigation or what percentage of their
dower land required recourse to the courts. Nevertheless, dower was a
popular plea, and many widows brought a number of suits for dower.[7]

Securing a writ of dower, as in other common law actions, initiated a

legal process requiring determination, knowledge, persistence, and probably hired expertise. The quest for dower in the law courts shaped an
important aspect of the widow's experience within the mold of court
dates, procedural stages—many of which were determined by the defendant's response or recalcitrance—and peculiar features of the English
law of dower. Widows, like other free tenants, in possession of or seeking
land, could not have been strangers to general common law process.
Such knowledge naturally included getting advice.

The greater reliance on the developing legal profession in the later
thirteenth century altered the nature of litigation. It also distinguishes
the dower claimants' experience from that of the period studied by Loengard. More and more widows, like male litigants, used an attorney to
stand in their place "to win or to lose" for some stages of their lawsuits.
Of course, not all attorneys were professional men of law. A number of
widows, discussed in this chapter, have no attorney listed on the plea
roll, and small dower claims continued. Yet royal courts were being
professionalized. While plea rolls list attorneys, the law reports indicate
that dower plaintiffs also retained pleaders or serjeants, the ancestors of
modern barristers, whose discussions with the judges are in the *Year
Books*.[8] Even if they used a legal advisor, most medieval relicts were
probably able to draw upon the "collective wisdom" of many other
widows who had gone to law to demand their dower. Age, health, personality, and sheer necessity too undoubtedly affected the degree to
which any widow could be considered her own best advocate in the
broad sense of doing all she could to secure her dower, including going
to law in the royal courts. The general question of what constituted
dower, how it could be lost and how one sued to get dower, had to be
of compelling interest to women. For many the stakes in a dower plea
might have been the widow's economic survival, perhaps that of her
children. A woman endowed with land of her late husband was not a
mere widow but enjoyed as well the socioeconomic status of doweress.

The lawsuit often brought opposition, which revealed facts or allega-
tions that were potentially deleterious to the success of the dower claim.
The contest between the claimant widow and the defendant denying the
obligation to grant her dower is valuable in understanding what it meant,
in personal terms, to sue for dower. Therefore, this essay will explore the
exceptions or defenses to dower pleas as a matrix in which we may see
the ways in which heirs sought to avoid granting dower and how widows
refuted such objections to their claim.[9] While the experience of going to

law included the whole course of the lawsuit, the portion in which the case was pleaded to issue is the most informative for social as well as legal history. When full particulars are given about the denial of dower, together with the widow's response, we can understand both the law and the ways in which the widow, in a sense, pitted her wits against her adversary. Personal knowledge about property arrangements, any lawsuits touching the estate, charters bearing upon it, and the details of her own marriage were necessary for the plaintiff, even with legal advice, to formulate a convincing rebuttal.

Because the widow brought her writ of dower against the occupant of each parcel of dower claimed, often that defendant was a tenant of the land in question, not the heir responsible for granting dower. Thus, the defendant's response usually was to vouch the heir to warranty, and the warrantor would, in a way, take the defendant's place to grant her the dower or support the denial of dower.[10] Therefore, in the common pattern the dispute initially or eventually came to be an intrafamilial struggle in which the person denying dower would have been her own adult child, her child represented by the guardian or stepchildren, or other relatives of her dead husband.[11] The strong element of family quarrel in dower pleas must have added to the emotional intensity of dower litigation. Even if she were represented by counsel or joined in the lawsuit by a new husband, they could not shield her from defenses to dower.

Pleas of dower in the royal courts were begun by the purchase of a writ from Chancery.[12] Served with a writ, some defendants came into court to render the widow her dower by license of the court.[13] If the defendant had no substantive objection to giving the woman her dower, why did he or she wait for the widow to sue? Naturally, some persons, then as now, never yielded anything undemanded. A royal writ was a "serious" demand. Additionally, the enrollment on the plea roll could serve as proof that the defendant endowed the widow with a life interest known as dower should her heirs try to treat the land as heritable. A good number of the cases that disappeared from the plea rolls were probably settled out of court.[14] Prompt response to the writ usually meant that no monetary penalty or amercement was owed to the Crown by the defendant.[15] A few lawsuits were quashed by the defendants' successful objection to the form of the writ, but the widow plaintiff could secure another writ. When the writ was incorrect, the court often forgave her amercement.[16] Because common law procedure was still flexible, on other occasions the defect in the dower writ was overlooked or amended by the court.[17]

Because a widow was entitled to dower from every parcel of land held by her late husband in such a way as to entitle her to dower, widows often brought a number of suits for dower.[18] Placed together initially on the plea roll, the variety of response or nonresponse on the part of the defendant meant that a plaintiff's several suits for dower often became separated as they progressed through the coils of court process. It took time to place successive pressure on recalcitrant defendants to get them into court and take the land claimed into the purview of the court.[19] Nonappearance often resulted in the widow plaintiff recovering her land by the default of the defendant. The widow of John Passey, for example, secured dower by default of all six defendants.[20] Default in dower, however, could be reversed later.[21]

Vouching to warranty, especially when heiresses and their husbands were summoned, extended the number of court appearances. Delays not only kept the widow from a decision regarding her dower, but she or her attorney also had to be present in court every time the case came up or else the suit was lost by the plaintiff's failure to prosecute. One widow and her new spouse failed to appear late in the process of the case and lost;[22] this may indicate an out-of-court settlement or a realization that they would not win.[23] Even after a jury had determined a widow's right to dower, the defendants often delayed in turning over the land or paying any damages awarded. Writs of final process were created to mobilize the sheriff to get the victor her due from the lawsuit, but they took time to work.[24] Persons who lost lawsuits also owed the Crown a payment known as an amercement. Securing dower, like the employment of other legal remedies, was an engrossing and time-consuming business. The importance of the widow's portion meant that it was rarely optional litigation.

The most compelling objection to a dower claim, though infrequently found, must be the insistence that no dower was owed because the plaintiff's husband was not dead. Widows of men slain in battle needed witnesses or royal records to establish their husband's death. A widow whose husband died in the battle of Stirling was allowed to produce three witnesses "who were sworn and examined by the justices" to prove "sufficiently and suitably that he was slain in the first clash of the battle."[25] Another "widow" was denied dower because her husband was not dead but, rather, a "monk professed." Justice Bereford blamed her advisor, exclaiming, "he who counselled the woman to bring this writ must have wished the woman to lose her labour."[26] Yet not all monastic vocations ended dower rights. In a 1281 case the unfortunate plaintiff was denied dower on the ground that her husband was alive and living in France. She demanded a jury, but the verdict confirmed the defense and added the information that her husband was living in Paris.[27] That woman was an abandoned wife, not a widow. She had at least discovered the whereabouts of her errant husband and might have been able to secure maintenance from an ecclesiastical court. Meanwhile, probably in view of her bleak prospects, the court at least forgave her the amercement for failure to win a lawsuit.

Widows more often met the objection that they had not been validly married to the man from whom they claimed dower. If the woman persisted in her assertion that she had been validly married, and most did, she frequently accompanied her rejoinder with particulars about the marriage: where and when the exchange of consent had occurred, witnesses, possible prenuptial agreements, and wedding festivities. Charles Donahue, Jr., discusses marriage litigation in the church courts later in this volume.[28] At that point the dower case in the royal court was adjourned while a request to "prove the marriage" was sent to the episcopal court governing the area in which the marriage was alleged to have taken place. The ability to contract marriages privately meant that the validity of many marriages was called into question. The failure to follow the rules of the Church in regard to consanguinity or the proper age to consent to a marriage—twelve for girls, fourteen for boys—could result in "annulments" whereby new, licit marriages might be contracted.[29] The material in these dower pleas indicates that some people seem to have "married" and "divorced" without reference to the rules of the Church and only later, perhaps desirous of a legitimate heir or in fear of death, sought to "work out" their matrimonial affairs in accordance with canon law.[30]

The report of the ecclesiastical court affirming or denying the validity of the plaintiff widow's marriage was enrolled with her dower case on the royal court's plea roll. In a 1314 case, for example, Matilda, the widow of Robert Kent of Calneton, sued one Benedict who promptly vouched to warrant Geoffrey the son of Nicholas Kent. That adult heir came into court to deny the validity of the plaintiff's marriage to Robert. Matilda continued to insist on the validity of her marriage, and a mandate went to the court of the archbishop of York. After several proddings from the royal court York certified by letters patent that Matilda and Robert had been validly married. The Court of Common Pleas awarded her dower and ordered a jury to set the damages due to Matilda for the detention of her dower.[31] Similarly, Agnes, the widow of Robert Rikeman of Staunford, won her dower and damages of thirty shillings from the defendant who had denied her marriage. The marriage had been proved valid in the court of the bishop of Lincoln and the letters enrolled on the record of the royal court proceedings. A common law jury was then ordered by the royal judges to set the damages for the detention of her dower.[32] The cooperation between the canon and common law jurisdiction is a marked feature of dower pleadings. Conversely, of course, if the Church court had found that the widowed claimant was not married to the man from whom she claimed dower, she lost her case in the royal court.

A few defendants tried to get out of providing dower by attacking the character of the widowed plaintiff; proven adultery had come to be a bar to common law dower. The determination of the question of her alleged adultery involved recourse to a common law jury of neighbors, not a canon law court. Chapter 34 of the Statute of Westminster II (1285) stated that a widow would lose her dower if she became an adulteress and had not freely been forgiven by her spouse.[33] In modern terms this may be seen as equivalent to the statement that the marital relationship has broken down completely. Adultery while in the household of the husband might also have implied that he condoned his wife's conduct. Whatever the intent of the 1285 statute, the requirement that the wayward wife had to have gone to live with her lover made it easier for a jury to decide the matter of her alleged infidelity. In one such case the widow said that the husband had refused to allow her to live with him. The jury stated, however, that the husband had forgiven his wife two days before his death and, thus, the widow was entitled to her dower. It was obviously prudent that the reconciliation be fairly public.[34]

One widow met her adversary's charge of adultery by saying that her late husband had driven her to live elsewhere. She denied that she went off and set up housekeeping in various counties with Robert Chaumberlayn, the man named by the defendant as her lover. The widow, Joan, explained that she did not leave her husband, Simon de Percefoil, "spontaneously of her own free will" but that, due to his "harshness," she had gone to live with Philip le Lou and Margery, his wife, in Warwickshire. This case went to a jury, but, because the defendant, John, son of Roger

Percefoil, gave Joan her dower of Simon, the verdict merely stated her husband "died seised." The heir, probably the nephew of her late husband, may have made inquiries himself before conceding her demand. The reason for his concession is not mentioned in the court record. Joan responded to the offer of her late husband's kinsman by waiving her damages.[35] Another widow denied the charge of adultery with the pathetic story of her husband's poverty, which had driven her home to her mother: her husband sold all his land and could not "sustain" his wife. The absence of land during the marriage makes it all too probable that there was nothing left to provide dower for her, though I do not know the outcome of the case.[36] Personal hostility may have motivated some of these accusations of adultery; it was, however, within the competence of the common law jury to determine their validity.

Because a valid marriage was based on consent,[37] not carnal consummation, the age at which dower could be received came to be nine, well beneath the age of puberty.[38] Therefore, another defense was the denial that the widow had reached that mandatory age of nine years. To show exception to my general conviction that teenage marriage was normative for non-nobles,[39] there is a case in which the defendant's objection on the ground of insufficient age was met by the very young widow's and her guardian's assertion that it was her second marriage and that she had already received dower of the endowment of her first husband. The defendants, however, reiterated their insistence that the girl was only eight and three-quarter years of age at the time of her most recent spouse's death and claimed to base their assertion on royal administrative records. The verdict, alas, has not been found.[40] Yet, in a 1348 case in which the defendants claimed that the plaintiff was too young to merit dower, the jury said that she was nine years old and more at the time of her husband's death, and she won her dower plus damages.[41] In a 1280 dower case the widow was met with two objections to her demand: that her late husband was only six years old when he died in custody as a minor heir and that the plaintiff, Margery, herself was too young to deserve dower. The court ignored the age of the husband of whom dower was claimed. As for the widow's age, the record states "that Margery was present in court and seen by the judges to be seventeen years old." "Questioned" about her age at the time of her husband's death, it was said—by whom we do not know—that she was then eleven years old. The case never went to a jury because her adversary capitulated and rendered her dower by license of the court.[42] While the decided cases that I have found are not very numerous, the practice in dower pleas gave some credence to the "rule" that the claimant widow had to be at least nine years old.

A larger number of defendants alleged that no dower was owing because the widow had quitclaimed her right to the dower, sometimes for a stated consideration. A quitclaim in her "free widowhood" would have been a bar to a common law dower. In cases of that exception to dower the court often ordered an examination of the record of the royal court. A widow in 1291 was proved to have made a concord in which she had given up her dower rights for an annuity in wheat.[43] In confrontations of this sort the defendants often displayed the "writing" in court. Some widows were noted as "unable to deny" and lost their suit for dower.[44] One widow, however, successfully pointed out that the charter shown by the defendant did not contain the words that she had "remised and quitclaimed her dower." At that point her adversary was unable to deny it, and she got her dower.[45] Unscrupulous persons probably took occasional advantage of the widow's grief to have her make a bad bargain. It is difficult to know what redress she would have had, unless it were to try to void a contract made under duress or diminished capacity.[46]

Some parties tried to deny a widow dower rights on the ground that she had accepted less dower than she now demanded and was "satisfied" with the lesser endowment. Such assertions brought forth some lively response by the widows in question. When Alice, the widow of William Gerberge, sued Ralph, son of Richard, for dower of half of forty shillings rent; John Herebrond for half of two messuages; and John Coston for half of twenty-eight shillings rent, all three defendants vouched to warrant the heir Thomas Gerberge. Thomas argued that she ought not to be dowered therein because she had received one hundred shillings rent in another place as "her whole dower." He claimed that the assignment was made by him and that she had "held herself to be content." Alice disagreed: the rent was to be her whole dower in that one place, and she now sued in regard to the other properties of her late husband. Furthermore, the widow insisted that rent was not assigned by Thomas but was, instead, won in the royal court by his default. The jury confirmed her assertion, and the heir Thomas was ordered to grant her dower of one-half, as she claimed. The defendants were to hold their lands in peace and were not liable to provide the dower.[47] Here the extreme animosity between Alice and her stepson is well documented in other royal records:

Thomas had brought an appeal against her for causing the death of his father, William, the spouse from whom she derived her dower. Thomas had been imprisoned at Norwich and fined for his failure to pursue his appeal.[48] In 1285 Alice had offered fealty to the Crown for certain of her dower lands in Yarmouth. By the grant of the king and the heir, perhaps as part of the pacification of the quarrel, on the widow's death the land would go to the friars preachers of that town.[49]

Accusations of murder are rare accompaniments to refusal to grant dower. A husband who had been convicted of felony, however, would have forfeited his property. Dower rights were thus extinguished. As Britton's treatise succinctly declared, "the wives . . . of felons shall not hold in dower any tenement assigned by such husbands."[50] When a widow and her new husband sought her dower in two suits in 1292 the two defendants argued that she ought not to have dower because her first husband, Henry Warde, was hanged for robbery at Castle Barnard. Whether this was true or not, the plaintiffs failed to prosecute that dower plea.[51] In a report in the *Year Books* touching the impact of the husband's felony on dower, Malore observed that, "when a woman has an action to demand dower, the husband cannot bar her by any act except his felony."[52] When English civil strife involved the penalty of treason the pacification often included specific provision of dower for widows of combatants, as did the Dictum of Kenilworth.[53] Being unable to rebut the charge that her last husband was a felon cost the widowed plaintiff her bid for dower in the royal Court of Common Pleas. Edward I's trenchant stand against the widows of Scotland, as Cynthia Neville discusses in this volume, cost some of the women their freedom as well as the property rights flowing from their marriages to rebels.

Much more common were disagreements about what constituted the widow's "whole dower" of several parcels of land. The widow of Richer de Docking brought two writs claiming dower in Norfolk. The writs were for lands and rents held by tenures that would sustain "dotation" of one-half and one-third, respectively. One defendant, John Lovel, made different responses to the several parcels claimed. In regard to two portions he offered to render her dower of one-third by license. The widow rejected this offer because the lands in question were socage and should yield her one-half. That issue went to a jury. The result was a split verdict in which she recovered half of some of the land and a third of a few acres, and, concerning the residue claimed from John, she was in mercy for false claim.[54] The outcome of the proceedings against the second defendant who appeared by an attorney has not been found. Even with good intentions apportioning dower was a fairly complex art, and disputes of that sort are not uncommon. The guardian of the heir tried to deprive an Essex widow of part of her claim because she received half of a nineteen-pound rent in Stanburne. She would not accept the assignment because it was not equal to her proper share of all her late husband's lands. The jury agreed. That plaintiff and her new spouse were awarded seisin of her whole dower and sixty-three pounds in damages.[55]

The most frequent objection to the widow's demand for dower was that her late husband was not seised of the property either at the marriage or afterward.[56] When Lucy, the widow of Philip de Satcheverill, and her new husband claimed a third of two messuages, two carucates of land, sixty acres of woods, and forty shillings rent in Devon as dower of Philip, the defendants argued that Philip was not seised. The plaintiffs were unable to deny it. Therefore, Henry and Lucy took nothing by their writ and were amerced for false claim.[57] In another dower plea of the same law term the widow sued a chaplain with the same surname as her late husband for a third part of twenty-three acres in Derbyshire. That defendant also refused dower because her late husband had not been seised at the time of the marriage or after. The case went to a jury that found against the plaintiff.[58] A compromise resolved the plea of Margery, the widow of William de Appleford, for dower in fifty marks rent in Grantchester near Cambridge, brought against the warden and scholars of Merton in Oxford. The warden argued that Merton held only ten marks rent in the property and, furthermore, that the rent ought not to provide dower because a "long time before their marriage" her late husband had granted the land to two brothers for ten marks rent and then, in a royal court, conveyed the rent to the scholars. The widow rejoined that the warden and scholars held the whole rent of fifty marks and that her husband had been seised on the day of their marriage. She included a long history of the property that was inherited from her husband's mother. The issue went to a jury, but before the verdict the parties came to an agreement whereby the scholars of Merton were to pay her two and a half marks a year, and she remitted the rest of her dower claim.[59]

A variant of the husband's "not being seised" defense was to argue that the nature of his right was not one that could provide dower for his wife: he could have been only a tenant for term of years or for life.[60] The defendant might make that objection to only part of the demand. In a report of a 1294 dower plea in which the defendant's response was that concerning "two parts of her demand we readily grant her dower; but as to the third part of the whole, we say she ought not to have dower." The reason for denial was that her late husband had never held that one-third in demesne. It came out in the *Year Book* dialogue, although the outcome is not known.[61] The objections to granting dower to the plaintiff based on the nature of the property holding reveal the incredible complexity of the medieval law of tenures and estates and the relish with which freeholders exploited the nearly infinite possibility to rent, grant, sell, and resettle the property, even though feudal tenures could not be willed.[62]

The quest for dower by Alice the widow of Simon le Constable illustrates the difficult situation of the heir of a father with an unusually complicated marital career, which even involved the death by poisoning of the heir's mother. The late-thirteenth-century legal treatise called *Britton* devoted a great deal of space to plural spouses,[63] a concern the Constable dower saga also bears out. In 1297 the royal court received a writ of dower from an Alice, who claimed to be the widow of Simon le Constable. The defendant named was Katherine, who was described as the daughter of Philip de Wyvlesby, but she would claim to hold the property in question as the widow of the same Simon. Katherine vouched to warrant Simon's adult son and heir, Robert. At the outcome of the case Alice would get dower and damages as the legitimate wife of Simon, Katherine would hold in peace the lands Robert had given her, and Simon's unfortunate son seems to have been left with little inheritance due to his father's penchant for what might now be called "serial monogamy." Katherine was represented by an attorney; Paul Brand is editing a law report of the case that indicates that all the parties were spoken for in court by one or more serjeants. The opening of her defense was carefully worded to describe her claim to the lands demanded by Alice as "tenant for life by the grant of Robert," Simon's son, to settle a dower claim Katherine had brought against him. Much of the pleading is about Robert's obligation to warrant. It was important to avoid warranting unnecessarily, as the warrantor frequently ended up granting the dower, while the defendant went "quit." The plaintiff Alice's claim is ignored, while the argument raged about warranty. Robert insisted that Katherine should have vouched him as a doweress, not a tenant for life by grant.

On Katherine's behalf the court was shown written evidence touching her demand that Robert warrant the "reasonable dower" that he had granted to Katherine from Simon's "free lands" in the counties of York, Lincoln, and Norfolk. Robert countered that Katherine, in her "free widowhood and full legal power," had remised the dower lands to Robert and received other tenements from him. He also claimed that she had received a hundred shillings rent from a prior and convent in Lincoln at the order of Robert and his heirs to be paid for the whole life of Katherine. Robert asserted that Katherine held those lands and received the rent to that date. The plea roll noted that Robert "read and heard" the "writing" put forward by Katherine. Robert claimed that she held as "doweress," not as life tenant, and asked judgment of the court about whether he should warrant. If Katherine were dowered of Simon's land, Robert would still have had to be her warrantor. As only one widow of each generation could claim dower, however, if Katherine held land as dower, Alice need not be dowered by Robert. If it came to a quarrel between the two "wives," only one would get dower.

Katherine may have been described as life tenant in her initial defense to Alice's dower plea because Katherine knew her marriage to Simon was open to question. In fact, the proof of Alice's claim to be the legitimate wife of Simon had been established in another plea of dower. Katherine perhaps chose to think of her endowment as her dower. Meanwhile, the seemingly ignored plaintiff Alice was given another day before the court while the warranty issue was settled. Robert was eventually amerced for failure to warrant. Now at last we get to the heart of Alice's bid for dower as Simon's widow. The ecclesiastical court of Norwich's determination of the validity of the marriage between Simon and Alice was copied onto the enrollment of this case on the plea roll of the Court of Common Pleas. Because the plaintiff's marriage to Simon was valid, Robert rendered Alice dower of the free tenures that he had inherited from Simon, and inquiry was to be made about what damages Alice should receive.[64] Katherine, the erstwhile wife of Simon le Constable, was to hold her lands in peace.

The social context of litigation, while always germane, often is not recoverable.[65] Yet the sensational Constable history left tantalizing traces in royal legal and administrative records. Alice had been married to Simon for ten years, and after Simon's death Robert had inherited Simon's property as an adult of twenty-nine years.[66] Katherine was not Robert's mother; his mother was Joan, who had been murdered. In 1294 a Katherine, "wife" of Simon le Constable, received a royal pardon for her indictment before a royal court for having prepared a poison for

John de Danethorp, at some time her husband, Joan, the wife of Simon, and a Henry de Thornleye.[67] Despite her exoneration, could Katherine have borne some responsibility for the poisoning of her previous husband and Simon's wife, Joan, the mother of Robert? Had Katherine lived as Simon's wife in a union not recognized by the Church but in which Simon's son would provide her with life maintenance, believing her to be his father's widow? When did Simon form a valid marriage with Alice? Simon, accused of procuring the poisoning of his wife and the abduction of Katherine from her husband and various thefts, had refused to put himself on the verdict of a jury and died in prison while undergoing *fort et dure*.[68] Unfortunately, the documents do not reveal all the answers. Katherine kept her property, but, thanks to his settlement of an earlier dower plea of his father's erstwhile wife, Robert also had to endow his father's legitimate wife, Alice. Emotions as well as property were often on trial in dower pleas. The dramatic Constable family saga sets it apart, however, from the usual background of dower pleas. Katherine may have preferred her neighbors to think the land was hers as Simon's widow, not as a well-provided mistress; few could have considered her typical of the many doweresses of their acquaintance.

The royal court again sought ecclesiastical court cooperation in resolving a dower plea of 1291 in which the defendant, the abbot of Fountains, denied the obligation to dower Sibilla with a small-holding in Yorkshire on the ground that she was not a widow but, instead, the medieval equivalent of a divorcée. The abbot alleged that the marriage of Alan de Whixley and Sibilla had ended in a "divorce celebrated" in the court of the prior of St. Andrew of Northampton, commissary of Robert de Kilwardby, late archbishop of Canterbury, in his last visitation of the bishopric of Lincoln. Sibilla denied the divorce, and the request went from the Court of Common Pleas to the canon law court at Canterbury to search its records. Despite the great specificity of the exception to dower, no record of the divorce was found. The abbot rendered Sibilla her dower, though the payout to her is further complicated by the abbot's getting equal land from the warrantor. But Sibilla finally got her dower of Alan de Whixley as well as damages from the abbot who had produced such a circumstantial, though seemingly untrue, account of a divorce in order to deprive a widow of her small dower. There were, however, some doubts about her marriage to Alan, who was a professional canon lawyer, because Sibilla had been sued for debt as the widow of another, although she then claimed to be Alan's wife.[69] Sibilla would probably have identified herself with Donahue's female litigants in the canon law court. Sibilla, at any rate, won her dower suit in Common Pleas thanks to the negative report of the church court about a divorce.

When Alice, the widow of Gawan le Butler, brought two claims for dower against Walter de Hopton, she won one suit and lost the other. Split results were quite common. But in one of her cases the jury verdict reveals an attempt to alter tenurial arrangements to try to provide a life interest for a husband of a childless marriage. Alice had sued Walter de Hopton, who was a former royal justice but by then was disgraced, for a third part of two manors. Her claim for each manor appears separately on the plea roll because juries from each locale might be required. In regard to the first manor, Alkementon, the jury supported the defendant in the familiar assertion that her husband, Gawan, was not seised of the manor at the time of the marriage or thereafter. Thus, Alice lost her suit for dower therein.

Concerning a similar denial of dower from the manor of Hinstock, however, the jury declared Alice was entitled to her dower of that manor. The verdict gave a history of the properties of Walter's late wife. Walter had been married to Matilda, the lady of Wem, who had held the manor of Hinstock and other manors of her own inheritance. The law was such that Walter would do homage and hold the land during Matilda's life. If a child had been born of Walter and Matilda's marriage, even if the infant lived only for a few minutes, Walter would have continued in seisin after Matilda's death. He would have had a life estate in her property as the tenant by curtesy,[70] and Walter's control of the land would have kept Gawan le Butler, relative and heir of Matilda and spouse of the plaintiff Alice, out of the property until the death of Walter. Matilda may have been older than Walter, unable to have children, or just eager to secure Walter's control of her lands. Whatever their motive, Walter and Matilda engaged in conveyancing to turn her property, or some of it, into a joint estate for themselves, with either spouse enjoying the right of survivorship.

Joint tenancy was commonly used to provide for the wife and deprive the lord of some "taxation" due to a minority succession. To that end the couple used the customary grant and regrant pattern so an estate passed to Roger le Rous and back to Walter and Matilda as joint tenants. This joint estate, however, was created in the manor of Tirley, not Hinstock, the manor of which Alice claimed dower. Nevertheless, to confuse the situation Walter, after Matilda's death, stayed in Hinstock, perhaps because of the neglect of the escheator. The jurors were uncertain but stated that Walter was not seised of the manor of Hinstock. Later the king granted him the wardship of Gawan, who was a minor heir in the king's gift, and Walter's presence in the property probably continued in his role as guardian. The jury verdict, like the history of the property, is long and tortuous. The outcome favored Alice, since the jury declared that "it appeared sufficient and manifest" that the manor of Hinstock was of the free and feudal tenure of Gawan and, therefore, that Alice was to receive her dower in the manor of Hinstock and sixty shillings damages. Gawan le Butler's heir was his brother William. Alice's successful bid for dower revealed the resettlement of Tirley and gives us a glimpse of how property resettlement could affect dower pleas.[71]

The custom of curtesy, the "male dower," was involved in a dower plea in which the daughter of a London merchant sought half of a property in Holborn. The burgess father, in arranging the marriage, demanded several charters to protect his daughter in widowhood, but he misunderstood the prospective groom's standing in regard to his London property. When the daughter was widowed and brought her writ of dower it was discovered that her late husband possessed no land, save by curtesy from his previous wife. Because curtesy was only a life interest, it was extinguished by his death, and there was nothing left to provide for his widow. Perhaps her father was less credulous in trade than in dealing with the lies of potential sons-in-law, or his dowerless daughter might have been bereft of support. She had already, it is true, remarried by the time her case came before the court. Yet her new spouse may well have counted on having the Holborn dower as well as the bride.[72] Getting another husband was easier if one held dower of a previous one; a handsome aggregation of cumulative life interests made even the quite mature widow a very pleasing prospect for matrimony, as the research of Barbara Hanawalt and Joel Rosenthal suggests. The widow may have distrusted her claim to dower of that Holborn property and have chosen any available spouse before her day in court. Royal court records cannot assure us, however, about such personal calculations.

Defendants also couched their offer to grant the dower demanded with the condition that the widow turn over the charters or other muniments that she detained.[73] In one such case the records of the late husband's tenure as royal sheriff were assumed to be in the widow's care.[74] In feudal tenures the lord, not the mother, was the legal guardian of the heir, and a few defendants met the widow's demand for dower with the counterdemand that she yield up the ward in her possession in order to get dower. The *Year Book* for Michaelmas term of 1343 has an example in which the heir was under age, and his guardian pleaded that the widow demandant had "eloigned [withheld] the heir," but, "if she would render the heir, he [the guardian] was ready, and always had been, to render dower."[75] The putative guardian could have brought a writ of wardship against a widow detaining the heir.[76]

My examples have been chosen to indicate the range of defendant response that the dower claimant confronted in the royal court. These situations formed a part of the practical and emotional experience of going to law. But what of the knowledgeable and effective personal component in their quest for dower? How immediately were late-thirteenth-century dower plaintiffs involved in the prosecution of their own lawsuits? Frequent remarriage meant, of course, that some widows had acquired a spouse who must be joined in the dower plea. The new husband may have taken an active interest in the process as well as looked forward to the fruits of victory in the lawsuit. On occasion the marriage took place during pending litigation. In the case of Margaret, who claimed dower of Richard de Bordeston, the warrantor refused to respond on the ground that Margaret married again, and her husband was not named in the writ. She was allowed to recede, but the new couple had to begin their joint suit for dower of her previous husband.[77] But most plaintiffs in dower were still widows. Prospective husbands may have preferred the litigation in the royal courts to have been successful before the marriage. Having dower made the Church's mandate requiring marital "free consent" a practical possibility: some widows remarried; some did not.

Loengard begins her account of early-thirteenth-century dower with the remark that, if a woman was ever in court in her life, it was to seek dower. A vast number of women claimed their dower in the Court of Common Pleas from 1272 to 1350. The evidence is not clear, however, about how many women "acted" for themselves or, if they had an attorney, were even actually present in court. The increasing professionalization of royal court process and personnel changed the texture of dower litigation. Indeed, it changed the nature of "going to law" for both male and female litigants in the civil pleas. Even though medieval English-women did not require an attorney or a male relative in order to bring a suit in the royal court, increasingly it became convenient and probably both prudent and usual for dower claimants to consult a lawyer. Whether or not widows secured legal advice, they still had to know the properties that might arguably provide dower and who held them at that time. The plaintiff's version of the "facts" was necessary to refute a denial of dower as well as to facilitate the actual award of dower.

The image of a widow alone—but legally potent—seeking dower before the impressive royal court, perhaps guided on technical points by the advice of serjeants and the justices or drawing upon the clerks' experience to shape her tactics, is not impossible. It is, however, probably far from normative by the end of the thirteenth century. I have indeed found a few cases in which the widowed plaintiff, without an attorney listed, made astonishingly technical objections to the defendant's denial of their dower.[78] One widow argued that, if the defendant really had a charter that could deny her dower, he would have shown it in court. That defendant caved in and admitted that he had no charter, an admission that won her dower;[79] it also may have enabled her to pay a pleader who, in the conventions of the plea rolls, would not have been named. Brand has suggested that, even if a widow did not have an attorney, she, like most common bench litigants, had a serjeant to speak for her, and the court record is telling us what he had to say in court on her behalf.[80]

Litigant experience was changing, and the added expense of going to law affected men as well as women. Remarried dower plaintiffs may well have heard their new husbands comment about the complexities of law and the need for greater professional advice—would that they had written it down for the convenience of historians. Despite the increase in legal learning and mass of surviving parchment relating to royal justice, much about basic common law procedure remained part of an oral tradition. Long ago W. C. Bolland, trying to explain the absence of an elementary treatise of legal procedure, wisely speculated that "as in those days everyone who was interested in such matters knew all about them, it seemed worth nobody's while to write down what was common knowledge."[81] Knowledge of the law was still essential for women, especially widows, who were a part of that broad group of property holders for whom recourse to the law courts was a familiar part of life. Litigants of both sexes found themselves distanced from the course of their own lawsuits, however, as lawyers were used more frequently. "Being your own best advocate" for dower claimants in common pleas meant knowing well the property claimed and then getting the best professional or quasiprofessional advice possible. The report of a dower plea of 18 Edward III reign noted "the woman who was a demandant was a poor woman, and had no counsel."[82] Litigant access is difficult to gauge, but small dower claims continued to come before the royal courts. Widows could proceed *per fidem* if they could not produce pledges for prosecution,[83] and paupers were forgiven amercement in dower pleas.[84]

One of the resourceful widows wishing to become doweresses is known to have had a professional pleader because the ten pounds and forty shillings damages in her dower plea are particularized to include two marks as a "salary" for Roger de Higham, a serjeant in the Court of Common Pleas and on Eyre.[85] Brand has identified him as a king's serjeant in this particular eyre and suggests that Roger's share in the damages was noted because he had been compelled to act for her by the court; it is a very early example of official notice of the assignment of damages to a serjeant in England. Forty shillings for the clerks also came out of her damages. Professional pleaders appear active in dower litigation, though they are usually invisible on the plea rolls. Using such legal services shows well widows' ability to prudently manage their litigation. Legal cunning was not limited to widows, for some of the heiresses who tried to avoid granting dower out of their inheritances also seem to have "studied" how to use the law courts.[86] Once in possession of dower the doweress often had, of course, to deploy a variety of legal remedies to protect her rights from challenge. At that point many successful widowed plaintiffs became determined defendants.[87] The vast evidence of the legal and administrative records offers considerable testimony that women could do what was necessary in their quest for dower.

NOTES

This chapter is part of the preparation of a book-length study of dower. I wish to acknowledge with gratitude my Newberry Library/National Endowment for the Humanities Fellowship, 1990–91; Northeastern Illinois University; and the university's Committee on Organized Research (COR) research grants, which have helped to support my research in the Public Record Office (PRO), London. I wish to thank the officers and staffs of the Newberry Library and the PRO. Thanks are especially due to David Lea. I am grateful to Paul Brand, James A. Brundage, Richard H. Helmholz, Janet S. Loengard, and Joel Rosenthal for reading various drafts of this chapter and to the 1990–91 Newberry fellows for their questions and constructive ideas. Brand's generosity has included sharing information from his yet unpublished volume of manuscript law reports and giving me the opportunity to read his fine article "'Deserving' and 'Undeserving' Wives: Earning and Forfeiting Dower in Medieval England." A far larger number of historians have discussed the law of dower with me. I am grateful to them all but naturally hold them blameless for the use I have made of their work and their suggestions.

1. See Robert C. Palmer, *The Whilton Dispute, 1264–1380: A Social-Legal Study of Dispute Settlement* (Princeton, 1984), 5–13, for discussion of the statistics regarding population and use of the Court of Common Pleas; 8, for his "prudent guess" that 10 percent of the population was involved in litigation.

2. Palmer, *Whilton*, pp. 9–10. In Palmer's calculations, for sound legal reasons, women appearing with their husbands were not counted as separate individuals (7–8). This minimizes the possible litigation experience of wives and undercounts the number of people involved in lawsuits.

3. The implications of feudal tenure, otherwise termed military or knight tenure, for the family are described in the pioneering work of T. F. T. Plucknett, *Legislation of Edward I* (Oxford, 1949). For the earlier period, see S. Painter, "The Family and the Feudal System in Twelfth-Century England," *Speculum* 59 (1960): 42; and J. C. Holt's four-part "Feudal Society and the Family," *Transactions of the Royal Historical Society,* 5th ser. 32 (1982): 193, 33 (1983): 193, 34 (1984): 1, and 35 (1985): 1. R. M. Smith discusses a broader tenurial context, including that of the peasants, in his article "Women's Property Rights under Customary Law: Some Developments in the Thirteenth and Fourteenth Centuries," *Transactions of the Royal Historical Society* 36 (1986): 165. For an introductory survey of law of tenures, see A. W. B. Simpson, *A History of the Land Law,* 2d ed. (Oxford, 1986), chaps. 1 and 2 and index (for "dower"). Simpson's frequent references to Lyttleton suggest, however, that many of his generalizations are appropriate to a period later than that discussed in this chapter.

4. In PRO ms., Court of Common Pleas CP 40/225 m 73 d (1318), the claim was for dower of a third part of a mill, ten acres of land, and thirty shillings of rent; in CP 40/227 m 17d (1319) the widow and her new husband demanded a third part of a messuage, sixteen acres of land, forty acres of meadow, and twelve-pence rent.

5. Palmer (*Whilton*, 6) observed that no cases came to Common Pleas from "London, Cheshire or Durham, of course." London dower cases, however, certainly do "appear" on royal court records in considerable numbers and broaden the social, economic, and geographic coverage of this article.

6. Sue Sheridan Walker, "Feudal Constraint and Free Consent in the Making of Marriages in Medieval England: Widows in the King's Gift," in *Canadian Historical Association: Historical Papers, 1979,* ed. Terry Cook and Claudette Lacelle (Ottawa, n.d.), 97.

7. For Bedfordshire in two years, e.g., there were 9 dower cases identified among 168 cases; for Berkshire, 25 dower among 209 cases; for Buckinghamshire, 20 dower among 211 cases; for Cambridge, 22 dower among 344 cases; for Cornwall, 30 dower among 198 cases; for Cumberland, 7 dower among 64 cases; for Derby, 19 dower among 201 cases; for Devon, 25 dower among 390 cases; for Dorset, 11 dower among 193 cases; for Essex, 29 dower among 532 cases; for Gloucester, 11 dower pleas among 215 cases (PRO [London], *Index of Placita de Banco A.D. 1327–1328 Lists and Indexes,* vol. 32 in 2 pts. [New York: Kraus Reprint Corporation, 1983]). This index, however, seems to under count dower pleas. I am collecting case counts at intervals from the manuscript plea rolls of the Court of Common Pleas 1272–1350, and the initial "hand count" indicates more than 550 entries relating to proceedings in dower for Michaelmas term of 1294 (CP 40/106). Some dower litigation is cloaked in the form of a request to an ecclesiastical court to determine the validity of a marriage, voucher to warranty, a suit between the defendant and a recalcitrant warrantor, compurgation to prevent default, or mesne or final process in dower. Nevertheless, when compared to the other actions listed in the *Index to Common Pleas 1327–1328,* dower is still a frequent plea.

8. Information about legal advisors appears in our sources in a variety of ways. The legal records called plea rolls name the parties to the action and indicate whether the plaintiff had an attorney; if the defendant answered the writ, the roll will indicate the use of an attorney. In CP 40/118 m 106d (1297), e.g., Beatrice, the widow of Anselm de Gyse, per attorney (name of attorney not given) demanded dower of one-third from Walter de Helyun, a former royal justice. Walter had an attorney although his name was not given. In CP 40/274 m 148 (1328) Eleanor, the widow of Herbert, son of John, had an attorney, Walter de Sandwich, in her demand for dower of one-third from Robert de Sapy, who appeared by his attorney, Peter de Edgeworth. Similarly, in CP 40/246 m 59d (1323) both the widow plaintiff and the defendant had a named attorney. A number of widows claiming dower have no attorney indicated on the plea roll: in CP 40/100 m 12 (1293) Matilda, the widow of William Deveraux, without an attorney mentioned, won her two pleas for dower of one-third from Edmund Mortimer, who was noted as having an attorney although he was not named in the plea roll. Several widowed plaintiffs with no attorney listed are mentioned in the text of this article. The pleaders who figure in the *Year Books,* however, are not mentioned in the plea rolls in that routine fashion. Law reports, many of which are still in manuscript, are crucial to understanding the question of legal representation in dower pleas. A fuller discussion will appear in my essay "The Widow and the Men of Law: An Exploration of Litigant Agency in the Dower Pleas in the Royal Courts of Medieval England," presented at International Medieval Family Law Seminar at the Faculty of Law, University of British Columbia, Nov. 1992, and a revised version given at the annual meeting of the

American Historical Association, Dec. 1992. The research of John H. Baker, Paul Brand, Paul Hyams, Robert C. Palmer, G. O. Sayles, and Wilfrid Prest forms an essential background to the subject.

9. Henry de Bracton, *Bracton on the Laws and Customs of England,* ed. G. E. Woodbine, trans. and rev. Samuel E. Thorne, 4 vols. (Cambridge, Mass., 1968–77), ff. 301b–312b (3:370–99; hereafter *Bracton*); *Fleta,* ed. G. O. Sayles, Selden Society, vol. 99 (1983), bk. 5 and chaps. 26 and 27; *Britton,* ed. Francis Morgan Nichols, 2 vols. (1865; reprint, Holmes Beach, Fla., 1983), V, I–XIII (2:235–96).

10. I intend to discuss warranty in dower pleas elsewhere.

11. On defenses to dower and family interests in an earlier period, see Janet S. Loengard, "'Of the Gift of Her Husband': English Dower and Its Consequences in the Year 1200," in *Women of the Medieval World,* ed. Julius Kirshner and Suzanne F. Wemple (London and New York, 1985), 215–37. See, generally, Joseph Biancalana, "Widows at Common Law: The Development of Common Law Dower," *Irish Jurist,* n.s., 23 (1988): 255–329; "The Writs of Dower and Chapter 49 of Westminster I," *Cambridge Law Journal* 49 (1990): 91–116.

12. *Early Register of Writs,* ed. Else de Haas and G. D. G. Hall, Selden Society, vol. 87 (1970), see index for commentary and many examples of dower writs. In the early thirteenth century dower pleas could also be begun by plaint or bill, but this practice appears to have become uncommon by the reign of Henry III; see *Select Cases of Procedure without Writ under Henry III,* ed. H. G. Richardson and G. O. Sayles, Selden Society, vol. 60 (1941), ciii–iv, clxiv.

13. E.g., CP 40/54 m 44 dorse (1284); CP 40/118 m 106 (1297).

14. On out-of-court settlements, see M. T. Clanchy, *Civil Pleas of the Wiltshire Eyre,* Wiltshire Record Society, vol. 26 (1970), 27–28.

15. E.g., PRO ms. Court of the Justices Itinerant, JUST 1/48 m 18 (1284).

16. E.g., JUST 1/1061 m 11 (1279), JUST 1/1102 m 36 (1294).

17. E.g., JUST 1/1061 m 45 (1279).

18. One widow, e.g., brought five separate writs of dower (CP 40/91 m 316 [1291]) and another four writs of dower (CP 40/80 m 192 d [1289]); in *Placito de Banco,* 1:19, Agnes, widow of Geoffrey de Okhangre, six writs of dower for land in Berkshire and one plea of land; 235, Roesia, the widow of Nicholas de Criel, five writs of dower in Kent; 249, Alice, widow of John de Serdynden, brought seven writs of dower in Kent; 312–13, Margery, the widow of John de Haryngton, thirteen dower and one plea of land in Lincolnshire; 325–27, Lucy, widow of John Martel, brought eight writs claiming dower in Lincolnshire. But one to three pleas per widow is the average. As cases appear on plea rolls by county, the same widow could have been seeking dower of lands in other counties.

19. For an example of the writ "cape in manum nostram," see *Early Registers of Writs,* Selden Society, vol. 70, 315–16. Because of the failure to appear in

court by both defendants and warrantors, orders for the cape are legion; see, e.g., CP 40/106 mm. 48, 53, 57, 5 d, 32d, 36d, 59 d, 64 d (two cases, different plaintiffs), 65 d, 66 d, 69 d, 166 d, 179 d, etc. (1294); CP 40/189 m 219 (1311).

20. CP 40/204 m 80 d (1314). Other recoveries by default: CP 40/221 mm 27 and 161 d (1318), and CP 40/389 m 150 (1357).

21. See my essay "Wager of Law and Judgment by Default in Pleas of Dower in the Royal Courts of Late Thirteenth and Fourteenth Century England," which is chapter 3, in *The Life of the Law: Select Proceedings of the Tenth British Legal History Conference Oxford, 1991,* ed. Peter Birks (London, 1993).

22. CP 40/304 m 479 (1336).

23. CP 40/78 m 18 (1289), concord enrolled; CP 40/80 m 181 d (1289), defendant's concession after jury called.

24. The writ of *elegit* was provided by chapter 18 of the statute of Westminster II (1285), *Statutes,* 1:82. It was far more expeditious than the writ of *fieri facias. Elegit* is discussed in connection with the collection of debts by Plucknett, *Legislation of Edward I,* 148–50. What a defendant or warrantor owed as a result of litigation was a judgment debt. I will discuss the final process in more detail in my monograph on dower.

25. See comments on *Mace v. Prat* in *Year Book 9 Edward II, 1315–1316,* ed. G. J. Turner and W. C. Bolland, Selden Society, vol. 45 (1928), xxv and 78 (case).

26. *Year Books 32 and 33 Edward I,* ed. Alfred J. Horwood RS 31a (London, 1864), 4:166–67. Paul Brand has found cases and reports suggesting that the wife might still be dowered if the couple were not formally divorced.

27. CP 40/42 m 72d (1281).

28. See *Select Cases from the Ecclesiastical Courts of the Province of Canterbury, c. 1200–1301,* ed. Norma Adams and Charles Donahue, Jr., Selden Society, vol. 95 (1981), for rich materials and introduction illustrating the many aspects of marital litigation. The introduction refers to the frequent cooperation between the royal and ecclesiastical jurisdictions in cases such as dower (98). A case with details about the marriage festivities is D. 14 (1291–92) (535–67). Royal court dower records rarely have much detail, as they only wished to establish the "public" character of the marriage that the defendant was denying; of course, marriage contracts made privately were enforceable as well. See n. 39 and discussion in Donahue essay in chapter 8 of this volume.

29. See Michael M. Sheehan, "The Formation and Stability of Marriage in Fourteenth-Century England: Evidence of an Ely Register," *Mediaeval Studies* 33 (1971): 228; and "Theory and Practice in Conciliar Legislation and Diocesan Statutes of Medieval England," *Mediaeval Studies* 40 (1978): 408.

30. Helmholz comments upon the freedom of marriage practice and persistence of the "idea that people could regulate marriages for themselves" (R. H. Helmholz, *Marriage Litigation in Medieval England* [Cambridge, 1974], 4–5).

31. CP 40/204 m 80 d (1314).

32. CP 40/221 m 113 (1318).

33. *Statutes of the Realm*, 1:87.

34. CP 40/136 m 108 (1301). Some cases refer to the dower plaintiff as having subsequently married "her adulterer." Brundage discusses the canonists' view on adultery and subsequent marriage, in *Law, Sex and Christian Society in Medieval Europe* (Chicago and London, 1987), 245–47.

35. CP 40/80 m 101 (1289).

36. CP 40/169 m 56 (1308).

37. Charles Donahue, Jr., "The Policy of Alexander III's Consent Theory of Marriage," in *Proceedings of the Fourth International Congress of Medieval Canon Law*, ed. S. Kuttner (Vatican City, 1976), 251; and "The Canon Law on the Formation of Marriage and Social Practice in the Later Middle Ages," *Journal of Family History* 8 (1983): 144.

38. *Bracton*, f. 92 (2:265) gives no exact age but refers to when she "is mature enough to take a husband"; or f. 302 (3:372), "at that time she was of such a tender age that she could not receive a husband, so as to deserve dower." *Fleta* (bk. 5, chap. 23, p. 73, and chap. 25, p. 81) states that the required age is nine and one-half. *Britton* (2:280–81) gives no precise age but asserts that the widow must have been "capable of deserving dower in the lifetime of her husband," even if she were a "maid" of "twenty or a hundred years old." See Brand, " 'Deserving' and 'Undeserving' Wives."

39. See evidence about the age of marriage of wards cited in Sue Sheridan Walker, "Free Consent and the Marriage of Feudal Wards in Medieval England," *Journal of Medieval History* 8 (1982): 123; and "Common Law Juries and Feudal Marriage Customs in Medieval England: The Pleas of Ravishment," *University of Illinois Law Review*, no. 3 (1984): 705.

40. CP 40/209 m 47 (1319).

41. CP 40/354 m 73 (1348).

42. JUST 1/763 m 5 (1280).

43. CP 40/89 m 129 (1291); other cases in which the widow lost because she quitclaimed her right to the dower (CP 40/189 m 174 [1311]) or "remised and relaxed her rights" (CP 40/354 m 354 [1348]).

44. E.g., CP 40/189 m 174 (1311) and CP 40/354 m 356 (1348).

45. JUST 1/1102 m 21 (1294).

46. Research in both the plea rolls of the common law courts and chancery materials is necessary in order to try to establish the practice in regard to attempts to undo such agreements and link the cases to an earlier dower plea.

47. CP 40/78 m 56 (1289).

48. *Calendar of Fine Rolls*, 1:165 (1282).

49. *Calendar of Patent Rolls, 1281–1292*, 167.

50. *Britton*, I, VI, 5 (1:37).

51. JUST 1/985 m 16 (1292).

52. *Year Books Michaelmas 33, 34, 35 Edward I*, ed. Alfred J. Horwood, RS 31a (London, 1879), 5:174–77 and 198–201 (another case).

53. Concerning the dictum, or "Award of Kenilworth," in 1266, see R. F. Treharne and Ivor Sanders, *Documents of Baronial Movement of Reform and Rebellion: 1258–1267* (Oxford, 1973), 57–60 (discussion), 334–35 (text). Chapter 31 provided: "Women shall have their heritages and dowers of their first husbands. They shall have the lands of their husbands in the manner in which the king has ordained, and the lands shall be ransomed." C. H. Knowles in "The Resettlement of England after the Barons' War, 1264–67," noted that this "humane treatment of the womenfolk contrasts with the plight of some of their counterparts" in later reigns (*Transactions of the Royal Historical Society*, 5th ser. 32 [1982]: esp. 28).

54. CP 40/116 m 85 (1297).

55. CP 40/80 m 138d (1289).

56. Loengard discusses the argument about using the day of death or day of marriage in the calculation of dower; my evidence raises questions about normative usage after 1273. A common defense was "not seised at marriage or after," but the plea roll entries do not always write it out completely.

57. CP 40/247 m 70 d (1323).

58. CP 40/27 m 25 d (1323); similar defense with jury verdict supporting plaintiff in CP 40/79 m 16 (1289); in CP 40/492 m 283 d (1383) the plaintiff and her new husband were unable to deny the defendant's reason for denying her dower and lost their plea.

59. JUST 1/86 m 2 (1286).

60. Such as a life estate as "tenant by curtesy" discussed below and cited in n. 72.

61. *Year Books 21–22 Edward I*, ed. Alfred J. Horwood, RS 31a (London, 1873), 2:406–11.

62. See John H. Baker and S. F. C. Milsom, ed., *Sources of English Legal History: Private Law to 1750* (London, 1986), esp. sec. 3 on "Family Interests and Settlements at Common Law"; J. M. W. Bean, *The Decline of English Feudalism* (Manchester, 1968).

63. *Britton* mentions plurality of spouses in the context of dower at several places in the treatise (V, II, 2 [2:241]; V, VII, 1–2 [2:263–65]; V, VIII, 1–4 [2:271–74]; V, X, 10–11 [2:284–86]).

64. CP 40/118 m 66 (1297).

65. We urgently need more serious scholarly accounts of family history based on manuscripts in order to understand the social facts behind litigation. An excellent example of this genre is David Crook, "Hardwick before Bess: The Origins and Early History of the Hardwick Family and Their Estate," *Derbyshire Archaeological Journal* 107 (1987): 41–54.

66. *Inquisitions Post Mortem* (hereafter *CIPM*), 3, no. 1931.

67. *Calendar of Patent Rolls, 1292–1301, 76.*

68. Regarding CP 40/188 m 66, Paul Brand, who is editing the parallel report found in the British Library, discovered more of the melodramatic details in the records of the 1293–94 Yorkshire Eyre (JUST 1/1098, mm 80 d and 95). One Beatrice de Vere of Sproatley had been condemned and burned for the poisonings of Joan. Katherine was also indicted for her alleged part in the poisonings but managed to persuade a jury that she was innocent.

69. CP 40/90 m 99 (1291). Brand called my attention to the debt case, which is JUST 1/622 (1285).

70. For a discussion of curtesy, see *Lyttleton, His Treatise of Tenures,* ed. T. E. Tomlins (London, 1841), 44, 45, 49. This treatise is from the fifteenth century, but curtesy, the male dower, is much earlier, as mentioned in the late twelfth-century treatise *Glanvill* (92–93 and 183). See the useful discussion of tenancy by the curtesy in Simpson, *Land Law,* 68–70.

71. CP 40/89 m 49 (1291). Maud the lady of Wem was the daughter of Walter Pantolf, and her first husband was Ralph Butler. For the descent of the barony of Wem, see I. J. Sanders, *English Baronies* (Oxford, 1960), 94–95. Maud's inquisition postmortem is in *CIPM* 2, no. 774, where she is described as the deceased wife of Walter de Hopton, the defendant in the cases discussed here. The conveyance of Tirley is in *Cal. Close Rolls 1279–88,* 234.

72. CP 40/161 m 254 (1306).

73. E.g., CP 40/163 m 67 (1307). A similar situation can be found in *Year Books Michaelmas 33, 34, and 35 Edward I,* RS 31a, 5:206–7 and 232–33; *Year Books 20 Edward III,* ed. Luke Owen Pike, RS 31b (London, 1908), 14:568–71.

74. *Eyre of Northamptonshire A.D. 1329–1330,* vol. 1, ed. D. W. Sutherland, Selden Society, vol. 97 (1981), 17–18.

75. *Year Book 17–18 Edward III,* ed. Luke Owen Pike, RS 31b (London, 1903), 10:256–57, in which the widow denied having eloigned the heir; see also *Underwood v. Furneaux* in *Year Books 1 and 2 Edward II (1307–1309),* Selden Society, vol. 17 (1903), 24–25, in which the widow's denial contains a history of the custody; and *Le Veel v. Berkele, Year Book 6 Edward II (1312–1313),* eds. P. Vinogradoff and Ludwik Ehrlich, Selden Society, vol. 34 (1917), 31–32. No results have been found for these cases.

76. Wardship pleas often brought widows into court as plaintiffs, defendants, or warrantors; see Sue Sheridan Walker, "The Feudal Family and the Common Law Courts: The Pleas of Wardship in Thirteenth- and Fourteenth-Century England," *Journal of Medieval History* 14 (1988): 13–31.

77. CP 40/106 m 245d (1294).

78. Seemingly without attorneys, Alda Martin, a London widow, successfully argued about the law of attorneys (CP 40/100 m 2 dorse [1293]); and some

widows promptly forgave a default and won dower by a jury verdict (CP 40/305 m 312 d [1336]; CP 40/226 m 119 [1319]).

79. CP 40/89 m 122 (1291).

80. Paul Brand's comment was made in a letter concerning a related subject. As he pointed out, without a copy of the report one cannot be certain, but the hypothesis that the serjeants assisted the widow is more likely than the alternative that she spoke for herself. Now see his splendid *The Origins of the English Legal Profession* (Oxford, 1992); his concluding remarks are useful in this context (158–60).

81. Intro., *Year Book 6 Edward II (1313)*, ed. W. C. Bolland, Selden Society, vol. 43 (1926), ix.

82. *Year Book 18 Edward III*, ed. Luke Owen Pike, RS 31b (London, 1904), 11:406–7.

83. See, e.g., PRO ms. Court of Common Pleas, Bench Writ files CP52, Trinity term 7–8 Edward II (1314) (Warr.); in 1294 it came to the attention of the court that the sheriff had not acted on a writ of dower because the widow was unable to get pledges; justice Mettingham provided them (CP/40 106 m 127).

84. See, e.g., CP 40/42 m 59d (1281); CP 40/91 m 316 (1291); CP 40/189 m 60 d (1311).

85. JUST 1/1102 m 21 (1294).

86. E.g., CP 40/73 m 41 (1288); CP 40/89 m 122 (1291).

87. As in CP 40/42 m 5 (1281), in which a widowed defendant was able to deny dower to another widow.

Chapter 5

Widows of War: Edward I and the Women of Scotland during the War of Independence

Cynthia J. Neville

One of the most constant features of life in later medieval England was the presence of war, with its attendant costs in human life and material goods. Women had little active role to play in campaigns, but they were touched in innumerable ways by the effects of conflict. Sue Sheridan Walker, in "Litigation as Personal Quest," shows that a distant war could impinge on a female plaintiff's case in the law courts; widows of English rebels and other felons faced the fact that forfeiture canceled dower rights. More immediately, and more obviously, war was often responsible for changing a woman's status in English law from that of wife to widow. The essays in this volume, especially those by Joel Rosenthal, Janet Loengard, and Barbara Hanawalt, explore the means by which women adjusted to the distinct status accorded in English law to widowhood when their husbands died as a result of accidental or natural circumstances. Women who lost their husbands in war similarly faced difficult periods of adjustment. But their choices in widowhood were often severely complicated or limited, especially if wartime conditions had transformed their former spouses from loyal liege subjects into avowed enemies of the Crown.

In the early fourteenth century two chroniclers, commenting on the death of Edward I of England, eulogized the character of the former king: "he was the most just of lawgivers, the most merciful comforter to the poor and the wronged"; "of chivalry, after king Arthur, was Edward the flower of Christendom ... of vigour and worth, and full of understanding, he had no equal in ruling a lordship."[1] From the perspective of his less competent son's reign Edward's years on the throne were recalled by his English subjects with enthusiasm and even wistfulness.

The king's Scottish enemies, however, remembered him chiefly as an oppressor who came to counter their struggle for independence with what one of his modern biographers has acknowledged as "unprecedented savagery."[2] For the women of Scotland the legacy of war against Edward was particularly bitter. Long after his death Edward I was still portrayed in Scottish historical writing as a ruler whose ambitions had left scores of women bereft of their husbands, their sons, and their lands.[3] And, while English chroniclers fondly recalled the man who had expressed heartfelt grief at the loss of his first queen and tender concern for the health of his second,[4] Scottish patriots remembered only the tyrant who had deliberately withheld his mercy from their women kin. The two faces of Edward I remained, for them, irreconcilable.

The English conquest and domination of Scotland effected in 1296 signaled the commencement of more than thirty years of hostilities, a conflict known to historians as the War of Independence.[5] The fate of the hundreds of Scottish noblemen who defied England during the War of Independence has been the subject of careful study by Scottish historians.[6] Less well served, however, is the history of the treatment that befell the women of Scotland in this same period; as wives, widows, daughters, and sisters of rebels, they, too, came to experience the wrath of the English Crown, to suffer wholesale forfeiture and imprisonment for their loyalty to the cause of Scottish independence. This essay attempts to remedy this deficiency by examining the fate of several Scottish women whose husbands opposed English domination during the most virulent phase of the war, which coincided with the energetic last years of Edward I's reign, 1296–1307. It looks chiefly at what happened to the widows of slain Scottish patriots but also takes into account women whose husbands were taken captive and led away to lengthy imprisonment in England—women who, for all intents and purposes, were widowed by the events of the war. Not surprisingly, most of the extant evidence relates almost entirely to the lives of noblewomen. But, fortuitously, there have also survived several petitions from "less substantial" women pleading for clemency in spite of their husbands' treasons. These reveal that the English Crown's reprisals against rebellious subjects were not reserved exclusively to wealthy and influential ladies but that they extended far down the social scale.

Warfare in the late thirteenth and early fourteenth centuries was heavily influenced by a series of conventions and customs. The law of arms, which governed relations between warring princes, was clear, for example, on the matter of prisoners taken both on and off the field. In a war defined as "just and lawful" it was permissible for a man to capture an enemy and hold him as a hostage for, and guarantor of, his prince's good faith, so long as the confinement was honorable, as befitted the prisoner's station.[7] Edward I, perhaps the most legal minded of all later medieval English kings, was familiar with these conventions of war and seems, indeed, to have been closely in touch with contemporary treatises on the subject.[8] The authors of this genre of literature, however diverse their origins, were unanimous in their exhortation that the ravages and dangers of war must not directly injure noncombatants. Within this general category were included old men, infirm persons, children, clerics, and, most comprehensively, women. These authors were also all of the opinion that a just commander in war was one who practiced freely the Christian virtue of charity.[9]

Edward I, however, invoked a higher authority in his dealings with Scotland than the mere conventions of war, no matter how soundly based these were in Christian theology. He firmly refused to consider the war with Scotland an "open" war in the contemporary sense of that term, that is, as a licit conflict between sovereign Christian princes.[10] Long before the campaign of 1296 he had his men of law construct for him a legal claim to lordship over the smaller kingdom,[11] a claim that had its foundation in the repeated acts of homage and fealty that the Scots king, John Balliol, had performed before Edward.[12]

From the point of view of the English Crown the specific legal status of hostilities against Scotland as a just war was crucial;[13] in essence it gave license to Edward to conduct unlimited war in pursuit of his territorial ambitions. More important, it played a key role in defining relations between Edward I and those individuals who chose to remain in the Scottish allegiance. As long as Scottish landholders refused to perform formal and genuine acts of homage and fealty—and sometimes even when they did—the English king considered and treated them as rebellious, obstinate, and contumacious vassals. And, because he succeeded in upholding this claim that interference in Scottish affairs was lawful, the king was able to act against the Scots with a ferociousness that put paid to all the normal conventions of war. This fact was made shockingly evident in his treatment of Scottish women.

Balliol proved both a difficult vassal and an ineffectual ruler in the years after his election. When in 1295 a Scottish parliament deposed him and the new Guardians of Scotland effected a truce with England's enemy, France, Edward moved swiftly. He justified his invasion of the kingdom on the bulwark of feudal law and custom. Just as he had done two decades earlier with respect to Wales, he adduced the traditional right of a lord to punish his defiant vassal. And, without a doubt, breach of the fealty owed by a vassal to his lord was the most treasonable of all medieval offenses. Edward argued throughout the war that in such a conflict observance of the norms of chivalric conduct must take second place to the prerogative of the offended lord. Few of his countrymen dared challenge the assertion.

In the course of the conflict, then, Edward I occasionally allowed the conventions of war to temper the punishment he meted out to the widows of Scottish patriots. But he remained obstinately convinced that feudal law endowed him with an awesome authority. Landholders in Scotland, both great and small, male and female, even those under the age of majority,[14] were held liable to the severe consequences incumbent upon unlawful defiance and were granted pardon and restitution of their forfeited lands only if Edward chose to exercise the lordly prerogative of mercy. The Scots, therefore, very quickly found themselves at war with a foe whose single-minded ability to use the law for his own ends had prepared him to act with uncommon fury against them.

The treatment meted out to Scottish rebels in the years after the outbreak of hostilities in 1296 followed a clearly discernible pattern: increasing severity on the king's part and a corresponding willingness to disregard the conventions enjoined on the Christian prince as victor in war. As previously argued, this was largely a reflection of Edward's firm conviction that his war against a rebellious Scotland was lawful and justifiable. But the trend is especially relevant with respect to his relations with the womenfolk of disgraced families. Where pragmatic considerations dictated time and time again that Scottish noblemen should be restored to lands that they had forfeited for their rebellious activities, the women of Scotland, as less substantial landholders, were generally of less pressing political concern. Consequently, they were treated with noticeably less tolerance.

Even among the women themselves Edward distinguished between those of the magnatial ranks and those of more modest social and economic standing. Wives he considered to be of greater import and, indeed, of greater value, than widows. Any hardship inflicted on the former was likely to influence a husband's actions as the war progressed, or so he hoped. The widows of Scottish patriots, because they were less valuable as political hostages, were the most expendable of all pawns, and the decline of the king's magnanimity toward Scotswomen in general is particularly evident in his treatment of these women. Moreover, by the early years of the fourteenth century, with the war showing few signs of a speedy conclusion, Edward had come to think of all Scots as devious and unrepentant rebels.[15] The time for clemency and fair-mindedness was, in his opinion, long gone; so, too, had the requirement to make a clear distinction between male and female offenders.

Several months before he crossed the River Tweed at the head of an army of conquest Edward I had begun to take action as a lord unlawfully defied. Immediately following the sealing of the Franco-Scottish treaty in October 1295, he commanded the seizure of lands held in England by Scots of all stations; by December a muster of the feudal host at Newcastle-upon-Tyne had been ordered. In mid-February 1296 another writ commanded the attachment of all Scottish goods and chattels found in England, and, finally, in April word was sent out that any Scottish persons found in the southern kingdom should be arrested and held until the king's pleasure should be made known.[16]

The effects of these far-reaching measures were not only to deprive summarily a large number of Scottish landholders of estates that many had acquired through English wives but also, more onerously, to force these same women to make difficult choices between marital and feudal loyalties. The peril consequent on such a dilemma is well illustrated in the case of Sir William Douglas and his wife, Eleanor Ferrers, dispossessed of estates that they controlled in Essex, Hertfordshire, and Northumberland in right of Eleanor, the widow of William Ferrers.[17] When Douglas was taken prisoner in the summer of 1297 and sent to confinement in England, his wife was compelled to seek Edward's generosity for her sustenance. She was granted only a portion of her former English lands and continued to live precariously on a small income after her husband's death in 1298. Eleanor was not fully restored to the English estates she held as dower of her first marriage until 1299, and her claims concerning dower lands that had been held by William Ferrers within Scotland were not settled until 1305.[18] For some years, then, as far as the Crown of England was concerned, her relationship with a proven Scottish rebel overrode all considerations of her personal loyalty.

Similar circumstances befell women of lesser means and so caused them perhaps greater distress. When in 1295 the Cumberland estate that the Scottish knight Sir David Torthorald had held of his wife's heritage was taken into the king's hand, Christine Torthorald was left destitute. Although the sheriff was ordered to give her seisin of the lands in the spring of 1296, she was still attempting to enter them in September. It was only after she had appealed to Edward I personally that the king directed the sheriff to insure that the lands had been seized solely by virtue of the royal command of 1295 concerning Scots lands in England, and, if this were the case, to restore her.[19] Another woman, a widow known only as Godava, lost the third part of a small rent of ten marks in Lincolnshire and appears to have died destitute.[20]

The losses that Eleanor Ferrers and Christine Torthorald experienced in the months leading up to war were sufficient to convince them that opposition to the might of the English Crown was futile and dangerous. Eleanor's third husband was an Englishman firmly in the allegiance of Edward I, while the Torthorald family likewise abandoned the Scottish cause. Its members were to manifest themselves as staunch opponents of Robert Bruce's ambitions in the early years of the fourteenth century.[21]

The opening stages of the campaign of 1296 saw the town of Berwick fall to the English, after a siege that lasted only one day. The slaughter that followed the surrender of the garrison was sufficiently fearful to earn Edward lasting infamy among the Scots. The chronicle accounts that record the event are, with one exception, predictable: the English writers are unanimous in their reports that townswomen were spared the king's anger,[22] while Scottish versions of the event contradict them and accuse Edward of indiscriminate violence.[23] Alone among the English accounts, the Lanercost chronicler records the fact that "persons of both sexes perished," though the friar responsible for this portion of the work clearly intended that Edward's harshness be weighed against the savagery that accompanied a Scottish raid into England on the very same day.[24]

Following this initial display of determination at Berwick, the king was prepared to act with unusual moderation. Confident after a leisurely progress around the kingdom that his conquest of Scotland was complete and enduring, Edward convened a parliament at Berwick on 28 August. Here he set about shaping a new government for Scotland; here, too, he addressed himself in methodical fashion to the future relations between the Crown of England and Scottish landowners.

Edward's first concern was the formal acknowledgment by landed persons of his overlordship. Accordingly, he caused to be drawn up a document that became known as the Ragman Roll. Dated at Berwick on 28 August, the roll records the fealty and homage of some two thousand Scottish freeholders, great and small, male and female—persons, that is, representative of Scottish landholding society as a whole.[25] The comprehensiveness intended of the document is well demonstrated by its inclusion of the names of some seventy women, ranging from the widows of fallen patriots to women whose husbands had died prior to the outbreak of hostilities to unmarried female tenants, lay and religious. The differing ranks of Scottish society are similarly well represented. Thus, "Isabel who was the wife of John the tailor" performed homage for the modest lands that she held in Forfar;[26] so, too, did Mary queen of Man, widowed three times over by 1296, for lands that she had acquired in Perthshire from her second husband, Malise, earl of Strathearn.[27] Annabella Graham, whose husband, Sir Patrick, had been slain fighting Edward at the battle of Dunbar in April, also performed homage for the Perthshire estates of her late spouse, although she was aware that her title to those lands had become precarious at best.[28]

By early September, with the fealty and homage of landowning Scotland formally on record and the appointment of new royal officials completed, Edward was free to turn his attention to the fate of individual landowners and their kin. In the course of the next few days careful provision was made for the restoration or punishment of women as well as men. On this occasion Edward could afford to display the magnanimity and even-handedness enjoined by the conventions of his day. Two writs issued on the first day of the month referred specifically to widows. The former took into account women whose husbands had died before the deposition of King John by the Scottish parliament in July 1295 and, therefore, still "in the king's peace"; the other was intended to deal with widows whose spouses had remained in, or come to, the English allegiance when the Franco-Scottish treaty of alliance had been made, in late October 1295. These men and their kin were also held to be guiltless in the matter of the Scottish rebellion; consequently, their widows were to be restored in full, and immediately, to all the landed estates and tenements that they held in Scotland as dower or as of hereditary right.[29] Two days later, when their names had been duly checked against the record of the Ragman Roll and the fact of their spouses' loyalty carefully confirmed, more than thirty widows received seisin of their lands, saving to the king all castles and fortified strongholds.[30]

For most of these women one brush with the anger of King Edward I was sufficient; they retired gratefully to their estates, and their names do not appear again in the English records of the war. A few of the women caught up in the business of the Berwick parliament took deliberate care to remain aloof from the treasonable activities of the male members of their families, when the latter subsequently chose to carry on the struggle against the English. Others, such as the widow Mary of Argyll, made a conspicuous effort in the years after 1296 to reassure the English Crown of their loyalty.[31] Some, however, were made of stronger mettle. Margaret lady of Penicuik was mentioned by name in 1298 in a dispatch from the constable of Edinburgh castle, concerning a raid on the outskirts of the town by the notorious rebel Simon Fraser. She was accused therein of receiving and sheltering Scottish miscreants, among them her son Hugh. Her tenants, who insisted that they remained loyal to the English Crown, suffered reprisals for her actions, but Margaret herself managed to escape the constable's men and to remain active in support of the Scottish cause.[32] Another Margaret, widow of Malcolm Ramsay, similarly remained steadfast to the Scots, in spite of the trouble she experienced in 1296. Her Berwickshire estates, valued at twenty pounds per annum, were still in King Edward's hands in the spring of 1299, "for her rebellion."[33]

Having assured himself of the goodwill of some Scottish widows, Edward next began consideration of the more delicate and complex matter of manifest Scottish rebels—that is, men and women who were indisputably guilty of open rebellion against the English Crown. The first to be dealt with were the subtenants of the former King John, whom Edward chose to adjudge guilty merely by association, rather than intent. He therefore decreed that, as soon as they had performed homage and fealty for the lands that they had held of Balliol, they should be restored to them but that they should now hold them directly of the English Crown.[34] Specifically excluded from Edward's magnanimity, however, were Balliol himself, the dozens of magnates who had been sent to English prisons, and those persons who remained in open rebellion. These individuals, and their kin, were to be considered separately, each according to his or her degree of culpability.

The women of the large and influential Comyn family were of particular concern to the English Crown. John Comyn of Badenoch, John Comyn, earl of Buchan, and Alexander Comyn had acted as chief architects of the Scottish revolt, and, although in September 1296 they were safely confined in English prisons, their prominence in Scottish landholding society meant that their tenants and sympathizers were both numerous and well distributed throughout the kingdom. The wives of such men must be treated with some care. Moreover, in the absence of their husbands the Comyn women might be manipulated to good advantage in the settlement of the newly conquered Scotland. John Comyn of Badenoch's wife, Joan, was the daughter of Edward's old friend William de Valence, earl of Pembroke; the countess of Buchan was the daughter of the earl of Fife, and Alexander Comyn's wife, Joan, was the sister of Sir William Latimer.[35] As members of influential Anglo-Scottish magnatial families, these women had every reason to hope for, and to expect, favorable treatment at Edward's hands.

Joan Comyn was most generously dealt with, for she was the king's cousin. As early as 4 September, provision was made, "of the king's special grace," for her to receive two hundred marks of land in Tyndale for her sustenance,[36] and a week later she was granted permission to transfer herself and her household to England in order to be closer to her husband, then in confinement in the Tower of London.[37] The courteous tone of the king's instructions belies his wish to have Joan Comyn safely within his reach. Alexander Comyn's wife, though she petitioned Edward for one hundred marks of land, was allotted a more modest thirty marks for her sustenance and was similarly instructed to come to England.[38] Isabel, countess of Buchan, was permitted to remain in Scotland; with both her husband and her brother in his custody Edward had little reason to be overly concerned with her.[39]

Less prominent women were also invited to present petitions requesting restitution, and at the Berwick parliament alone more than two dozen of these were proffered.[40] Edward was in no hurry, however, to rule on the case of the widows of less conspicuous men, and some waited several months before their requests were even considered.[41] Among the appeals presented in September were those made on behalf of wives whose spouses were in prison and who had no way of knowing the length of time they would have to fend for themselves. These women had in effect been widowed by the events of 1295–96 and were now compelled to make their own way in the world. Edward's eventual answers to the women's requests varied according to the severity of their husbands' offenses and to his own whim. Annabella Graham, who openly acknowledged Sir Patrick's rebellion, was summarily dismissed and told to plead her cause before the newly appointed Keeper of the Realm, John de

Warenne, earl of Surrey, and his council.[42] The Siward women were treated more leniently. Mary, whose husband, Richard, had been sent to the Tower,[43] traded on an earlier friendship with the king to ask for fifty marks of land in order to sustain herself and her nine children as well as her daughter-in-law, Elizabeth.[44] Richard Siward was to remain in prison until the end of July 1297, his son an additional seventeen months.[45] Mary, living on the annuity granted to her by Edward, awaited her husband's return in Scotland, but Elizabeth went to England and spent the rest of her life there.[46] Margaret, wife of Edward de Lathum, and Christine, wife of Stephen Pessun, whose rebel husbands were no longer in the kingdom, likewise applied for sustenance during their enforced solitude but were told abruptly: "the king wills that they shall have nothing."[47]

Five hundred years after the events of 1296 Lord Hailes commented that Edward I's conduct toward Scottish widows "in all things bore the semblance of moderation,"[48] and few of the king's modern critics find cause to disagree with this verdict. On the other hand, the king had no reason to be anything other than a stern but forgiving conqueror. The invasion of the kingdom and the subsequent appointment of a new treasurer and keeper of the realm had been undertaken with surprisingly little opposition, and there seemed little reason to doubt that Edward might not with a clear mind turn his attention to other pressing matters, both at home and abroad—to assume, in other words, as one historian has opined, that "the Scottish problem was solved."[49]

A more accurate picture of the king's treatment of Scottish widows should be sought in the decade after 1296, and especially the years 1298 and 1306, when the ephemeral nature of the conquest of Scotland was made evident to the English. On both occasions the Scots rose in revolt, and on both occasions Edward openly displayed his anger against the chief conspirators and their families. Whereas in 1296 his punishment of rebels was in general characterized by even-handedness, as the years thereafter wore on, the harshness, and more particularly, the vindictiveness of the king's judgments were made manifest, both to chroniclers who wrote of events and to Scottish women of all ranks who experienced them at first hand.

In the summer of 1298 Edward again mustered an offensive army, but some weeks before leading it into battle he began to exert pressure on the families of men whom he knew had assumed, or resumed, a prominent role in the Scottish opposition. Chief among these were members of the Comyn family. In March, immediately after John Comyn of Badenoch had deserted the king's army in Flanders and set sail for Scotland,[50] Edward wrote to "his dear kinswoman," Joan, requesting politely that she and her children come to London without delay.[51] Perhaps anticipating ambivalence, he simultaneously sent a message to one of his officials, commanding the latter to compel the lady's obedience should she hesitate or refuse to accede to the summons.[52] Edward, however, need not have been concerned with Joan de Valence in this renewed phase of the Scottish struggle. She duly traveled south and, mindful now of her late father's loyalties and the future concerns of her own family, chose to abandon her husband's cause altogether. She remained in England as a political widow, at Edward's peace, and eventually her children married into families with strictly English interests.[53] Her kinswoman Joan, the wife of Alexander Comyn, similarly chose political widowhood to the vagaries of the Comyn fortunes: though her husband remained in Scotland, Joan Latimer moved her household and her two young daughters to England.[54] Alice and Margaret married the English noblemen Sir Henry de Beaumont and Sir John Ross, respectively, and eventually became the heiresses of their uncle John Comyn, earl of Buchan.[55] Joan Latimer outlived her husband by many years. She was granted the Templar manor of Faxfleet in Yorkshire as sustenance, in recompense for the lands she had lost in Scotland, and in 1315 the Yorkshire manor of Malton.[56] A petition presented to Robert Bruce in 1320 for restitution of Comyn lands forfeited in Scotland was unsuccessful, and Joan once again returned to England.[57] From 1327 until her death in 1340 she was in receipt of an annuity of forty pounds from the English Crown, a reward that the Crown felt was suitable for her steadfast opposition to Scottish independence.[58]

These women had a difficult choice to make, and, given the nature of the surviving evidence, we cannot hope to discover fully the reasons that dictated their compliance with Edward's commands. But, clearly, the king's firm resolve to keep them apart from their troublesome husbands and their own concerns for their families were sufficient to make them abandon their spouses and homes, however reluctantly, for the duration of their married lives.

The expedition of 1298 culminated in an overwhelming victory for the English army at Falkirk on 22 July. This time Edward chose to act more decisively than he had in 1296 in the matter of the punishment of Scottish rebels. He was especially determined that the middling and lesser ranks of society—those men and their families who had so whole-heartedly committed themselves and their arms to Sir William Wallace—should feel the lasting influence of the royal anger. According to one chronicler, the king expressed a wish to parcel out the entire kingdom to his own followers and made it known that henceforth his soldiers "should take English wives and produce heirs who would possess that land forever, so that never again should there be any cause for intermingling with the Scots."[59]

The effect of Edward's policy was, indeed, felt strongly by the lesser landowners of Scotland, perhaps nowhere more severely than by the women whose husbands had opposed the English at Falkirk. Among the records of the priory of Coldingham is preserved a list of freeholders of the barony of the same name, probably compiled very soon after the battle, which includes the names of several hundred persons forfeited for their adherence to the Scots. The widows of fallen patriots are well represented in the rental, and the description of the modest estates that they lost by Edward's command reveals just how sweeping was the king's order: Alice, the widow of one John Ridel, lost her dower, the third part of the tiny manor of Flemington, while the widow of Bertram le Marshal lost the income from a toft and croft because of her spouse's forfeiture.[60] Edward was clearly uninterested in the profit, however small, that might have accrued to his coffers from the Coldingham estates, for the lands were taken into the hands of the bishop of Durham.[61] The hardship and dislocation that they caused were sufficient to fulfill his intentions.

The years 1299–1302 were characterized by periods of intermittent war and truce, in which Edward's relations with Scotland were complicated by his interests in France. By 1303, however, English diplomatic maneuverings and Continental events had succeeded in dismantling the Franco-Scottish alliance, and Edward prepared once more to move against his enemies with a strong army. After a campaign lasting less than a year he presided once more as victor over a parliament (convened at St. Andrews) in which Scottish magnates submitted to an English conqueror. As in 1296, a few penitent rebels were restored to their estates within several months, though the full extent of the forfeitures remains unknown.[62] A parliament held at Westminster in 1305 promulgated a lengthy ordinance for the future government of Scotland, henceforth referred to in English records as the "land," rather than the "realm" or "kingdom," of Scotland.[63]

The magnanimity that Edward displayed toward the Scots on this occasion has been applauded by historians,[64] but closer inspection reveals that his fairness and generosity were, in reality, little more than political astuteness. In 1304–5 Edward enjoyed the support of the papacy, which had, until very recently, been favorable to the Scottish cause. In France King Philip IV no longer had the means or the will to assist his former allies. Finally, at home the constitutional problems that had so disturbed the king in the late 1290s had abated by the opening years of the fourteenth century.[65] Even more than in 1296, then, Edward could afford to be forgiving. The restoration of the magnates and the leading role assigned to John Comyn of Badenoch in arranging a new government for Scotland were deliberately and shrewdly designed to win over by suasion the Scottish landowners and their followers. Among the landed persons thus fortuitously reinstated in their lands was Marie widow of Sir Alexander de Stirling, who had lost estates in Lanark and Dumfries.[66] The widow of Sir Thomas de Soules, however, was able to enjoy the king's generosity only after several years of troublesome legal wrangling, during which her claims were much hampered by the manifest treason of her late husband and his brother.[67]

The Scots were by no means defeated in 1304–5. Early in 1306 they were once again in arms against England, this time under the energetic leadership of a new king, Robert Bruce. Edward, at first incredulous, quickly sought and was given information on the sequence of events that had brought Bruce to the Scots throne—that is, the murder of John Comyn on 10 February, Bruce's seizure of several key fortresses, his coronation as king of Scots on 25 March, and a second inauguration two days later, when Isabella, countess of Buchan, performed the ceremony of enthroning the new monarch, a role traditionally reserved to the earls of Fife.[68]

The depth of Edward's anger when confirmation of Scottish events reached him is attested both in official record and chronicle accounts. A royal commission appointed Sir Aymer de Valence, earl of Pembroke, as the king's lieutenant in Scotland and granted him unusually extensive powers to wage war on the rebels.[69] John Barbour's chronicle notes that the earl was instructed to raise the banner of death over the realm, to burn and to slay—to unleash, in other words, the terrible effects of the *guerre mortelle*.[70] The Brut chronicler is even more explicit: he states that, when Edward heard of Bruce's enthronement, "he swore þat he wolde þerof bene avenged, and saide þat 'alle þe traitours of Scotland shuld bene hongede and draw, and þat þai shulde neuer bene raunsonede.' And Kyng Edward þouzt oppon þis falsenesse þat þe Scottes hade done."[71]

Pembroke's skill as a military commander won the day at the battle of Methven in June 1306. Bruce fled the field and went into hiding, but many of the noblemen who had fought on his behalf were taken prisoner and compelled to experience what one historian has described as the "brief reign of terror" that followed.[72]

The grisly executions of the earls of Atholl, Simon Fraser, Christopher Seton, Neil Bruce, and other friends and supporters of Robert Bruce have been extensively discussed and assessed by historians;[73] all are unanimous in their opinion that, even by contemporary standards, Edward treated these Scottish rebels with unusual severity. The chivalric conventions of the day enjoined a victor always to temper his anger with clemency, to have a proper regard for the merciful qualities of a virtuous prince. In 1306, however, Edward exhibited a grim disregard for the niceties of chivalric conduct. Nowhere was his abandonment of conventions more vividly evident than in the treatment he reserved for the wives and widows of defeated Scotsmen. The womenfolk of those who, in the king's opinion, had offended him most grievously were punished in a fashion intended to be commensurate with their spouses' perfidy. In the process the families of almost all Scottish landholders, great and small, came to feel to some degree the wrath of the English Crown.

Typical of the middling sort of landowners punished as a result of the events of 1306 were the widows Maud de Carrick and Margaret Fraser. Forfeited and restored once already since the outbreak of war a decade earlier,[74] Maud petitioned the king immediately following her dispossession for restitution of her considerable lands and appurtenances in Cumberland,[75] but to little avail. Angered by what he considered her evident contumacy, Edward dismissed her request, and she was not, in the end, restored to her estates until just before her death late in 1307, by a more forgiving Edward II. Her son was not permitted to succeed to his mother's lands until he had performed homage and fealty before the king in person.[76] Margaret, the widow of Gilbert Fraser, fared even more poorly: because of her kinship with the hated traitor, Sir Simon Fraser, her modest estates were granted to an English petitioner, together with her marriage.[77]

The most severe punishments of all, and those for which he has been most heavily censured, Edward reserved for the women of Robert Bruce's immediate entourage. In the confused weeks following the rout of the Scots at Methven, Bruce made arrangements for the safety of the womenfolk of his retinue, including his wife, Queen Elizabeth, his two sisters, Christian and Mary, his daughter, Marjorie, and Isabel, daughter of the earl of Fife and countess of Buchan.[78] The women were sent first to Kildrummy, whence they fled to the sanctuary of St. Duthac at Tain. Here, however, they were seized by William, earl of Ross, and sent under escort to England.[79]

Edward dealt with each of the women according to the degree of her complicity in Bruce's treason. He found himself in something of a quandary with respect to Bruce's wife, Elizabeth. According to one chronicler, she had derided her husband's pretensions on the occasion of their coronation,[80] and Edward regarded her attitude as deserving of some consideration. She was, moreover, the daughter of his faithful vassal, Richard de Burgh, earl of Ulster. But her support of Bruce in his rise to power was evident and could not be regarded in anything other than a stern and unforgiving light. Accordingly, arrangements for the custody of "the wife of the earl of Carrick," as she was still referred to, were made before Elizabeth had reached England: she was to be sent to the royal manor at Burstwick in Holderness and lodged there in comfort.[81] There was no mistaking the fact that the countess's confinement was to be anything other than strict imprisonment. Detailed instructions were set out regarding the household she was to be permitted—two members of which were to be "a maid and a woman for her chamber, who shall be of a good age and not cheerful"—but she was at all times to be watched carefully by male servants, chosen for their loyalty to Edward's own person. Moreover, the length of her term of confinement was deliberately left vague.[82] More distressing still was the fact that, almost as soon as she was settled at Burstwick, King Edward forgot all about Elizabeth de Burgh. Within months she wrote to him to report that her keepers "will not find for me [clothes] for my body, nor attire for my head, nor bed, nor ought that pertains to my chamber, save only a suit of three changes of apparel by the year," and to plead that she be assigned regular monies for her sustenance.[83]

Elizabeth became, in effect, a widow of the Scottish war, for she spent eight long years in strict confinement. Though Edward II granted her the pension that she had sought from his father, as well as occasional gifts of provisions,[84] her value as a hostage made her particularly vulnerable to the changing fortunes of the war with Scotland. As Bruce's position in Scotland improved and the strength of Scottish resistance increased in the years after 1308, Edward II found it necessary to keep Elizabeth's person at a safer distance from the Scottish border than Holderness. In 1308 she was transferred from Burstwick to the abbey of Biddlesdon in Buckinghamshire, to Windsor castle in 1312, to Shaftesbury in 1313, to the convent of Barking in Essex also in 1313, and finally, early in 1314, to Rochester castle, with careful provision made for her custody at each new stage of this peripatetic existence.[85] It was not until October 1314 that she was released from captivity, in an exchange involving several valuable English prisoners taken at Bannockburn.[86]

Christian Bruce, the sister of King Robert, was also sentenced to lengthy captivity in England, but not until after she had been widowed as a consequence of the brutal retaliation that Edward exacted upon her husband, Christopher Seton.[87] She was sent to the Gilbertine nunnery of Sixhills in Lincolnshire, where she was allotted a modest three pence per day for her sustenance. Like Bruce's wife, she was not finally released from the king's custody until 1314.[88]

Elizabeth de Burgh and Christian Bruce were treated harshly but not in unusually cruel fashion, for Edward recognized their value as hostages in future negotiations with the rebel Scots. Bruce's other female retainers, however, were shown no such mercy: just as he chose to spare Elizabeth and Christian, so did Edward fully intend that the punishment of the other noblewomen convey to Robert Bruce and the whole Scottish nation the full impact of the wrath of an aggrieved English Crown.[89] Isabel, countess of Buchan, who had assisted in enthroning the rebel king, and another royal sister, Mary Bruce, were dispatched to Berwick and Roxburgh, respectively, both castles chosen deliberately for their location within conquered Scottish territory. There elaborate arrangements were made for their imprisonment in cages of wood and iron.

Edward's instructions regarding the cages were clear. A royal writ commanded:

> that the chamberlain of Scotland, or his deputy at Berwick upon Tweed do, in one of the turrets of the said castle, cause construct a cage strongly latticed with wood, crossbarred, and secured with iron, in which he shall put the Countess of Buchan. And that he take care that she be so well and safely guarded therein, that in no sort she may issue therefrom. And that he appoint one or more women of Berwick, of English extraction, and liable to no suspicion, who shall minister to the said Countess in eating and drinking, and in all things else

convenient, in her said lodging place. And that he do cause her to be so well and strictly guarded in the cage, that she may not speak with any one, man or woman, of the Scottish nation, or with any one else, saving with the woman who shall be appointed to attend her or with the guard who shall have custody of her person. And that the cage be so constructed that the Countess may have therein the convenience of a decent chamber, nevertheless, that all things be so well and surely ordered, that no peril shall arise touching the right custody of the said Countess.[90]

One chronicle account adds further detail to this description: when informed of the countess of Buchan's capture Edward reputedly commented:

Because she did not smite with the sword, she shall not perish by the sword. But because of the unlawful crowning which she made, let her be kept most fastly in an iron crown, made after the fashion of a little house, whereof let the breadth and length, the height and the depth, be finished in the space of eight feet; and let her be hung up for ever at Berwick under the open sky, that all they who pass may see her, and know for what cause she is there.[91]

Mary Bruce was ordered confined under similar conditions in Roxburgh castle,[92] and Edward apparently intended that a third cage be constructed in the Tower for the incarceration of Bruce's twelve-year-old daughter, Marjorie. The latter order was almost immediately rescinded, however, and the girl was sent under guard to the priory of Watton in Yorkshire. There she remained under the watchful eye of King Edward II until 1314.[93]

G. W. S. Barrow has suggested that the king's inspiration for the punishment of Mary Bruce and the countess of Buchan may have originated in Continental conflicts of the mid-thirteenth century,[94] but Edward himself was not unfamiliar with this form of imprisonment. Only one year earlier he had had a similar cage built at Bristol castle to house Owen, son of David ap Gryffudd.[95] Indeed, the general nature of the punishments meted out in 1306 closely resembled the treatment of Welsh women and children following the execution of David in 1283. His elder son, Llewelyn, had also been closely confined in Bristol castle, while his daughters and niece spent the rest of their lives in English nunneries.[96]

Mary Bruce and the countess of Buchan remained in their cages for almost four years. In the spring of 1310 arrangements were made to exchange Mary for an English prisoner then in captivity in Scotland, but the king was not yet ready to release her.[97] Another exchange was mooted early in 1312, when Edward II suggested that the sheriff of Northumberland secure what ransom he could for her, but once again Mary's release was postponed, and she was returned to the custody of the sheriff. She was not finally permitted to leave England until the victory of the Scots at Bannockburn in 1314 provided her brother with the political leverage he required for her release.[98]

The "faithless conspirator,"[99] Isabel, countess of Buchan, was released from her cage just a month after Mary Bruce. Edward II, perhaps in recognition of her ill health, permitted her to take up residence in the Carmelite house in Berwick, but, although by now widowed, she was still considered too dangerous and outspoken a patriot to merit her freedom.[100] In 1313 she was committed to the custody of Sir Henry Beaumont, who, together with his wife, Alice Comyn, now claimed the earldom of Buchan. She spent the rest of her life under their watchful eyes.[101]

The harsh retribution that Edward I exercised on the women of Bruce's immediate entourage has always provoked comment and criticism among historians; indeed, condemnation of the king's actions has elicited a rare degree of consensus among scholars otherwise deeply divided in their assessment of this English ruler.[102] Edward treated Bruce's female followers in brutal, highly exceptional fashion. While he was aware that the vindictiveness and lack of moderation that he exhibited were very much at odds with the conduct expected of a Christian prince, he refused to permit custom or convention to temper his actions.

In 1306 Edward was well into the second decade of a war that he continued to claim was nothing less than the rebellion of a contumacious vassal against his lawful lord. The face of the vassal had undergone significant transformation since 1295, from that of John Balliol to those of the self-appointed Guardians of the Realm of Scotland, to that of Robert Bruce. But for Edward the nature of the rebellion had not significantly altered, and his determination to crush the rising had not diminished. Indeed, it had now become imperative, for the would-be king of Scots now claimed a sovereignty that, in Edward's unwavering opinion, was utterly and indisputably illegal. The king's views on the

Scottish situation closely paralleled those that had governed his harsh treatment of the leaders of another, earlier rebellion, the Welsh uprising of 1294–95.[103] On this occasion, too, continued refusal to accept Edward's rights as overlord had signaled the end of any inclination he might have felt toward clemency or generosity.

Edward's single-minded belief in the righteousness of his cause and his consequent determination to punish in appropriate fashion rebels of all stations were also given expression in the treatment he meted out to men and women other than those of Bruce's immediate entourage. The earl of Menteith, forfeited in May 1306, was imprisoned at Abergavenny, while his wife, Marjory, was committed for life to the manor of Wooton, Northamptonshire.[104] Mary de Graham, the widow of a prominent Scottish patriot, lost all claim to her husband's lands in Scotland and was permitted to regain seisin of the considerable lands she had inherited in England through her mother only on condition that she and her son remain forever in England. Under such pressure Mary accepted the realities of her situation. She duly became a sworn tenant of the English Crown and never again returned to Scotland.[105] The wife of William Wysman, who had presumably taken an active part in assisting Robert Bruce, was rounded up in the aftermath of Methven. Though hardly a serious threat to the settlement of Scotland, she was placed in the custody of the constable of Roxburgh castle and lodged there indefinitely.[106]

Edward I chose to deal with the widows of important Scottish landholders according to their individual offenses and merits. "Lesser folk" were nevertheless not permitted to escape the consequences of his wrath. An ordinance issued at Lanercost in 1307, while the king lay gravely ill, bears witness to Edward's enduring determination to punish all of Bruce's supporters, great and small. It commanded that such persons be pursued "with the hue and cry . . . as forcibly as may be from town to town, region to region, county to county, until they come to the king's peace as of right or are taken alive or dead"; those who refused to submit were to be adjudged traitors and forfeited. Persons involved in any way in the murder of John Comyn were to be hanged and drawn; those who had assisted or advised Bruce in his seizure of the throne of Scotland were likewise to be drawn, hanged, and also beheaded. Those who surrendered to the English, "be they clerks or otherwise," were to be forfeited and committed to indefinite imprisonment. A final clause stated grimly: "And the poor commons of Scotland, who were compelled to rise against the king in this war, shall be put to ransoms . . . each according to the gravity of his trespass."[107]

These were the words of a ruler driven by intense anger. They were also the commands of a king who, extremely ill, though he was, and no doubt conscious of the imminence of his death, nevertheless continued to manifest a grim determination to punish a people whom he adjudged to be persistent, unrepentant rebels. This was no "open" war, fought between sovereign Christian princes, in which the conventions and customs governing chivalric conduct must needs be taken under consideration and for his actions during which each king would have to account before God. Edward left little room in his war against the Scots for the qualities of mercy and forbearance. His obsessive conviction in the justness of his cause was translated into the acceptance that women, too, irrespective of their noncombatant status, must suffer the same castigation as male rebels.

Contemporary English opinion was apparently in agreement with Edward I's. Though some chroniclers commented on the increasing rage that characterized Edward's relations with the Scots in the years after 1296, few dared to be openly critical of the savagery that he demonstrated toward Bruce's followers in 1306. Remarkably, none considered his treatment of the female kin of Scottish rebels undeservedly harsh. In his account of the countess of Buchan's capture, Walter of Guisborough states simply that the lady was placed in a cage, "so that all passersby might look upon her and recognize her,"[108] and other writers describe the countess's punishment in equally laconic fashion.[109] To some observers the king was guilty not of unchivalric conduct but, rather, of an excess of generosity: two chroniclers suggest that the countess's husband wished to have her put to death for her treason but that Edward declined to take such action.[110] The Scottish chroniclers were not so sanguine or forgiving. John of Fordun, writing in the later fourteenth century, soundly condemned Edward's actions in outlawing the wives of men who had joined Bruce and decried the treatment he meted out to defenseless noncombatants throughout the war.[111]

Women's experience in war during the medieval period was seldom as detached as the writings of military theorists would have modern readers believe. While they were everywhere considered noncombatants, the deprivations they suffered both to home and property were as real as if they themselves had taken part in campaigns. Indeed, those losses were in a sense more profound than those that afflicted the soldiers who fought actively. For dozens of Scottish women the death of a husband and the forfeiture of family estates, which were the legacies of war against Edward I of England, represented the loss not only of emotional and material well-being but also of the very elements that gave them protection under the law of the land and a claim, however tenuous, to the governance of the kingdom. For others condemnation to a life in foreign nunneries as political widows was equally devastating, for such sentences deprived them just as effectively of participation in a normal life.

Edward I's death wrought little change in the harsh conditions that Scottish women had experienced for more than a decade. Edward II granted no general amnesty to Scottish women (or anyone else) in the weeks following his father's death in July 1307; indeed, no formal amnesty was ever forthcoming for the likes of Bruce's wife and daughters, who remained in captivity until Edward II was able to trade on their value as political hostages, or for the countess of Buchan.[112] Many of the women whose husbands perished in the course of the war were still in England long after 1307, seeking compensation for their losses or living as unwilling guests of the English Crown.[113] Edward II displayed little reluctance, however, in accepting and perpetuating the decisions made by his father with respect to these women. Like Edward I, he considered them rebels against their rightful overlord, and for the duration of his own lifetime Edward dealt with forfeited widows in as unforgiving a fashion as his father had. It was not until 1328, when the war was brought to a conclusion by the Treaty of Edinburgh-Northampton, that England recognized the sovereignty of the Scottish kingdom. By then many of the widows of the earliest participants in the war had died. It was left to their children—the so-called Disinherited—to settle with another, the third Edward, the claims for restitution and compensation that had been bequeathed to them.

NOTES

The author wishes to acknowledge the assistance of the Social Sciences and Humanities Research Council of Canada in the preparation of this essay.

1. *Commendatio Lamentabilis in Transitu Magni Regis Edwardi,* in *Chronicles of the Reigns of Edward I and Edward II,* ed. W. Stubbs, 2 vols., RS 76

(1882–83): 2:61; *The Chronicle of John de Langtoft,* ed. T. Wright, 2 vols., RS 47 (1866–68), 2:381, 383.

2. M. Prestwich, *Edward I* (London, 1988), 508.

3. See the descriptions of Edward's reign in *Johannis de Fordun Chronica Gentis Scotorum,* ed. W. F. Skene (Edinburgh, 1871), 344 (English version in *John of Fordun's Chronicle of the Scottish Nation,* ed. W. F. Skene [Edinburgh, 1872], 336); and Hector Boece, *The Chronicle of Scotland, 1571,* ed. E. C. Batho and H. W. Husbands, 2 vols., Scottish Text Society (1938–41), 2:268, 269.

4. *Johannis de Trokelowe, et Henrici de Blaneforde monachorum S. Albani, necnon quorundam anonymorum, Chronica et Annales,* ed. H. T. Riley, RS 28 (1866): 49–50; *Willelmi Rishanger quondam monachi S. Albami Chronica et Annales,* ed. H. T. Riley, RS 28 (1865): 120–21; *The Chronicle of Walter of Guiborough,* ed. H. Rothwell, Camden Society (1957), 227–28; P. Chaplais, "Some Private Letters of Edward I," *English Historical Review* 77 (1962): 79–86.

5. The most comprehensive study of the War of Independence is found in G. W. S. Barrow, *Robert Bruce and the Community of the Realm of Scotland,* 3d ed. (Edinburgh, 1988), 62–261; but see also R. Nicholson, *Scotland: The Later Middle Ages* (Edinburgh, 1974), 44–122; and M. Prestwich, *Edward I* (London, 1988), 356–75, 469–516; and G. W. S. Barrow, "A Kingdom in Crisis: Scotland and the Maid of Norway," *Scottish Historical Review* 69 (1990): 131–34.

6. E. M. Barron, *The Scottish War of Independence: A Critical Study,* 2d ed. (Inverness, 1934), 224–35. Barron's arguments are revised and reassessed in Barrow, *Robert Bruce,* 154–60; "Lothian in the First War of Independence, 1296–1328," *Scottish Historical Review* 55 (1976): 151–71; "The Clergy in the War of Independence," in *The Kingdom of the Scots,* ed. Barrow (London, 1973), 233–54; and Alexander Grant, *Independence and Nationhood: Scotland, 1306–1469* (London, 1984), 3–18. For an account of the troubles experienced by a single noble family, see C. J. Neville, "The Political Allegiance of the Earls of Strathearn during the War of Independence," *Scottish Historical Review* 65 (1986): 133–53.

7. M. Keen, *The Laws of War in the Late Middle Ages* (London, 1965), 70, 79–80.

8. Edward I is known to have owned a French translation of the fourth-century writer Flavius Vegetius Renatus's treatise *De Re Militari* (*L'Art de chevalerie, traductiion du "De Re Militari" de Végèce, par Jean de Meun,* ed. U. Robert, Société des Anciens Textes Français [1897], vi–viii; D. Legge, "The Lord Edward's Vegetius," *Scriptorium* 7 [1953]: 262–65). On the influence of military treatises on the conduct of war, see P. Contamine, *War in the Middle Ages,* trans. M. Jones (Oxford, 1986), 210–18; and P. Contamine, "The War Literature of the Late Middle Ages: The Treatises of Robert de Balsac and Béraud Stuart, Lord

of Aubigny," in *War, Literature and Politics,* ed. C. T. Allmand (Liverpool, 1976), 102–3.

9. Contamine, *War in the Middle Ages,* 305. In the fourteenth century Honoré Bonet included a brief discussion of noncombatants in his own version of Vegetius' treatise. *The Tree of Battles of Honoré Bonet,* ed. G. W. Coopland (Cambridge, Mass., 1947), 144–45, 168. See also C. T. Allmand, "The War and Non-combatant," in *The Hundred Years War,* ed. K. Fowler (London, 1971), 163–83.

10. Keen, *Laws of War,* 82–104.

11. Between June 1291 and Nov. 1292 Edward I sat in judgment over the disputed succession to the throne of Scotland, an episode known as the Great Cause. A month after he ruled in favor of John Balliol's claim King John performed homage for, and received seisin of, the kingdom of Scotland (Nicholson, *Scotland: The Later Middle Ages,* 36–43; Barrow, *Robert Bruce,* 30–38; Prestwich, *Edward I,* 356–75). The voluminous documents arising from the Great Cause are collected in E. L. G. Stones and G. G. Simpson, eds., *Edward I and the Throne of Scotland,* 2 vols. (Oxford, 1978).

12. Balliol performed homage and fealty to Edward in "unambiguous terms" several times over, most notably after judgment had been given in his favor in Nov. 1292, in Dec. 1292 following his enthronement, and in Oct. 1293, when he appeared before the English parliament (Stones and Simpson, *The Great Cause,* 2:260–63; *Rotuli Parliamentorum . . . ,* 6 vols. [n.p., n.d.], 1:113; Prestwich, *Edward I,* 370).

13. On the subject of the just war, see F. Russell, *The Just War in the Middle Ages* (Cambridge, 1975), 213–57; and Keen, *Laws of War,* 63–81.

14. In 1296 the two-year-old son of William Douglas, found at Stebbings, was arrested and held captive pending Edward's instructions (*Calendar of Documents relating to Scotland preserved in Her Majesty's Public Record Office,* ed. J. Bain, 4 vols. [Edinburgh, 1881–88], 2, no. 736; *Calendar of Fine Rolls 1272–1307,* 372).

15. William Rishanger records an oath sworn by Edward in the year 1300 in which the king threatened to lay waste "the whole of Scotland, from sea to sea" (*Chron. Rishanger,* 447). At the great Feast of the Swans in May 1306 Edward is said to have vowed that, once he had taken his vengeance on Robert Bruce, he would never again bear arms against a Christian prince (Nicholas Trivet, *Annales,* cited in N. Denholm-Young, "The Song of Carlaverock and the Parliamentary Roll of Arms as Found in Cott. MS. Calig. A. XVIII in the British Museum," *Proceedings of the British Academy* 47 [1961]: 258).

16. Barrow, *Robert Bruce,* 69; *Parliamentary Writs and Writs of Military Summons, Edward I and Edward II,* ed. F. Palgrave, 2 vols., Record Commission (1827–34), 2:275–78; *Calendar of Close Rolls, 1288–96,* 473; *Documents Illustrative of the History of Scotland from the Death of King Alexander the Third*

to the *Accession of Robert Bruce, MCCLXXXVI–MCCCVI,* ed. J. Stevenson, 2 vols. (Edinburgh, 1870), 2:22–23. Further instructions concerning the recruitment of troops followed in Feb. 1296 (*Cal. Docs. Scot.,* 2, no. 727; *Cal. Patent Rolls, 1292–1301,* 184). For a specific command, relating to the lands of Edmund Comyn of Kilbride, see Stevenson, *Documents,* 2:20–21.

17. *Cal. Fine Rolls, 1272–1307,* 372; PRO E 352/94. Douglas had already had a brush with Edward I's anger when, in 1289, he abducted Eleanor and married her without the king's license (E 371/52 m 3); Stevenson, *Documents,* 1:83, 85, 154, 155; *Illustrations of Scottish History from the Twelfth to the Sixteenth Century,* ed. J. Stevenson, Maitland Club (1834), 35. A decade and a half later Eleanor was still negotiating with the Crown regarding the fine that Douglas had been compelled to pay for the offense (*Cal. Close Rolls, 1302–7,* 240; PRO E 159/76 m 25d, E 159/78 m 81d).

18. *Cal. Fine Rolls, 1272–1307,* 356, 386; *Cal. Close Rolls, 1296–1302,* 225; PRO E 159/71 mm 63, 67d; C 81/20 (1898), C47/22/4(6).

19. *Cal. Fine Rolls, 1272–1307,* 372; *Cal. Close Rolls, 1288–96,* 492.

20. *Cal. Fine Rolls, 1272–1307,* 372.

21. *Cal. Patent Rolls, 1301–7,* 161; Barrow, *Robert Bruce,* 358 n. 80; *Parl. Writs,* 1:284; H. Gough, ed., *Scotland in 1298* (London, 1888), 196; *Cal. Docs. Scot.,* 3, nos. 406, 691, 789, 839, 935; *Cal. Close Rolls, 1318–23,* 188; *Cal. Close Rolls, 1327–30,* 39, 166, 268, 323, 454.

22. *Chron. Guisborough,* 275; *Chron. Rishanger,* 157, 373–74; *Chronicon Henrici Knighton,* ed. J. R. Lumby, RS 92 (1889), 304; *Flores Historiarum,* ed. H. R. Luard, 3 vols., RS 95 (1890), 3:96–97.

23. John of Fordun, writing almost a century after the event, states that, "sparing neither sex nor age, the aforesaid king of England, in his tyrannous rage, bade them put to the sword 7500 souls of both sexes," and Andrew of Wyntoun, writing later still, reports that neither cleric nor lay person, old or young, master or servant, maid or wife escaped the king's wrath: "þe liffis al þai tuk þaim fra" (*John of Fordun's Chronicle of the Scottish Nation,* 318; *Johannis de Fordun Chronica Gentis Scotorum,* 324; Andrew of Wyntoun, *The Orygynale Cronykil of Scotland,* ed. D. Laing, 6 vols., Scottish Text Society [1903–14], 5:283–85).

24. *The Chronicle of Lanercost, 1272–1346,* trans. H. Maxwell (Glasgow, 1913), 135.

25. *Instrumenta publica sive processus super fidelitatibus et homagiis Scotorum domino regi Angliae factis, 1291–96,* ed. T. Thomson, Bannatyne Club (1834), 118–74, calendared in *Cal. Docs. Scot.,* 2, no. 823. The complicated procedures whereby individual fealties, some sworn personally, others by proxy, were recorded on the Ragman Roll are discussed in Barrow, *Robert Bruce,* 76–77.

26. *Instrumenta publica,* 156.

27. *Instrumenta publica,* 164. Mary appears in the records relating to the War of Independence under a bewildering variety of names. She is sometimes, as in 1296, styled queen of Man, for she was the widow of King Magnus of Man. She appears also as countess of Strathearn, widow of earl Malise II (d. 1271), whom she had married in 1265; in the 1280s as the widow of Hugh of Abernethy; and in the 1290s as wife, then widow, of the Englishman Sir William FitzWarin. But in petitions to King Edward I she also recalls her paternal origins by styling herself Mary of Argyll: she was the daughter of Ewen of Argyll. She remained loyal to King Edward until her death in 1302 (*The Scots Peerage,* ed. J. Balfour Paul, 9 vols. [Edinburgh, 1904–14], 7:400–401, 8:246–47; *Extracta e variis cronicis Scocie,* ed. W. B. D. D. Turnbull, Abbotsford Club [1842], 109; *Acts of the Parliaments of Scotland,* ed. T. Thomson and C. Innes, 12 vols., in 13; Record Commission [1814–75], 1:446; *Vetera monumenta Hibernorum et Scotorum historiam illustrantia,* ed. A. Theiner [Rome, 1864], no. 277; PRO E 159/73 m 32d; E 159/78 m 62d). See also C. J. Neville, "The Earls of Strathearn from the Twelfth to the Mid-Fourteenth Century, with an Edition of their Written Acts" (Ph.D. diss., University of Aberdeen, 1983), 112–13.

28. *Instrumenta publica,* 146.

29. Stevenson, *Documents,* 2:86–87.

30. *Foedera, conventiones, literae, etc.,* ed. T. Rymer, 10 vols., fac. ed. (The Hague, 1739–45), 1, 3:164. On 2 Sept. the Scottish religious houses were similarly restored to their lands. The writs commanding restitution included the names of several Scottish prioresses. Unmarried women were accorded similar courtesy. Thus, Ela de Ardross, Christine Lockhart, Agnes de Twisel, and others, "who have never been married . . . and who have remained loyal to us," received seisin of their Scottish lands, also after their homage and fealty had been confirmed in the Ragman Roll (*Rotuli Scotiae in Turri Londinensi et in domo capitulari Westmonasteriensi asservati,* ed. D. MacPherson, 2 vols., Record Commission [1814–19], 1:24–25, 26, 29; PRO E 370/1/10).

31. Mary, the wife of William FitzWarin, traveled to Scotland in Apr. 1299 to visit her husband, then in captivity. As "former queen of Man," she was in receipt of a royal gift of wine and victuals in 1300; she died in the king's peace in 1302 (Stevenson, *Illustrations,* 37; *Cal. Patent Rolls, 1292–1301,* 407; PRO E 159/73 m 32d; E 101/8/10). Although her allegiance to the English Crown was genuine, Mary nevertheless petitioned the king in 1299 as "a friend of the Scottish prisoners in England," for an exchange of Englishmen and Scotsmen then being held in captivity (Stevenson, *Illustrations,* 36). A few women made a much more conspicuous commitment to the English side. Euphemia, countess of Ross, whose husband was taken prisoner in 1296 and sent to the Tower, abandoned the Scottish cause altogether and later actively assisted the English forces with men, arms, and horses (*Cal. Close Rolls, 1288–96,* 481; Stevenson, *Documents,* 2:210–11, 214; PRO SC 1/16/33; SC 1/15/138; SC 1/20/47).

32. Stevenson, *Documents,* 2:303–4; PRO C 47/22/8(3); Barrow, *Robert Bruce,* 106.

33. C. Moor, *Knights of Edward I,* 5 vols., Harleian Society (1929–32), 4:112.

34. Stevenson, *Documents,* 2:87–91; *Rot. Scot.,* 1:26–27.

35. *Scots Peerage,* 1:508–10, 2:255–58; Moor, *Knights of Edward I,* 1:229–32; J. R. S. Phillips, *Aymer de Valence Earl of Pembroke, 1307–1324* (Oxford, 1972), 2, 15, 16.

36. *Rot. Scot.,* 1:28; PRO E 370/1/10; Stevenson, *Documents,* 2:97–98. Joan's father, Sir William de Valence, had been the half-brother of King Henry III (Phillips, *Aymer de Valence,* 2).

37. *Cal. Patent Rolls, 1292–1301,* 200, 202; *Cal. Close Rolls, 1288–96,* 480.

38. Stevenson, *Documents,* 2:93; *Foedera,* 1, 3:164; *Cal. Patent Rolls, 1292–1301,* 395.

39. John Comyn had been sent to the Tower in May 1296. Duncan, the young heir of the earl of Fife, had been under Edward's close guardianship from the time of his infancy (*Cal. Close Rolls, 1288–96,* 481; Barrow, *Robert Bruce,* 45).

40. Stevenson, *Documents,* 2:92–98.

41. One commission of inquiry was assembled at Berwick on 3 Sept., presided over by Hugh Despenser, Walter de Beauchamp, the king's steward, John de Droxford, keeper of the Wardrobe, and John Benstead. Another commission, empowered to hear similar petitions, was not, however, convened until Jan. 1297 (Stevenson, *Documents,* 2:96–97; *Rot. Scot.,* 1:38). Barrow's comment that Edward "was willing to give ear to" the pleas of several widows at Berwick obscures the fact that not all were adjudicated immediately and that several women never received restitution of Scottish dower lands. See G. W. S. Barrow, "The Aftermath of War: Scotland and England in the Late Thirteenth and Early Fourteenth Centuries," *Transactions of the Royal Historical Society,* 5th ser. 28 (1978): 115.

42. Stevenson, *Documents,* 2:92.

43. *Cal. Close Rolls, 1288–96,* 481. Siward's estates in Scotland and England were forfeited immediately after his capture at Dunbar (*Cal. Fine Rolls, 1272–1307,* 371; PRO E 352/94). His role in the events of 1296 are described in *Chron. Langtoft,* 2:241–49.

44. Stevenson, *Documents,* 2:93; PRO E 370/1/10. In 1294 Mary had received a gift of twelve does from the king's forest at Fakenham (*Cal. Close Rolls, 1288–96,* 406). Elizabeth's husband, Richard, Jr., was lodged in Bristol castle after the battle of Dunbar (*Cal. Close Rolls, 1288–96,* 483).

45. Moor, *Knights of Edward I,* 4:254–55.

46. *Foedera,* 1, 3:164; PRO E 370/1/10; E 159/80 m 96. The Siward family

thereafter remained loyal to the English Crown. See *Calendar of Chancery Warrants, 1244–1326,* 358; *Cal. Patent Rolls, 1301–7,* 503; Stevenson, *Illustrations,* 44; Barrow, *Robert Bruce,* 281.

47. Stevenson, *Documents,* 2:94–95.

48. Sir David Dalrymple Lord Hailes, *Annals of Scotland from the Accession of Malcolm surnamed Canmore to the Accession of the House of Stuart,* 2d ed., 3 vols. (Edinburgh, 1797), 2:267. Contemporary opinion supports the sentiment: a letter of Lady Margaret de Soules, dated early Jan. 1297, notes that the king "has granted all the ladies of Scotland their terces and dowries" (PRO SC 8/6983).

49. Barrow, *Robert Bruce,* 78.

50. *Chron. Rishanger,* 414; *Chron. Langtoft,* 311; Barrow, *Robert Bruce,* 98, 345 n. 41.

51. Gough, *Scotland in 1298,* 83; *Cal. Close Rolls, 1296–1302,* 204.

52. Stevenson, *Documents,* 2:272–73; *Cal. Patent Rolls, 1292–1301,* 337.

53. In Feb. 1299 Joan Comyn was granted safe conduct to visit her husband in Scotland, but she returned to England and spent the rest of her life there. (*Cal. Patent Rolls, 1292–1301,* 395). Her son, John, married the English heiress Margaret Wake of Liddel and fell fighting on the English side at the battle of Bannockburn (*Scots Peerage,* 1:509–10; Moor, *Knights of Edward I,* 1:232; *Cal. Patent Rolls, 1307–13,* 510; *Chron. Lanercost,* 208; *Cal. Patent Rolls, 1313–17,* 164, 657). Joan Comyn, the daughter of John Comyn of Badenoch, married David de Strathbolgie and was still alive in 1328; the other daughter, Elizabeth Comyn, married Sir Richard Talbot. They eventually succeeded as coheiresses to the estates of their uncle, Aymer de Valence, and their brother, John Comyn (*Scots Peerage,* 1:510; Moor, *Knights of Edward I,* 1:232; *Cal. Close Rolls, 1323–27,* 244; *Calendar of Inquisitions Post Mortem,* 6, no. 697 [hereafter *CIPM*]).

54. Joan returned to Scotland briefly, early in 1299, "to have a colloquy with her husband," but she did not remain there beyond Whitsuntide (*Cal. Patent Rolls, 1292–1301,* 395).

55. *Scots Peerage,* 2:259; Moor, *Knights of Edward I,* 1:229–30; *Cal. Docs. Scot.,* 3, nos. 201, 249, 296; *Cal. Close Rolls, 1307–13,* 409.

56. PRO C 47/22/5(22); SC 1/14/104; *Cal. Fine Rolls, 1307–19,* 112, 267, 272; *Cal. Close Rolls, 1307–13,* 391, 395; *Cal. Patent Rolls, 1307–13,* 569; *Cal. Close Rolls, 1313–18,* 259; *Cal. Patent Rolls, 1313–17,* 539.

57. *Cal. Patent Rolls, 1317–21,* 512; *Foedera,* 2, 2:10.

58. *Cal. Docs. Scot.,* 3, no. 1006; *Cal. Close Rolls, 1327–30,* 174, 260, 279, 334, 457, 496; *Cal. Close Rolls, 1330–33,* 21, 85, 214, 494; *Cal. Close Rolls, 1333–37,* 28, 74, 257, 389–90, 616; *Cal. Close Rolls, 1337–39,* 48, 207, 377, 603; *Cal. Close Rolls, 1339–41,* 66, 198, 389, 541.

59. *Chron. Rishanger,* 388. While there is little doubt of the exaggerated

nature of Rishanger's account, the sentiments it represents were nonetheless genuine.

60. *The Correspondence, Inventories, Account Rolls, and Law Proceedings of the Priory of Coldingham,* ed. J. Raine, Surtees Society (1941), ciii, cii.

61. G. T. Lapsley, *The County Palatine of Durham* (New York, 1900) 43; *Historiae Dunelmensis scriptores tres: Gaufridus de Coldingham, Robertus de Graystanes, et Willelmus de Chambre,* ed. J. Raine, Surtees Society (1839), app. no. ccclii. The confiscations and forfeitures effected by Edward I in Coldingham following the uprising of 1298 are discussed in Barrow, "Aftermath of War," 116–19.

62. As Barrow has remarked, "We have no Ragman Roll for 1304," but two lists recording some of the submissions have survived. See Barrow, *Robert Bruce,* 133–34; *Documents and Records Illustrating the History of Scotland,* ed. F. Palgrave, Record Commission (1837), 194–97, 299–301.

63. A translation of the ordinance for the government of Scotland is reproduced in *Anglo-Scottish Relations, 1174–1328,* ed. E. L. G. Stones (Oxford, 1965), 241–59. The discussions in parliament that preceded its promulgation are narrated in *Flores Historiarum,* 3:124–25. The settlement of 1304–5 is reviewed in Barrow, *Robert Bruce,* (132–36). The constitutional implications of the change of terms are briefly reviewed in M. Prestwich, "Colonial Scotland: The English in Scotland under Edward I," in *Scotland and England, 1286–1815,* ed. R. A. Mason (Edinburgh, 1987), 15.

64. Barrow, for example, characterizes Edward's actions in 1304–5 as prudent and lenient and describes the settlement as "both mild and statesmanlike" (*Robert Bruce,* 132). Prestwich also writes in favorable terms about the settlement; see Prestwich, "Colonial Scotland," 9–10.

65. For a discussion of the crisis of 1297 and its aftermath, see Prestwich, *Edward I,* 410–35, 517–55; and *War, Politics and Finance under Edward I* (Totowa, N.J., 1972), 247–81.

66. PRO C 47/22/5(65).

67. *Cal. Close Rolls, 1301–7,* 129; PRO C 47/22/5(68); *Calendar of Inquisitions Miscellaneous, 1307–49,* no. 395; *Cal. Close Rolls, 1318–23,* 38–39.

68. The events of Feb. and Mar. 1306 are reviewed in Barrow, *Robert Bruce* (145–53), and Stones, *Anglo-Scottish Relations* (261–69).

69. *Foedera,* 1, 4:49; *Cal. Patent Rolls, 1301–7,* 426; *Parl. Writs,* 1:374.

70. *John Barbour: Barbour's Bruce,* ed. M. P. McDiarmid and J. A. C. Stevenson, 3 vols., Scottish Text Society (1980–85), 2:31–32. The significance of the dragon banner in war is discussed in Keen, *Laws of War* (105–9).

71. *The Brut or the Chronicles of England,* ed. F. W. D. Brie, Early English Text Society (1906–8), 200. Matthew of Westminster likewise speaks of Edward's grim determination in 1306 to crush the Scots once and for all (*Flores*

Historiarum, 3:324). The king's most recent biographer concurs: "Edward responded to the events of Scotland with unprecedented savagery" (Prestwich, *Edward I*, 508).

72. Barrow, *Robert Bruce*, 161.

73. See especially Barrow, *Robert Bruce*, 161–62, which discusses the chronicle accounts of the executions; and Prestwich, *Edward I*, 508.

74. *CIPM* 3, no. 583; *Cal. Fine Rolls, 1272–1307*, 430; *Cal. Close Rolls, 1296–1302*, 524–25; PRO C47/22/9(104).

75. Palgrave, *Docs. Hist. Scot.*, 316.

76. *Cal. Fine Rolls, 1307–19*, 6, 21; *CIPM* 5, no. 9; PRO C81/59 (162); E159/83 m 80d.

77. Palgrave, *Docs. Hist. Scot.*, 310.

78. Isabel's husband was John Comyn, earl of Buchan (d. 1308). She stole away from her husband in order to be present at Scone for Bruce's enthronement (*Chron. Guisborough*, 367; *Chron. Knighton*, 108–9).

79. Barbour, *Bruce*, 2:57–59, 74; *Chron. Fordun*, 2:334–35.

80. Marquess of Bute, "Notice of a Manuscript of the Later Part of the Fourteenth Century Entitled *Passio Scotorum perjuratorum*," *Proceedings of the Society of Antiquaries of Scotland*, n.s., 7 (1884–85): 172–73. Abbreviated versions of the story are also found in *Flores Historiarum*, 3:130, and *Chron. Guisborough*, 369–70.

81. She was permitted, e.g., three hounds for those occasions when she wished to hunt, ample venison and fish, and was given "the nicest house on the manor" (Palgrave, *Docs. Hist. Scot.*, 358; *Foedera*, 1, 4:58).

82. Palgrave, *Docs. Hist. Scot.*, 357–58; *Foedera*, 1, 4:58. The household was also to include a butler, two valets "advanced in age" (including one from the earl of Ulster's retinue), and a page boy, "who shall be sober and quiet."

83. *Facsimiles of the National Manuscripts of Scotland*, 3 vols., Record Commission (1867), 2, no. xvi.

84. PRO E 101/382/15 (misdated in *Cal. Docs. Scot.*, 3, nos. 299, to 1313); E 159/84 m 97d; E 159/87 m 146d; *Cal. Close Rolls, 1307–13*, 284, 511.

85. *Cal. Close Rolls, 1307–13*, 39, 284, 394, 511; *Cal. Close Rolls, 1313–18*, 43, 49; *Foedera*, 1, 4:204; 2, 1:64; PRO E 159/87 mm 146d, 147.

86. *Vita Edwardi Secundi*, ed. N. Denholm-Young (London, 1957), 58; Barbour, *Bruce*, 3:76; *Chronica Monasterii S. Albani Thomae Walsingham*, ed. H. T. Riley, RS 28 (1863), 142; *Chron. Lanercost*, 211; *Cal. Patent Rolls, 1313–17*, 160; *Foedera*, 2, 1:69, 72; PRO E 101/14/22.

87. Seton was drawn, hanged, and beheaded at Dumfries in the summer of 1306 for his part in the murder of John Comyn (*Chron. Guisborough*, 369). Christopher Seton's widowed mother also suffered grave material loss as a result of her son's rebellion. She petitioned parliament in 1306 for restitution of a

portion of her dower lands and was still suing for their recovery the following year (*Rot. Parl.*, 1:206; *Cal. Patent Rolls, 1301–7*, 465; PRO SC 8/2[57]; *Calendar of Charter Rolls, 1300–26*, 84).

88. Palgrave, *Docs. Hist. Scot.*, 359; *Chron. Guisborough*, 369; *Cal. Patent Rolls, 1301–7*, 503; *Cal. Close Rolls, 1307–13*, 14; *Cal. Close Rolls, 1313–18*, 108.

89. Prestwich argues that "Edward obviously decided to make a public spectacle of Mary Bruce and the countess of Buchan" (*Edward I*, 509).

90. Palgrave, *Docs. Hist. Scot.*, 358, trans. in Hailes, *Annals*, 11–12. See also *Foedera*, 1, 4:58–59.

91. *Passio Scotorum*, 175–76. These details are also found in *Flores Historiarum*, 3:324.

92. Palgrave, *Docs. Hist. Scot.*, 358–59; *Foedera*, 1, 4:59.

93. Palgrave, *Docs. Hist. Scot.*, 359; *Foedera*, 1, 4:59; *Cal. Patent Rolls, 1301–7*, 503; *Chron. Guisborough*, 369. Marjorie was the daughter of Bruce's first wife, Isabel of Mar.

94. Barrow, *Robert Bruce*, 162.

95. Prestwich, *Edward I*, 203.

96. Prestwich, *Edward I*, 203; F. M. Powicke, *King Henry the Third and the Lord Edward*, 2 vols. (Oxford, 1947), 2:684.

97. *Cal. Close Rolls, 1307–13*, 203; *Foedera*, 1, 4:166; PRO E159/87 m 13d. There is no reason to believe, as Barrow suggests, that Mary had been released from her cage at an earlier date; see Barrow, *Robert Bruce*, 162.

98. *Cal. Close Rolls, 1307–13*, 399, 406; *Cal. Docs. Scot.*, 3, no. 340.

99. *Flores Historiarum*, 3:324.

100. *Rot. Scot.*, 1:85. John Comyn, earl of Buchan, had died late in 1308 (*Scots Peerage*, 1:258; Moor, *Knights of Edward I*, 1:229).

101. *Cal. Close Rolls, 1307–13*, 409, 497–98, 529; *Foedera*, 2, 1:35. The earl of Buchan's heirs were his nieces Alice and Margaret, daughters of Alexander Comyn. Henry de Beaumont's claim was in right of his wife, Alice, who called herself countess of Buchan (*Scots Peerage*, 2:258).

102. Barrow states that the punishments bespoke a "peculiarly maniacal quality"; Prestwich similarly writes of the "savagery" and "highly unusual" nature of the king's orders. Even Sir Maurice Powicke, generally favorable to Edward, noted the "peculiar ferocity" of the sentences (Barrow, *Robert Bruce*, 162; Prestwich, *War, Politics and Finance*, 250; Prestwich, *Edward I*, 508; M. Powicke, *The Thirteenth Century, 1216–1307*, 2d ed. [Oxford, 1962], 716).

103. The punishment meted out to the leaders of the Welsh rebellion in 1295 are discussed in Prestwich, *Edward I* (224).

104. Marjory was left a widow in 1309, when her husband died in captivity. Only then was she permitted to depart, but, rendered landless by the earl's forfeiture, she chose instead to spend her remaining years at Wotton (*Scots

Peerage, 6:135; *Cal. Charter Rolls, 1300–26,* 68; *Cal. Patent Rolls, 1307–13,* 108).

105. In 1291 Mary inherited a moiety of the large barony of Muschamp, the lands of which were located chiefly in Northumberland. She performed homage and fealty to Edward I soon after the death of her rebel husband in May 1306 (Moor, *Knights of Edward I,* 2:135; *Cal. Fine Rolls, 1272–1307,* 394, 536; *Cal. Patent Rolls, 1292–1301,* 513; *CIPM* 3, no. 364; *Cal. Close Rolls, 1302–7,* 392; PRO C 81/1772; C 143/66[3]; E 159/84 m 32d; E 368/85 m 116d). For the division of Robert de Muschamp's inheritance, see also Neville, "Earls of Strathearn," 109–11, 107; *Foedera,* 1, 4:59.

106. *Foedera,* 1, 4:59.

107. Palgrave, *Docs. Hist. Scot.,* 361–63.

108. *Chron. Guisborough,* 367.

109. The chronicler William Rishanger notes simply that Isabella was placed "so that passers-by might look at her," and another writes that the countess was put in a little wooden chamber "so that all might look in from curiosity" (*Chron. Rishanger,* 229; *Scalacronica: The Reigns of Edward I, Edward II and Edward III,* trans. H. Maxwell [Glasgow, 1907], 31).

110. *Chron. Walsingham,* 108–9; *Chron. Guisborough,* 367.

111. *Johannis de Fordunn Chronica Gentis Scotorum,* 341–42.

112. A petition from Robert Keith requesting the release of Isabel of Buchan from her cage on compassionate grounds was rejected out of hand by Edward II (Barrow, *Robert Bruce,* 11).

113. Alice, wife of John de Caunton, former wife of Thomas de Soules, was typical of the sort of woman caught up in this dilemma. Although she performed homage to Edward I in 1306, she was compelled to sue the English Crown for her dower of Thomas's estates in Northumberland. She was not granted seisin of these lands until June 1310. The financial loss that she suffered in the years before she was restored is attested in a writ directed to the sheriff of Northumberland in Mar. 1310, to inquire into the dispersal and departure of numerous villeins since the time of the forfeiture (*Cal. Close Rolls, 1307–13,* 115, 203).

Chapter 6

Remarriage as an Option for Urban and Rural Widows in Late Medieval England

Barbara A. Hanawalt

Widows were an object of concern in medieval society. On the one hand, they could be vulnerable, but, on the other, they were potentially independent, powerful individuals. While a maiden, the woman's father had legal charge of her, and, while a wife, she was legally covered by the husband. But a widow could enter into contracts alone, sue for debt, run her business, till her land, and marry off her children. If she gained this economic and legal freedom of action, moralists worried, would she also exercise sexual freedom? Remarriage seemed a convenient solution to curb widows' freedoms and distribute their wealth to other males. In this chapter I will investigate the decision to remarry among peasant and urban widows. I will argue that in England generous dowers together with a widow's freedom to choose a new husband combined to emphasize horizontal, nonkin ties in urban and rural communities rather than vertical, patrilineal ones. Remarriage of widows thus undermined the strength of patriarchy among these groups in medieval England.[1]

My concern in this chapter, therefore, will be with widows' choice of remarriage as an option for spending their remaining days. These days might be short if they were widowed in plague times or if they were already over forty. But they might also be looking at a long widowhood if they were healthy and close to twenty. If they had minor children, they had needs that women without children would not have. If their marriage had been unpleasant or giving birth painful, then they might not want to remarry. On the other hand, they might not have children yet and hope to do so by remarrying. While widows had the legal freedom to continue cultivation, craft, or business, they may have found the prospect daunting and preferred to have a new husband handle the affairs. Other widows might respond with relish to their new independence. In addition to individual preferences and needs, all widows would face external pressures such as suitors' designs on their property and moral standards imposed by the Church, the community, and folk wisdom. Freedom in the Middle Ages always came with a price, and for widows the price could determine the limits on their freedom of choice.

Moralists' Advice to Widows

Medieval lay and ecclesiastical thinkers imbibed the concerns of Saint Paul and Saint Jerome that women's sexual appetites were voracious, particularly if they had already known sexual intercourse. While men mostly could keep a lid on women's sexuality through the father's control over his daughters, a husband's over his wife, and a bishop's over nuns, the one stage in a woman's life that defied such easy dominance was that of widowhood. Widows had independent financial means derived from marriage or inheritance. A widow probably did not have living parents, and, even if she did, their hold over their daughter and her property was tenuous, so that a widow might actually choose not to remarry; she might remarry whom she pleased; she might take her inheritance and dower to a nunnery; or she might realize the worst fears of the moralists and live wantonly. But what resources? Most men's real concern was with any material assets that the widow had available, but the moralistic literature seemed much more obsessed with her sexual resources. Sex did, indeed, have a practical side, since the heirs of a widow's body could insure inheritances and continuation of economic benefits, but the physical use, enjoyment, and disposal of her body was the main preoccupation of the moralists.

First, neighbors and friends expected the widow to wail and lament her loss, since failure to do so would indicate a hard heart. But the widow should not make an excessive show of mourning because that made others uncomfortable. She should bury her husband, see that his will was executed, and prepare to live a chaste life while rearing children and looking after her household. Somber clothing was commended:

> hit falleth to wedowes for to use symple and comune clothinge of
> mene colour and noght gay ne starynge, ne of queynte and sotil schap,
> and take ensample of the holy wedowe Judith, of whom holy writ

maketh mynde, that anone whan hir housbonde was deed sche lefte all hir gay attyre and apparaile.

Some moralists, however, could readily observe that black became the complexions of young widows, showing off the delicate tones of their skin and hair. Such vanity posed a threat to their chastity.[2]

Preservation of chastity came foremost in the minds of the moral advisors to widows. Now that her husband was gone, she would have to preserve her own good reputation. The advice followed the usual lines for women: keep to your house and surround yourself with honorable female servants. The moralists were particularly worried that these free women would dress well and wander about to tempt men and themselves with lust. One moralist concluded: "Of this Saint Paul complains. They go wandering about from house to house, and are not only idle but tattlers also and busy-bodies, speaking things which they ought not." He offers the solution that a neighbor had given to a man whose cat strayed: "Shorten her tail, cut her ears, and singe her fur; then she will stay at home." So too, he concluded, should immodest widows be treated so that "they will not then be so much desired of folk."[3]

Moralists had mixed views about remarriage of widows, as James Brundage has discussed in this volume. Marriage in itself was a sad necessity, for procreation and widowhood could not restore virginity in any case. For older widows the moralists recommended against remarriage. They were to educate their children and generously share their wealth with the Church and charities. But the younger widow, one whose traditional black garments set off the vermilion and white of her complexion, was a special problem. She must carefully observe humility and modesty to preserve her reputation. Since she would have more temptation to sin, her passions were still strong and she was attractive, she should remarry. If she did not have children, she should remarry soon. For some moralists the sad truth was that widows were likely to have wealth, and then it did not matter whether they were plain or beautiful: men would want to marry them.[4] With regret they realized that remarriage was likely.

Widows' Material Resources

We must, therefore, consider the resources available to widows in order to assess their options and decision about remarriage. I have elsewhere called medieval marriage a "partnership" marriage.[5] In both the urban and rural family the tasks of the husband and wife were well defined in order to make the family a viable economic unit. Nowhere was the partnership clearer than in negotiations to enter into marriage. Although no written contract might exist, family and friends arranging the marriage assumed that both partners to the venture would contribute a share to the financial success of the marriage and regarded their negotiations as binding. To insure that everyone else in the community or parish knew the arrangements the contract was recited at the church door when the couple married. Only the very wealthy, the very poor, or the very foolish would enter into such an important obligation without an agreement.

The usual arrangement was for the husband to contribute property and perhaps a trade or business, while the wife contributed money, goods, and perhaps livestock. The wife's contribution, the dowry, was to provide capital for establishing the family, and it would usually go to the children of the marriage. Because the wife was likely to outlive the husband and might well have young children to raise, the husband insured that his partner would receive a portion of his property that she could have for her use during her lifetime. Dower, or the later form of provision for widows called jointure, in English law was generous, for the widow could even take it into another marriage.[6] The woman was thus compensated for her contributions to the marriage. The dower's advantage in terms of perpetuating the family unit was that it guaranteed that the widow would be able to support and rear the children of the union. Janet Loengard and Sue Sheridan Walker have described common law governing dower and the many pleas in royal courts seeking it.

The terms of the settlement depended upon law and custom. In common law the widow received one-third of the husband's property for her life use if he predeceased her. London custom followed common law in giving widows one-third of the husband's estate for their life use, if the marriage produced children. In this case the children got one-third, and the testator disposed of his third for the good of his soul. If the couple had no children, then the widow was entitled to one-half. With the exception of the "free bench," that is, the house in which the couple dwelt while they were married, the widow could take this property into a new marriage for the duration of her life. For the most part the dower was real property—tenements and rents in London. In addition, the husband might make additional provisions in his will for movable property or even additional real property.[7]

The rural provisions for widows fell under customary rather than common law and, therefore, varied from region to region and manor to manor. On the whole customary law was even more generous than common law. A frequent ploy was for the husband, at the time of his marriage, to release his tenement to the lord and make fine with him so that the couple could hold it in joint tenancy. When the husband died the wife could continue on the tenement for the rest of her life without making a new fine to hold the land. She would be expected to continue working the land, providing for labor services, and paying rent. On some manors she would have to relinquish the land when her son reached the age of majority (twenty-one to twenty-four years), but in these cases some other provision would be made for her mature years. As in the urban environment, the husband could also make provision through a will that would tailor his bequests to his widow's requirements.[8] As in urban law, women did not have to remain in "pure widowhood" (unmarried) in order to enjoy life use of the land and other property.

In assessing widows' potential access to wealth, it is valuable to know how successful they were in realizing their dower. In the countryside the practice of recording arrangements for the widow in manorial court rolls insured that they were not only common knowledge in the village but also that they were written down. Although peasants did not own their land outright, they did have right by long-standing custom to rent familial holdings. Widows' rights were also well known in the village and manor and were recorded in the *custumals*. Nonetheless, manorial court rolls show that some widows took sons or their husbands' brothers to court to get their dower.[9]

In the urban environment the widow's position might be more tenuous, because dower arrangements were contractual between the two parties. Sometimes the arrangement was written and relatives and parishioners might remember the reading of the banns, but tenements set aside for the widow might change hands frequently. Thus, upon the death of her husband the widow might find herself in a legal battle with others, usually tenants, who claimed a prior right over the property. While it is impossible to know what percentage of widows in London had a difficult time recovering their dower, 53 percent of those widows who did have to go to court were able to retrieve their disputed dower.[10] We may assume, therefore, that for the most part both urban and rural widows did receive their dowers.

The material well-being of the new widow depended on a number of circumstances. The dower might have dwindled if the couple's fortune had been bad and they had been forced to sell off resources. On the other hand, the couple's economic partnership might have prospered, in which case the husband might enrich the initial dower with further bequests in the will. Broader economic and demographic events such as the plague might also influence the final size of the dower. If the widow had been an heiress in her own right or had her own business, then she would have her inheritance in addition to the dower. She might or might not have any of the dowry left that she brought to the partnership.[11] Then, too, the wealth of a widow depended directly on her social class or status in society. If she married the firstborn son of a wealthy peasant, she could assume to have a good dower, but, if she married a cotter, she might be as poor as the widow Chaucer described in the *Canterbury Tales.* A wealthy grocer's widow in London would have far more resources than the widow of an artisan or, worse yet, a laborer. Age was also a factor. An old woman, left a widow, might simply have a retirement contract, either one that the couple had negotiated together or one that the husband provided in his will. In this case her material condition might include only her "freebench," a dower cottage, a room in the guild almshouse, or a place by her son's hearth.[12]

We would like to know, of course, how many women became widows in a year and what their age and condition was. Medievalists know not to be choosy and would be happy to have this information for one village or one town for a single year. As usual, records do not permit such accurate demographic information. In spite of the dangers associated with childbirth, women in the Middle Ages seemed to have outlived their husbands on the average. Of the 326 wills of adult males I surveyed for fifteenth-century Bedfordshire, 235 (72 percent) had a surviving wife.[13] In her study of pre-plague Brigstock Judith Bennett found that 12 percent of the women identified were widows. In the London Husting Court wills, 1,743 out of 3,300 men's wills (53 percent) mention a surviving wife.[14] We may assume, then, that widowhood was a common occurrence in late medieval England.

We can also make some speculations about the average age of the widows among the peasantry. The best estimates suggest that couples would fairly routinely celebrate their twentieth wedding anniversary. Assuming that couples married when they were in their late teens or early twenties, a widow who had twenty years of marriage would be in her late thirties or early forties when she was widowed.[15] Bennett's study indicated that those widows who did not remarry survived their husbands by an average of nine years.[16] In London the age disparity between husband and wife might have been greater, with men making their first marriage in their late twenties or early thirties and women in their teens. Thus, London widows might have been younger on the average than rural widows.[17] We are talking here of averages based on slim evidence. The population of widows would, of course, contain young women with or without children, perhaps a predominance of middle-aged women, and some elderly ones as well.

Moralists lamented that men sought out widows for remarriage because they were wealthy. An analysis of provisions for widows in the rural Bedfordshire wills suggests generous land bequests: 63 percent granted the widow the home tenement for life, 3 percent had the tenement only until the oldest son reached his majority, 3 percent were given the house but not the lands, and 3 percent were allowed a room in the main house. Other provisions included one-third of the property (2 percent), return of dowry (5 percent), land other than the home tenement (15 percent), and a separate house (5 percent). In addition, widows were left money, animals, household goods, and the residue of the property after debts were paid (52 percent).[18] In London as well, widows were well endowed with rents and property: 86 percent of the testators left their wives real property as well as goods. This property included tenements, rents, shops, gardens, taverns, breweries, wharves, or land in the country. Only 13 percent left goods and money alone, and 1 percent set up annuities for their widows.[19] Wills, of course, represent the upper end of both the rural and urban status groups: those with sufficient land and wealth to make a will.[20] We can conclude from these figures that the majority of these well-off widows were not retired, living on pensions and retirement contracts, and might well be candidates for remarriage.

The Decision to Remarry

Medieval evidence does not permit a reconstruction of the percentage of widows who chose to remarry, but what evidence we do have shows wide variation depending upon the circumstances. Parish registers from the sixteenth century provide a better basis for such a calculation than do medieval records. They indicate that 25 to 30 percent of the widows remarried: for widowers it was higher. Remarriage was fairly rapid, with almost half of those remarrying doing so within the year. These figures come mostly from villages. Canon law required no mourning period in such cases.[21]

Few husbands recorded an objection to his wife's remarriage in their wills. In the London Husting wills only 3 percent of the husbands specified that their wives not remarry. In the rural Bedfordshire wills as well a husband rarely barred remarriage. Some explicitly mentioned that the amount of lands and goods would diminish if the wife remarried or that she would get a greater amount "providing that she did not remarry." But other husbands endowed their widows with land and goods that they could take with them to a subsequent marriage. For instance, William Spenser gave his wife four acres and three rods of land that she held in clear title and could alienate. Another husband instructed his son to keep his wife but that, if she married or moved, she was to have half of the movable goods.[22] In London, likewise, a husband might feel more comfortable about both his wife and his business if she remarried. A skinner in 1403 left his business and apprentices to his wife along with her dower, specifying that she continue the business or marry someone in the trade within three years.[23]

Medieval village studies offer some insight into remarriage that shows that local conditions were important in remarriage. In early fourteenth-century Halesowen (Yorkshire) six of every ten widows remarried.[24] Bennett found, however, that in Northamptonshire during the same period the economic resources of the manor made a great difference. Brigstock was on the edge of a royal forest that offered a variety of economic outlets, including forestry and poaching. Economic diversity undercut the marriage market for widows, since men had a number of options and did not need the dower lands. Thus, in Brigstock only about one out of every thirteen widows married a second time. Iver, which had a pastoral economy, had a similar low rate of remarriage.[25]

General economic conditions as well as those of the locality played a role in remarriage. The marriage market for widows appears to have fluctuated depending on the availability of land. In the tight land markets of the early fourteenth and the sixteenth centuries, when population exceeded the available arable land and no other economic outlets existed as they did in Brigstock and Iver, widows were in demand as marriage partners. J. Z. Titow described the marriage pattern on the late-thirteenth-century Winchester estates as a "marriage fugue." In that period of general scarcity of land and, consequently, of food, survival became an issue. By the early fourteenth-century bad crops meant severe hunger for some, and in the famines of 1315–17 and 1322–23 many people died of starvation. On manors that had no vacant land young men sought older widows for marriage partners. They lived on her land until she died, at which time the land reverted to her heirs or, quite frequently, continued with her new husband. The man might, at this point, remarry a younger woman, thus establishing a fugue pattern of a younger man marrying an older widow, remarrying a younger woman who, when she is widowed, would marry a younger man.[26] Thus, in the Malthusian conditions of the early fourteenth century and the sixteenth century widows with a life interest in lands were attractive marriage partners because land was in very short supply. For a young man, marrying a widow meant land for her lifetime and perhaps an opportunity to continue the arrangement thereafter, if there were no preferable heirs. During this period of land hunger the lords encouraged widows to remarry because they could then collect money from the marriage fines.

By contrast, Ravensdale has demonstrated that at Crowland Abbey, in the century following the Black Death, the marriage market for widows collapsed. Population was diminished, wages were high, and land was vacant. A young man who chose to remain on the land might easily inherit either his family land or that of a relative. Young men with land chose to marry women their own age. Indeed, after 1349 many widows refused to take their husbands' tenements because they could find neither a new husband nor laborers to work their land. Thus, widows were no longer desirable in the marriage market. Other court roll studies have shown a similar pattern in widows' marriages.[27] In the rural environment, then, the availability of land and other resources was one of the determining factors for widows remarrying. If land was readily available or the village economy provided other sources of livelihood, then widows might not find marriage partners should they want them.

Reconstitution of London's population is a formidable task that has not yet been undertaken, so that the measures of widows remarrying are indirect. The dower suits that appear in the London mayor's court of Common Pleas provide some indication of remarriage (see table 1).[28] These cases in which the widow is suing for disputed dower were initiated fairly quickly after the death of the husband and the probate of the will, as can be seen from comparing wills with the initiation of the dower case. While unmarried women could initiate these cases alone or with an attorney, about a third of the widows had remarried already and brought the suit with their new husband.

The percentage of widows who remarried increased to 50 percent following the Black Death in 1348–49 but then dropped again in the fifteenth century. Women appearing in dower suits were, for the most part, wealthy women who were suing to recover real estate and rents. As such, they would be very desirable marriage partners and may have been more in demand than poorer widows. On the other hand, they also had the resources to live on their own and not remarry if they chose.

Another series of records also gives some indication about the remarriage of widows. The mayor and aldermen of London were legally responsible for protecting the person, property, and marriage of the orphaned children of London citizens. When a London citizen died leaving minor children, the court appointed a guardian of the children and their property. The law stated that the guardian could not be someone who would stand to inherit should the child die. If the mother was alive, she was usually given the guardianship, because she had only a life interest in dower and could not inherit. Table 2 indicates the total number of widowed mothers who appeared before the mayor and aldermen with their orphaned children and the number who were already remarried at the time that they made this appearance. The cases are recorded in the *Letter Books*.[29] Remarriage of urban women with minor children, at 57 percent, is greater than the number of widows who remarried in the course of contesting their dower. Perhaps the widow with a contested dower was less attractive than one with minor children. As we shall see, the added incentive of having control over the property of the minor may have increased their desirability among suitors. What is interesting is that the pattern of remarriage is similar: relatively high in the beginning of the fourteenth century, increasing after the Black Death, then drop-

TABLE 1.   Remarried Plaintiffs in Dower Suits

Year	Total Number of Women	Number Remarried	Percentage
1301–6	113	38	34%
1327–32	72	11	15
1348–53	42	21	50
1374–79	30	16	53
1400–1405	16	6	38
1427–33	8	3	38
Total	281	95	34%

Note: These figures come from the mayor of London's Court of Common Pleas. The sample is in six-year intervals. The figures included here are those of all women who brought a plea of dower, regardless of whether or not it reached final completion.

ping off somewhat in the fifteenth century. In general, the percentage remarrying is greater than in the countryside, with the exception of the 60 percent that Zvi Razi found for Halesowen in the pre-plague period.

The comparison between the urban and rural remarriage patterns shows that both responded to the broader economic and demographic events that were so significant for England during the fourteenth and fifteenth centuries. During the first quarter of the fourteenth century, when Titow could demonstrate the marriage fugue on the Winchester estates in response to land and food scarcity, in London widows also were desirable marriage partners because of the cushion of wealth from dower. Perhaps also widows preferred the security of remarriage when the price of grain was very high and people were literally dying in the streets of London from lack of food. After the last famine in the early 1320s remarriage decreased. Unlike the pattern in the countryside, remarriage became even more important in the century following the Black Death. The period 1349–1458 was a time of recurrent visitations of plague and a variety of other diseases, so that population continued to be low. Nowhere was disease more prevalent than in the filth of London. Sixty-five percent of the widows with minor children there chose to remarry during this grim period.[30]

Statistics derived from medieval sources, as we have said, need the

TABLE 2.   Remarriage among Widowed Mothers of London Wards from the London *Letter Books*

Years	Number of Widowed Mothers	Number Remarried	Percentage Remarried
1309–18	21	15	71%
1319–28	13	6	46
1329–38	5	0	0
1339–48	15	3	20
1349–58	13	4	31
1359–68	9	3	33
1369–78	22	10	45
1379–88	17	11	65
1389–98	9	9	100
1399–1408	14	13	93
1409–18	20	14	70
1419–28	24	15	63
1429–38	13	6	46
1439–48	13	8	62
1449–58	4	3	75
Total	212	120	57%

usual warning labels. But, even if we are seeing only the tip of the iceberg, at least we know it is that and not a random ice cube, which is all that illustrative cases drawn from a sea of plea rolls provide. In both the dower cases and the appearances of widows as guardians of their children, we are speaking mostly of an elite group of women: citizens of London with some property, perhaps a great deal. The statistics only show those women who remarried very soon after the death of their husbands, although the more reliable sixteenth-century evidence indicates that widows who remarried tended to do so very soon. And, of course, widows who had neither minor children nor a disputed dower do not appear. It is also worrisome that the period of initial plague does not show more cases of wardship. Perhaps this defect in the records was the result of death of all family members (as much as 50 percent of the London population may have died), or perhaps a lapse in record keeping or court functioning explains it. Furthermore, the dower cases show a decline of remarriages following 1348–49, whereas the wardship cases show a rise. The discrepancy between the two might be explained by the greater degree of anxiety on the part of women with minor children to seek security in remarriage (we do not know in dower cases whether or not the women had minor children).

In addition to the more global worries of famine and disease, women had individual reasons to remarry or not. Children would be a primary factor in the decision to remarry. A peasant woman with children in their teens would already have an adequate work force for her tenement and likely would be in her thirties or older. She would be unlikely to remarry. But a widow with young children and the need to hire labor for the fields might find remarriage a secure option. Indeed, Cicely Howell found that in Kibworth in the fifteenth century, when a man had a mature son alive, 41 percent (with 193 men's wills in the sample) favored the son for inheritance. The thirty-three men who died leaving minor children tended to prefer providing the wife with the tenement and residue (42 percent of those with minor children). Men without children favored their wife with their tenement in 81 percent of the cases.[31] Thus, younger women with children and those without would have been more desirable on the marriage market given the structure of inheritance.

In London the wardship cases give us some indication of the role of minor children in the decision to remarry. One could imagine that the presence of children might work both ways in that decision. While the mother of minor children might find it as advantageous as the peasant woman to turn management of a craft or business over to a new husband, a prospective husband might react as some did in the countryside after the depopulation and prefer younger, unencumbered women. On the other hand, these women had property and so, too, did the wards; a new husband could manage the wards' property to his advantage until they came of age. Although over 50 percent of the widows remarried, the number of children did not appear to make a significant difference in the decision: 45 percent of those with one child had remarried compared to 43 percent of the unremarried; 24 percent with two children remarried compared to 18 percent not remarrying; and 17 percent with three children married again as opposed to 20 percent who did not. Fourteen percent of the remarried women had four or more children compared to 19 percent of those not remarrying. Thus, only slight and not very significant differences in numbers of children appear to have influenced either prospective new husbands or the women themselves. Of course, the mortality rate of children was very high, so perhaps their existence was not a significant factor.

Crass economic factors may have motivated the new husbands and account for the upswing in remarriage among urban women. In my research in the London *Letter Books,* from 1309 to 1368, the average wealth of the wardship property hovered around £20 16s. 7d. In the period 1369–78 it went up to almost £54 3s. 1d. It averaged £208 6s. 5d. for the rest of the period in table 2. Combining the third from dower with the third bequeathed to the children could provide a substantial influx of capital. Sylvia Thrupp quotes a case of a fifteenth-century grocer who married a widow with a dower of £764 and was then appointed guardian of her six children with permission to trade with their patrimony (an equal amount) until they came of age. Thus, he was able to use two-thirds of a profitable business for his own purposes.[32]

Changes in London society may have played the most significant role in the remarriage of city widows as opposed to peasant widows following the Black Death. Guilds became increasingly important in the regulation of London society and government following the Black Death. As these horizontal lines of trade and craft "brotherhoods" strengthened in the society, the changes in the selection of guardians is noticeable. Increasingly, men turned to members of their own guild or one closely related to be one of the guardians. Since the value of property put into both the widow's dower and the children's bequests had increased substantially by 1368, one can understand that guild brothers would want to keep the wealth among themselves. While most husbands may not have taken the precaution that the skinner did in requiring that his wife marry someone in the trade, guild brothers might have had an implicit understanding about the matter. If one may judge from the numerous and valuable bequests that widows left to their husbands' guilds, the loyalty must have extended to wives as well. The recirculation of widows and their wealth within the guild was another type of restriction in a period when guilds were becoming increasingly protectionist in their political and economic roles. Trade secrets would not leak out if the widow remained within the association.

Such evidence as we have suggests that, in the selection of a new husband, London women seem to have increasingly turned to the same or a related craft or business. Thrupp found that the mayor and aldermen, who had control over the marriage as well as the wardship of orphans, arranged for 84 percent of merchants' daughters to marry merchants. When widows remarried the proportion was even higher. In thirty-seven cases from the fifteenth century thirty-four widows chose husbands from the merchant class; twenty-two of these were from the same company as the former husband.[33] Goldsmiths' widows seemed to have preferred goldsmiths.[34] The same pattern may be observed for the crafts. Steve Rappaport was able to demonstrate that by the sixteenth century widows insisted on suitors joining their guild as a condition of marriage. In 1592 a Mr. Wilks appealed to the Merchant Taylors because Helen Hudson, a Vintner's widow, would not marry him unless he transferred to her company. The Merchant Taylors responded by sending a delegation to widow Hudson to see if she would join them, but she declared that she "will by no means assent to leave her trade." Finally, Wilks was allowed to leave the Merchant Taylors and become a Vintner.[35]

Although we know little about the courtship and remarriage of widows in the countryside, we do know something about the "marriage market" for widows in London (the term is selected with full cognizance of the implication). As Alison Hanham has observed: "Matchmaking was an enormously serious business for the parties and their relations, and a favourite sport for those less directly involved in the outcome."[36] George Cely, mercer and stapler, competed for the hand of Margery, widow of Edmund Rygon. She was a second wife, young and childless, and had been made chief executor of Edmund's estate, with the bulk of his property at her disposal for the good of his soul. Like the Celys, he was a Stapler and had property in Calais. Here was the classic opportunity to keep the considerable wealth within the select group of Staplers. George had considerable competition in his wooing. William Cely wrote in 1484 that a maternal relative of Margery's had arrived in Calais, apparently on a reconnaissance mission for the family, to find out what George's prospects were.

> it is said here by many persons here how that ye be sure ["contracted"] to her. With the which, sir, I am well content and right glad thereof. And sir, all those here that knoweth you, both merchants and soldiers, commend you greatly, saying "if that gentlewoman should be worth double that she is ye were worthy to have her." And as for making of search of your dealing here, I trow there is no man that maketh any. If they do, they need go no farther than the books in the treasury, where they may find that your sales made within less than this year amounts above [£]2,000 where that the person that laboured for to 'a be afore you, he and his brother had not in this town this twelve months the one half of that.

George not only had to prove his business success, but he also had to provide an attractive dower for widow Rygon and woo her with precious gifts. Dower, of course, was real estate, and he bought more than £485 worth at this period, along with jewels, plate, and a costly ring. Later his sister-in-law was to claim that he spent all of his proper share of the stock that he had inherited with his brother, Richard, her husband. In addition, he bore the cost of the wedding feasts.[37]

While George's wooing of a wealthy widow was successful, others, whose stories are preserved in the Chancery Petitions, show the pitfalls of wooing independent-minded widows. The market in the late fourteenth and fifteenth centuries favored the widow in London. A draper laid his case of investment in courting a widow before the mayor in the hopes of recovering something from her estate. He had, he claimed, made a contract of marriage before witnesses with the widow and had spent time and money on her business for three years because he assumed that it would all accrue to his profit when they married. He also spent some £20 on gifts for her and her friends and finally went off on a trading venture to Spain to buy merchandise for her worth £400. When he returned she was favoring a rival and would not see him. She died unmarried, and he was trying to reclaim his investment against the £2,000 estate she left behind.[38]

The marketing of widows appears in a petition brought by Nicholas Boylle, draper of London, complaining to the lord chancellor that John Walsale had run into Nicholas on Lombard Street and told him that he knew of a widow who was worth two hundred marks and more and that he would undertake to try to persuade her to favor, love, and show goodwill to Nicholas if he would give him a bond for twenty pounds to be paid if he succeeded in bringing about the union. John made the approach and told Nicholas that she wanted to know if young Nicholas had the goodwill of his father, and she also wanted it assured in front of his father that he would leave all his goods and livelihood to her and his son. He delivered her goods in earnest of his intent. She utterly refused him and married Richard Sebe, a mercer of London. She was apparently not interested, for she never made inquiries about his livelihood. Nicholas's complaint was not against the market-wise widow, who made her own matrimonial decisions, but, rather, against John, who wanted to collect his commission even though no marriage resulted.[39]

The independent widows, negotiating on their own, brought more petitions to Chancery than those negotiated by friends and parents. All parties had one complaint or another. There were the disappointed prospective husbands. Roger Radnore of Worcester, a chapman, complained that he had made a contract of marriage twelve months earlier with Alice George, a London widow, and she had sworn in church to the contract and had delivered goods to him. But a rival, William Whetehall, appeared and "subtelly labored with Alice," and she made another contract and married him. When Roger came to London to buy goods according to his occupation Alice and William had him arrested for the goods she had given him when they were engaged.[40] On the other hand, Elizabeth Baxter, late wife of John Croke, said that John "being of his own free will and liberty lawfully contracted matrimony" with her and "at his own cost caused the matrimony to be solemized in book before the Archdeacon and before many people." They lived together for half a year after that "with love and charity as husband and wife," but another woman, Elizabeth Cotton, claimed prior contract and was upheld in the consistory court. John had retained goods that she had brought to the marriage as well as those he had pledged to her; he had beaten her and had her and her mother arrested and put into prison.[41]

The widow's ambiguous position as an independent agent muddled marital arrangements among family members as well. While they assumed that they exercised control over the widows, their legal rights were so ambiguous that a basis of appeal existed. William Yong claimed that Elizabeth Kesten, "widow and well willer and lover" to him, would have married him, but her brother had interfered and had him put into prison. On the other hand, Margaret Wodevyld of London said that her brother-in-law was trying to marry her off to a country bumpkin and that she would not have him. The brother-in-law had her arrested and put into prison. Parents-in-law, who stood to lose control over the dower, also complained bitterly about the legally independent widow. Richard Rous of Cornwall complained that his widowed daughter-in-law was abducted and married while she was in the governance and rule of her uncle in London.[42]

Modern sympathies, like medieval ones, assume that widows would remarry because of a need for male companionship and economic security. But we must not overlook the possibility of the gold diggers as well. After all, a widow could continue to remarry, accumulating dowers as she outlived husbands. Take, for example, the case of Thomasine Bonaventure, who was born to poor parents in Cornwall about 1450. While she was tending the sheep one day, Thomas Bumsby, a London mercer who traded in Cornwall, saw her and was struck by her beauty and good manners. He asked her to come to London as his servant. Her parents consented after he produced witnesses to testify to his character and contracted to endow her if he died. The young woman might well have been mistress as well as servant to him. In any case his wife died several years later, and he married Thomasine. He died two years later, and, as they had no children, she got half of his estate. As a wealthy and beautiful young widow, she had many suitors and finally married Henry Galle. When he died she was about thirty and again without children, so that she got half of Galle's estate as jointure. She then married John Percival, a merchant tailor and later mayor of London. When he died in 1507 she was so wealthy that she fell victim to one of Henry VII's money-raising schemes. He pardoned her for a trumped-up offense in exchange for a payment of 1000 pounds.[43]

Other Options than Remarriage

Although the subject of this chapter is the remarriage of widows, at least a mention of other options gives some perspective on the choice to remarry. Where considerable property was involved, both rural and urban women faced pressure for remarriage: matchmakers, suitors, family, lords in the country, guildsmen, and city officials would pressure wealthy widows to remarry. What escape did a widow have, and what sort of life could she expect?

An option open to wealthy, free widows, noble and borough, was to become a vowess. Joel Rosenthal has described the mind-set that might have urged this choice. To take the vow the woman pledged herself to become a nun in all respects except for taking the veil. The veil would be left on the bishop's altar in case she wished to take the final step. It could be a frustrating business for potential suitors. Word came to the Celys on 29 March 1482 that Robert Byfeld had been buried on 27 March, "and on the morrow early his wife took the mantle and the ring." To the players on the marriage market this was a severe disappointment, since her husband had left her eighteen hundred marks as dower.[44]

Peasant women did not usually have this option open to them, since entry into a nunnery required the equivalent of a dowry, and peasant women did not have control over their lands. But they could choose not to remarry and keep their tenement for their heirs. Several advantages accrued from such a decision. They would not complicate the division of property by a second family, and, for those who preferred independence, they had the option of continuing the homestead on their own. Certainly, as mentioned, part of the decision would depend on the age of the children (should she have any) and the availability of labor to work the land. As Bennett has shown, only some women chose to exercise the option of active involvement with economic and community affairs. Alice Avice, during her twenty-four years as a wife, played the traditional, subordinate role in the public context, but during the subsequent eight years of her widowhood she took an active part in controlling her property and her public entry into the manorial court. She was, of course, a mature woman and not one of the hot commodities on the marriage market in a village that had a sufficiently diversified economy in the hard times of the early years of the fourteenth century. But other village women chose to shun the manorial court and opted for withdrawal from a public forum in their widowhood.[45]

In the urban environment widows of London citizens became free of the city and, as such, could carry on their husbands' trades.[46] Guilds allowed widows to continue the privileges of membership. They could have apprentices and be members of the guild, although they could not become guild officers. Although we do not have adequate guild records for the Middle Ages to determine how many women took this option, those from the sixteenth century indicate that very few women continued trading sole: under 2 percent of the apprentices worked for women.[47] In the Middle Ages the most common mention of widows engaged in their own businesses are innkeepers, brewers, silk workers, embroiderers, dressmakers, vendors of various sorts, and prostitutes.

Becoming an independent proprietor of either a London business or a peasant holding was fraught with problems. Hired, male labor might not respect women as proprietors. Apprentices, journeymen, ploughmen, and reapers might desert the widow or prove obstreperous when faced with her commands. When discipline of inferiors included physical chastisement women might be at a disadvantage. Reliable labor was hard to come by at the best of times, and the ambiguous position of the widow made her role even more difficult.[48] Our contemporary viewpoint makes us want to place the emphasis on the independent widows finally gaining independence from the legal and moral domination of men. But that perspective may not be one that a fourteenth- or fifteenth-century widow would share. The position was difficult, and one must consider that remarriage might have been preferable for the widow rather than dealing with the problems of a woman placed in a male-dominated work- and marketplace.

Consider, for instance, the insistent voice of moralists and neighbors whispering about the reputation of widows who did not remarry. Slurs on widows' chastity were bound to arise, especially for those who chose not to remarry. Widows had to fight in court and in appeals to the chancellor for their reputations. Jane Burton, a London widow, claimed that she was of good name and fame but that evil-disposed people of malice and ill will, without cause, had brought her before the ward moot, accusing her of having a house of misrule. They had her put into prison and were forcing her to leave her house. Another widow claimed that in a dispute over rent her opponent brought a charge in the ward moot of Farringdon Without the Walls, calling her a "common woman." She said that they had come while she was at high mass at St. Brides and that right after the Passion they had pulled her out of her pew and took her off to prison. She indignantly argued that she had been "a pure maiden and wife in the same parish for 14 years." Both women took their cases to Chancery.[49]

Was there no rest from lazy servants, disobedient apprentices, busy-bodies, nosy neighbors, and critical clergy? Yes, if the widows followed the prescriptions of the moralists. If they were old, looked dowdy or at least only handsome in their somber clothes, gave freely to charity, kept their chastity, managed to control their business affairs, or were wealthy or witty enough to command respect, then they could form a viable and respectable single life. Both rural and urban widows might choose, in ripe years, to continue to interact with the community and become the resource of friends, family, guild, and Church. In both the urban and rural environment wills indicate the close connections that widows maintained. But women could also escape these connections through remarriage.

Remarriage, as we have seen, was a common solution to the problem of widows. Problems existed both for themselves and for the society that surrounded them. Neighbors and moralists did not want independent women free to make their own, perhaps lascivious, decisions. Laymen were anxious to take control over their dowers. Widows, especially those who had young children or were young themselves, found remarriage a convenient solution for raising a family and getting either the field work or the urban business done. After all, the highest percentage of widows remarrying were those who appeared in the London court of orphans. Widows' chances of remarriage, in both the city and the countryside, depended on broad economic conditions as well as individual wealth and preference. What is apparent, however, is that, in choosing to remarry, they were forming strong ties horizontally across both urban and rural society. The dower distributed, for the lifetime of the remarried widow, property to the new husband. The new husband generally was selected from the same status group in the village and from the same business, craft, or guild in the city. Those who suffered from the freedom of a widow to remarry and take her dower with her were the heirs of the former husband or husbands. They could be denied access to that property for a considerable length of time. Furthermore, should a widow have children by a second marriage, some of the profit of a father's business or land would go to future children. Provision for peasant and urban widows thus undermined patrilineal ties and emphasized those within the same status groups. For the nobility, who had to be concerned with the patrilineage, such freedom of selection was curtailed.[50]

NOTES

1. I have explicitly excluded noble women from this chapter. For noble women lineage meant much more than it did in either the urban or rural peasant context, so that their decision to remarry would be quite different. Patrilineal lines meant much more to noble families.

2. G. R. Owst, *Literature and Pulpit in Medieval England*, 3d ed. (New York, 1961), 119; Ruth Kelso, *Doctrine for the Lady of the Renaissance* (Urbana, Ill., 1956), 126–30.

3. Owst, *Literature and Pulpit*, 388–89.

4. Kelso, *Doctrine for the Renaissance Woman*, 131–32; Owst, *Literature and Pulpit*, 381.

5. Barbara A. Hanawalt, *The Ties That Bound: Peasant Families in Medieval England* (New York, 1986), 205–19.

6. Caroline M. Barron ("The 'Golden Age' of Women in Medieval London," *Reading Medieval Studies* 15 [1989]: 38–42) has a fine discussion of London dower customs.

7. See Barbara A. Hanawalt, "The Widow's Mite: Provisions for Medieval London Widows," in *Upon My Husband's Death: Widows in the Literature and Histories of Medieval Europe*, ed. Louise Mirrer (Ann Arbor, 1992), 21–45, for a more complete description of dower provisions in London.

8. See Hanawalt, *Ties That Bound*, 221, for a fuller description.

9. Hanawalt, *Ties That Bound*, 225.

10. See Hanawalt, "Widow's Mite," for a complete discussion of court procedures and the success of widows. These cases are preserved in the Corporation of London Archives in the Common Plea Rolls (hereafter referred to as CP with the archival number).

11. See Judith M. Bennett, *Women in the Medieval English Countryside: Gender and Household in Brigstock before the Plague* (New York, 1987), 110–11, for a discussion of the dowry in peasant households.

12. Hanawalt, *Ties That Bound*, 227–35. Elaine Clark, "Some Aspects of Social Security in Medieval England," *Journal of Family History* 7 (1982): 307–20.

13. *Bedfordshire Wills, 1480–1519*, trans. Patricia Bell, Bedfordshire Historical Record Society 45 (1966); *Bedfordshire Wills Proved in the Prerogative Court of Canterbury, 1383–1548*, ed. Margaret McGregor, Bedfordshire Historical Record Society 58 (1979); *English Wills, 1498–1526*, ed. A. F. Cirket, Bedfordshire Historical Record Society 37 (1956).

14. *Calendar of Wills Proved and Enrolled in the Court of Husting, London, A.D. 1258–1688*, ed. Reginald R. Sharpe (London, 1889). Only medieval wills appear in this sample (until 1500).

15. See Bennett, *Women in the Medieval English Countryside*, 143–44; and also her footnote discussion of Zvi Razi's estimates in *Life, Marriage, and Death in a Medieval Parish: Economy, Society and Demography in Halesowen, 1270–1400* (Cambridge, 1980). J. Z. Titow (*English Rural Society, 1200–1350* [London, 1969], 87) found that 9 to 15 percent of the landholders on Winchester, Glastonbury, and Worcester estates were women, probably widows. R. H. Hilton (*The English Peasantry in the Later Middle Ages* [Oxford, 1975], 99) found one in seven tenants were widows in 1419 in Ombersley.

16. Bennett, *Women in the Medieval English Countryside*, 144. There is no comparable study for other villages.

17. Sylvia Thrupp, *The Merchant Class of Medieval London* (Ann Arbor, 1948), 192–93, 196, 213.

18. Hanawalt, *Ties That Bound*, 221–22.

19. Hanawalt, "Widow's Mite."

20. The wills recorded in London's Archdeaconry Court are less detailed but contain more wills of ordinary artisans of London. Of the 116 men who made provisions for their widows, only 18 percent mention real property, while 65 percent simply refer to the residue of their estate (Guildhall Library, Archdeacon's Court MS 9051/1, 9051/2; hereafter referred to as Archdeacon's Court with the manuscript number).

21. R. S. Schofield and E. A. Wrigley, "Remarriage Intervals and the Effect of Marriage Order on Fertility," in *Marriage and Remarriage in Populations of the Past,* ed. J. Dupaquier, E. Helin, P. Laslett, M. Livi-Bacci, S. Sogner (London, 1981), 212, 214; Michael M. Sheehan, "The Influence of Canon Law on the Property Rights of Married Women in England," *Mediaeval Studies* 25 (1963): 121.

22. *Bedfordshire Wills*, no. 183, 62 and 55; *English Wills*, 13–14.

23. Archdeacon's Court 9051/1 105v.

24. Razi, *Life, Marriage, and Death*, 63.

25. Bennett, *Women in the Medieval English Countryside*, 146.

26. J. Z. Titow, "Some Differences between Manors and the Effects on the Condition of the Peasant in the Thirteenth Century," *Agricultural History Review* 10 (1962): 7–13; Eleanor Searle, "Seigneurial Control of Women's Marriages: The Antecedents and Function of Merchet in England," *Past and Present* 82 (1979): 40. For the sixteenth century, see Margaret Spufford, *Contrasting Communities: English Villagers in the Sixteenth and Seventeenth Centuries* (Cambridge, 1974), 116–17, 163.

27. J. R. Ravensdale, "Population Changes and the Transfer of Customary Land on a Cambridgeshire Manor in the Fourteenth Century," in *Land, Kinship, and Life-Cycle,* ed. Richard Smith (Cambridge, 1984), 197–225. Judith Bennett ("Medieval Peasant Marriage: An Examination of Marriage License Fines in the *Liber Gersumarum,*" in *Pathways to Medieval Peasants,* ed. J. A. Raftis

[Toronto, 1981], 205) found that, on Ramsey Abbey estates from 1398 to 1458, only 47 of the 426 *merchet* payments recorded were from widows. Razi (*Life, Death, and Marriage,* 63, 136) found that only 10 percent of the widows remarried after the Black Death.

28. See Hanawalt, "Widow's Mite," for a more complete description of the court and the sampling method for this study.

29. *Calendar of Letter-Books Preserved among the Archives of the Corporation of the City of London at the Guildhall, Letter Books D-K,* ed. R. Sharpe (London, 1912). By *Letter Book L* the method of listing guardians changes so that it is not easy to follow the remarriages.

30. Comparisons with early modern figures are useful here. Steve Rappaport (*Worlds within Worlds: Structures of Life in Sixteenth-Century London* [Cambridge, 1989], 40) quotes N. Adamson ("Urban Families: The Social Context of the London Elite, 1500–1603," [Ph.D. diss., University of Toronto, 1983]) showing that only a third of 208 widows of aldermanic families chose to marry again. Charles Carlton (*The Court of Orphans* [Leicester, 1974]) discusses the remarriage of widows appearing in the mayor's court but does not do a calculation.

31. Cicely Howell, "Peasant Inheritance Customs in the Midlands, 1280–1700," in *Family and Inheritance: Rural Society in Western Europe, 1200–1800,* ed. Jack Goody, Joan Thirsk, and E. P. Thompson (Cambridge, 1976), 141–43.

32. Thrupp, *Merchant Class,* 107.

33. Thrupp, *Merchant Class,* 28.

34. Thomas F. Reddaway (*The Early History of The Goldsmiths' Company, 1327–1509* [London, 1975], 275–321) has reconstructed biographies indicating marriages, when known.

35. Rappaport, *Worlds within Worlds,* 40–41.

36. Alison Hanham, *The Celys and Their World: An English Merchant Family of the Fifteenth Century* (Cambridge, 1985), 309.

37. Hanham, *Celys and Their World,* 309–15.

38. Thrupp, *Merchant Class,* 106–7.

39. C1, Chancery Petitions in the Public Record Office, London. These are undated but come from the fifteenth century (C1/43/65).

40. C1/46/111.

41. C1/61/485.

42. C1/66/308; C1/158/35; C1/66/389.

43. Charles M. Clode, *The Early History of the Guild of Merchant Tailors,* pt. 2 (London, 1888), 11–13, 20–21.

44. Hanham, *Celys and Their World,* 310.

45. Bennett, *Women in the Medieval English Countryside,* 142–46.

46. Barron, (" 'Golden Age' of Women," 45–46) says that widows were expected to continue their husband's business.

47. Rappaport, *Worlds within Worlds,* 41.

48. See Hanawalt, *Ties That Bound,* (223), for the problems of peasant widows with help; see "Widow's Mite," for the problems of urban widows.

49. C1/123/6; C1/61/189.

50. Linda Mitchell, "Widowhood in Medieval England: Baronial Dowagers of the Thirteenth-Century Welsh Marches" (Ph.D. diss., Indiana University, 1990), chap. 3.

Chapter 7

Married Women's Wills in Later Medieval England

Richard H. Helmholz

This essay makes a modest contribution to the history of women's rights by examining the evolution of the testamentary capacity of married women in later medieval England. The subject is doubly appropriate for this volume. Not only does it touch directly on the volume's theme, dealing with the extent of women's legal control over property, it also takes up a subject that was treated and illuminated by one of Michael Sheehan's early articles.[1] Like Sheehan's article, this one is based largely on the canon law and the records of the spiritual courts.[2] Such concentration is warranted; indeed, it is required by the subject. The spiritual courts held primary probate jurisdiction in England well into modern times,[3] and it is to their records, rather than those of the common law courts, that historians must have recourse if they are to trace the story accurately. Sheehan was a true pioneer in this kind of tracing, and this essay carries on work he first undertook.

The Problem Stated

The question is whether English married women had a legal right to make a valid last will and testament and, if they did, whether they in fact made use of the right with any regularity. Widows and single women undoubtedly could and did leave personal property by will. That much is undisputed. Wives, however, stood in a rather different position. An Englishwoman was in some sense *in potestate* of her spouse.[4] Under the common law a woman's personal property normally passed under the control of her husband immediately upon their marriage. It followed that, although widows (as single women) could freely dispose of chattels by will, married women enjoyed no such right.[5]

According to English common law, the only circumstance that would permit a married woman to dispose of any property by will was the possession of the license of her husband. Early writers on English law— Glanvill,[6] Bracton,[7] and Fleta[8]—held that husbands *should* give such a license. They considered it a "pious and honest act" for a man to allow his wife to dispose of at least the third of their jointly held personal property that would pass to her by right if she outlived him. The argument was particularly cogent concerning those items that were given to her for personal adornment: what was called "paraphernalia" (though these writers did not use the exact word). For her, however, the grant of such a license rested in the husband's discretion. If he refused to give it, the married woman had no recourse. In effect, she simply had no property to will.

The position of the law of the Church, the canon law, was to the contrary. Following Roman law, medieval canonists held that married women were fully capable of making a testament of their separate property,[9] and English ecclesiastical legislation specifically prohibited husbands from impeding their wives from doing so. By the Council of Lambeth in 1261,[10] and by Archbishop Stratford's provincial constitution of 1343,[11] the English Church excommunicated ipso facto any husband who hindered his wife from making a valid testament. William Lyndwood, the great English canonist of the fifteenth century, glossed the latter at length, reiterating the canonical arguments in favor of the testamentary capacity of married women, at least about paraphernalia,[12] a term to which he gave an expansive reading.

In short, there was a clash between common law and canon law rules, and the question under investigation can be put in blunt terms: Which side won? It is anachronistic to assume that the common law *necessarily* did. We know that in some other areas of the law (e.g., contracts and benefices), the courts of the Church were capable of putting up spirited resistance to the rules of the royal courts, and even of prevailing in some instances.[13] The historian needs always to look impartially at the record evidence to come as close as possible to the reality of the matter.

So far, the only substantive study to have done this is the 1963 article by Michael Sheehan. Sheehan showed that the canonical position was not entirely a dead letter in medieval practice. Among other things he examined the only collection of probate acts then in print, that of the consistory court of Rochester for 1347, discovering that a meaningful proportion of the wills registered had in fact been made by women. Of seventy-one wills, twenty (28 percent) belonged to women, and thirteen of these (18 percent) certainly belonged to married women.[14] Sheehan concluded that, despite the common law rules, married women "very often managed to distribute property at death."[15] As the careful scholar he was, Sheehan did not push this finding any further than his evidence permitted. But he provided a benchmark, and he opened up the field to investigation of the manuscript sources from the later medieval period. The question here is: What does the later evidence demonstrate?

Married Women's Wills in the Court Records

The surviving evidence does in fact demonstrate several things. In the first place, the records of the spiritual courts show that some married women continued to make wills in later medieval England. Almost every diocese with any considerable run of surviving court books produces examples of the proof and enforcement of wills made by married women. Examples are found from the dioceses of Canterbury,[16] Chichester,[17] Ely,[18] Hereford,[19] London,[20] Rochester,[21] Salisbury,[22] and York.[23] Records from the archdeaconries of Buckingham[24] and St. Alban's[25] also contain litigation involving the enforcement of married women's wills. Moreover, a brief commentary written by a practicing English ecclesiastical lawyer early in the fifteenth century contended that women could make valid wills.[26] Evidently, by 1400 canonical notions on this score had not been entirely submerged by a rising tide of common law.

The conclusion is buttressed by the fact that, with only two possible exceptions (the case from the archdeaconry of St. Alban's and one from York), the records neither mention the assent of the husband nor treat its existence as a matter in dispute. This contrasts with late-sixteenth-and seventeenth-century practice, in which the husband's consent became a necessary feature, indeed the centerpiece, of such ecclesiastical litigation.[27] True enough, many of the instances record that the husband served as executor of his wife's testament, so that such assent might readily have been presumed.[28] Nonetheless, if the surviving records tell the truth, the judges in the spiritual court made nothing of it. They did not require that such consent be either pleaded or proved.

The conclusion is also supported by the cases in which husbands were cited by Church court judges for impeding their wives in the making of a will, cases brought to enforce the 1343 constitution of Archbishop Stratford. In the commissary court at Canterbury in 1470, for instance, John Aleyn of the parish of St. Nicholas in Canterbury was disciplined because he "impeded his wife from making a testament of her own."[29] Before the bishop of Ely's court in 1463 Roger Salter was similarly cited because he "impeded the last will of his deceased wife" by detaining clothing left to Margaret Tolle in her testament.[30] In 1445 at Rochester John Stock was summoned to appear before the diocesan court for a similar offense in the case of his wife's will. Indeed, the record states that Stock had "publicly proclaimed that women could not make any testament."[31] It goes on to note that Stock later submitted to the court's jurisdiction, so that Elena Stock's testament could be produced and probated.

Lyndwood's statement that women's testamentary freedom was achieved through allowing them to bequeath their paraphernalia also finds some support in the instance act books. At Hereford in 1479 Richard Spicer was brought before the commissary court for failing to probate his wife's, Agnes's, testament. At first he said that she had no right to make a testament, "because the goods of his wife were his own,"[32] but the act book records that he later appeared before the judge and "repented of his words," producing the will and inventory of "omnia bona paraphernalia sua" that had belonged to Agnes for approval by the Hereford court.[33] Unfortunately, the case does not say what these goods consisted of, so that we get no clue about whether the English Church took a particularly expansive view of the limits of paraphernalia in practice as well as theory.[34]

These examples suggest that the English Church courts resisted the common law rules and that, by hook or by crook, they managed to protect the rights of married women to control their separate property. Indeed, they would be dispositive, except for their scarcity. I have been able to discover only a few such examples in the surviving records, and the work that has gone into discovering them has not been that of a casual week or two. There are hundreds and hundreds of testamentary matters, both instance and ex officio, found in the surviving act books. They produce a very small harvest of cases showing active enforcement of the canonical position on freedom of testation by married women. If asked to produce cases brought for impeding the probate of a man's will, I could produce dozens. Of similar proceedings for impeding the probate of a married woman's will, seemingly a bigger problem given the likely attitude of many husbands, I can produce no more than a handful.

Moreover, at least some of the cases dealing with the ordinary probate of married women's wills can be explained by special factors. There are cases in which the woman's will was made to fulfill her responsibilities as executrix of someone who had predeceased her.[35] There are others in which the will had been made before her marriage.[36] And there are some in which the woman's will turns out to have been made jointly with her husband.[37] If one were to treat all cases in which the husband acted as executor as instances of spousal license, the number of cases in which a married woman made a valid last will and testament contrary to the rules of the common law during the fifteenth century would be small. The record evidence thus shows that the canonical rules were known. They were also sometimes enforced. It would be incorrect to conclude, however, that there was a general vindication of the canonical position on the basis of the surviving records of the spiritual courts.

Moreover, there is positive evidence of a slightly different sort to show that by the fifteenth century very few married women left last wills and testaments. This evidence comes from noncontentious probate *acta* found in the records. Such *acta* recorded all the wills proved by specific ecclesiastical courts and normally all cases of intestacy as well. Probably they were kept because the courts collected a fee for proving a will and for the ensuing estate administration,[38] and, although they certainly do not contain records of all persons who died in any one place, they do allow us a window on those who died with enough personal property to make it worth disposing of by testamentary disposition.[39]

Sheehan used just such *acta* for the 1340s to show that married women did in fact regularly make testamentary dispositions of their property. He found that a percentage of about 28 percent of wills probated were those of women. It turns out, however, that such relatively high percentages did not continue into the next century. At Rochester itself the 1457 act book contains 123 wills. Of these, only 18 (14.6 percent) belonged to women, and only 2 (1.6 percent) belonged to certainly married women.[40] At Canterbury, twenty years later in 1477, there were fifty estates administered at the Dover, Hythe, and Romney sessions, and only six of these estates (12 percent) belonged to women, with none belonging to a woman who was certainly married.[41] Similarly, in the commissary court for the diocese of London during the post-

Christmas term of 1497, only 10 of 72 testaments (13.9 percent) belonged to women, and none came from a woman who can be shown to have been married at the time of her death.[42]

The only exception so far discovered comes from the diocese of Hereford. During the fall of 1453 nineteen testaments were proved by the diocesan court sitting in the parish church of Pontesbury. Of these, six were from female decedents, and, of these, half were certainly married.[43] This is a very small sample, however, and is also quite unusual. Otherwise, low percentage figures, similar to those given above, were obtained in samples taken from the diocese of York in 1504,[44] Chichester in 1506–8,[45] and Lichfield in 1535.[46] In each case the percentage of women's wills proved by the ecclesiastical court was between 10 percent and 14 percent of the total, and the number of wills that can be proved to have come from women married at the date of their death approaches a figure of zero.

It is true that in each of these samples some wills continued to be made by women. Between 10 percent and 15 percent of women's wills was an average figure for the seventeenth century, however, when we know certainly that only unmarried women had an enforceable right to execute valid wills.[47] It therefore seems likely that the percentages found from earlier periods likewise reflect mostly the wills of widows, not married women. It is hard to escape the conclusion that, by the middle of the fifteenth century, wills of married women had become rarities in England. There were always some, perhaps more so among the wealthy or the powerful than among the middling sort most diocesan courts dealt with, and it is too strong to describe an attempt to leave personal property by testament as always an "exercise in futility."[48] Nonetheless, except for unusual situations, by the mid-fifteenth century the common law position had come to prevail.

Possible Factors in the Evolution

How are we to interpret and explain this development? At first blush the answer seems to be simple and, by now, familiar: a rise in the hardheartedness of men. Husbands and common lawyers deprived married women of a right that once had belonged to them. A moment's reflection, however, shows the difficulties inherent in this explanation. Other than the decline itself, there is no actual evidence in its favor, and the male dominance in the making and enforcement of legal rules upon which it rests is as demonstrable for the thirteenth century as it is for the six-teenth. The explanation is not wholly implausible, of course, and may even be correct at some level. It is certainly, however, too simple. One ought to seek an interpretation that takes account of change in light of other developments in the law and also of specific evidence found in the court records.

A second kind of explanation—substantive change in ordinary legal practice—presents even greater difficulties than the first. So far as one can tell from the surviving evidence, the judges of England's ecclesiastical courts did not change their minds about women's rights during the period under discussion. Nor could anyone who reads Charles Donahue's essay in this collection suppose that women were unwilling or unable to bring suit in the spiritual courts. In the courts at York, at least, they took a large part in the initiation of litigation. The canon law on the subject of the legal capacity of married women did not itself vary, and the views of these ecclesiastical lawyers seem to have remained constant. Quite aside from the subject of marriage, they continued to allow women full rights in other areas of testamentary practice, as, for instance, the right to act as an executrix or testamentary guardian.[49] They continued to allow married women to represent themselves in litigation, without the consent of their husbands.[50] They continued to allow women to serve as legitimate witnesses to wills, even though the practice appeared to contradict texts of the *ius commune*.[51] And, as noted, they continued at least occasionally to enforce Archbishop Stratford's constitution against impeding exercise of a wife's testamentary rights.[52] One must therefore look beyond the actions and opinions of ecclesiastical lawyers to explain what change there was.

One does not fare much better by concentrating upon the practitioners of the English common law. Initially, one might suppose that the common lawyers put increasing pressure on the courts of the Church to conform to the common law rules and that the number of married women's wills declined as a result. But this seems not to have happened in this instance. The time frame is wrong. There *did* come a moment when such pressure was exerted and when spiritual jurisdiction shrank drastically in consequence. But that moment arrived only toward the very close of the fifteenth century.[53] By that time the common law position over married women's wills had already been vindicated in daily practice. Again, for a satisfying explanation one must look elsewhere than at the activities of this particular set of lawyers.

In looking farther afield, I suggest that the explanation may lie in evolving ideas about the nature of married women's property generally. Specifically, it may lie in a growing social acceptance of the view that married women had no separate property and that what personal property they did have would normally have been held in trust for them. By 1450, that is, it was more widely assumed than it had been in 1300 that married women had no independent legal interests in chattels apart from their husbands. Therefore, married women were regarded as having nothing to will. My views on the subject are admittedly tentative, and I put the suggestion forward with diffidence. But the proffered explanation finds some support in the court records, and it also fits what we know about other developments in English law during the later Middle Ages. As the essays by Sue Sheridan Walker and Janet Loengard in this volume clearly show, widows both held and exercised legal rights over property. But the legal situation of married women was quite the reverse.

Part of the evidence from the fifteenth century act books supporting this explanation has already been mentioned in passing. In them one finds explicit statements by men that married women owned no chattels; instead, only their husbands did. Thus, at Canterbury in 1471 John Kynge, the executor named in the testament of Isabelle Parys, explained his failure to act by saying bluntly that Isabelle "had no property she could bequeath."[54] Or, as a Hereford man put it in 1479, "all the goods of his wife belonged to him."[55] This second man was subsequently rebuked for expressing his view, but such sentiments are mirrored in the surviving act books with enough frequency to suggest that they were not at all exceptional.[56] Increasingly by the fifteenth century, married women were regarded as having no separate property rights. The sentiment might even have been shared by many married women themselves. Their inability to make a valid testament followed as a consequence.

The development in attitudes tracked and was supported by two distinct legal developments: the rise in the testamentary freedom held by men and the growth of trusts for married women. The first of these is simply that by the fifteenth century husbands enjoyed greater power to bequeath their chattels. Their wives enjoyed correspondingly less. The second has to do with the ways in which married women commonly enjoyed any right to property. It worked to diminish the need for them to make a testament.

In the thirteenth century even a man's rights to bequeath his personal property were quite circumscribed if he were married.[57] For instance, in cases in which he left a wife and children, the wife was entitled to a third and the children also to a third of his estate. Only the other third of his chattels was the husband free to dispose of as he wished. By the fifteenth century, however, this restriction had largely disappeared from English practice.[58] We understand the mechanics and the reasons for this change imperfectly, and there were parts of England in which the older regime continued to hold sway into the early modern period. Nonetheless, it is true that, as a general matter, over the same period during which married women's wills disappear from the probate act books, the husband's power of testation over his chattels also became absolute.

The connection between these two developments may not seem obvious, but it is nonetheless logical. When the authors of *Glanvill, Bracton,* and *Fleta,* the early treatises on English common law, endorsed the principle that a man *should* permit his wife to make a will, they did so to enable her to bequeath the share that would come to her as a matter of right if she survived him.[59] It was not the woman's separate property brought to the marriage but, rather, an aliquot share of all the personal property owned by the couple during the marriage that these English common lawyers believed the married woman had a moral right to bequeath. Although the husband had power over it during the marriage, he could not by his own will deprive his wife of that portion. In such a regime the idea that a married woman enjoyed some real property rights—at least about this legitimate expectancy—would have seemed entirely natural.

With the loss of that expectancy that followed inevitably from the subsequent establishment of the husband's testamentary freedom, however, the reason for the wife's making a testament of her own would equally have been lost. Once this development had happened, as it had by the fifteenth century, the expectancy that had furnished the reason for married women to make wills in the first place would have vanished along with it. Simply put, because wives no longer had this expectancy, they no longer had anything to will, even as a matter of grace on the part of their husbands. And, thus, it would be natural to find exactly what one does find in the pages of the Church court records: the gradual decline and virtual disappearance of married women's wills.

A second factor that may have worked to diminish the number of married women's wills was the rise of the use, ancestor of the modern trust,[60] by which married women became the equitable beneficiaries of real and personal property rather than its owners. When a woman held only the beneficial interest in land or chattels, as she did under a medieval use, she was less likely to have made a will disposing of that interest than if she held legal title to the property. At her death the property would more often have passed under the terms of the original use, not by virtue of her will. Thus, when trusts became the normal way for married women to hold property, it would have been widely assumed that it was natural for them to hold only such beneficial interests. That was simply the way most married women owned property. And that form of ownership diminished the need for a will. When trusts became common, married women's wills would not have been *excluded,* of course. But they would have been less common, because succession to the property would more often have been taken care of in the original trust.

In time the married women's trust became an important way by which married women preserved control over their separate property. Historians have generally supposed that its beginnings can be traced back no further than the sixteenth century,[61] and it does seem likely that it did rise to real prominence at that time. The trust for married women was certainly known to common lawyers, however, during the fifteenth century.[62] And there are also many examples of such trusts for chattels to be found in the fifteenth-century records of the ecclesiastical courts.[63] Separation of legal from beneficial ownership of chattels in the interests of women and children would have been a familiar feature of practice in the spiritual forum. It is therefore a live possibility, although admittedly a speculative one, that the inception of trusts for married women led to a diminution in the frequency of their wills probated in the ecclesiastical courts, which undoubtedly occurred. This development worked, together with the establishment of men's freedom of testation, to end what Sheehan found for the mid-fourteenth century: that is, a regime in which a meaningful number of married women continued to exercise the canonical power to make a testamentary disposition of their property.

Conclusion

Any conclusion about the testamentary capacity of married women that does justice to the evidence must make room for, even if it cannot completely explain, seemingly contradictory evidence. On the one hand, the courts of the English Church were willing to probate the testaments of married women throughout the later medieval period, and at least there is some evidence showing that they would willingly act against men who impeded women in making such testaments. Married women's wills never disappeared completely. On the other hand, the ecclesiastical courts had fewer occasions to probate and enforce such wills by the fifteenth century than they had a hundred years earlier. It appears true that by 1450, at the latest, the married woman's testament had become a rarity in fact as well as a violation of common law rules.

In assessing this evidence, it is well to recall that the canon law did not regard the law of succession as an inherently spiritual matter. Unlike jurisdiction over marriage or simony, the existence of ecclesiastical jurisdiction over probate was a matter of English custom, not of canonical principle. Custom left room for development, and development there was. If the reasons for that evolution cannot be demonstrated with certainty, at least the balance of the evidence suggests that the likely explanation lies in the evolution of societal attitudes toward marital property rights. The victory of the common law regime over the more generous position of the canon law may have been as much the result as it was the cause of that development.

APPENDIX

The following discussion appears in an early-fifteenth-century ecclesiastical precedent book now in the British Library. Its author is anonymous, and the manuscript gives no hint of how an academic treatment of law came to appear in a text devoted to routine forms used in spiritual court practice. It is presented here simply as an example of contemporary interest in the question dealt with in this chapter, and as showing the continuation of the principles of the *ius commune,* tempered slightly by the author's familiarity with contemporary English practice. In parentheses, I have added modern references to the authorities that are cited in traditional civilian form.

MS. Reg. 11 A XI, fols. 7v–8
Quero nunquid mulier possit testari de bonis suis propriis invito marito? Dic quod de omnibus bonis que habuit ante matrimonium, ut puta parapharnalibus suis que iam possunt decerni, satis bene potest condere testamentum, quia in eis vir nullam habuit communitatem uxore prohibente, ut in l. hac lege C. de pactis conventis (Cod. 5.14.8). Et omnes res sunt parapharnales quas habet extra dotem, ut in dicta lege et ff. de iur. dot.

l. si ego § dotis (Dig. 23.3.9.2) usque in finem. Et ex istis legibus patet quod per matrimonium bona viri et mulieris non sunt communicata, ff. solut. ma. l. menia (Dig. 24.3.49) et C. de rei uxor. l. unica (Cod. 5.13.1). Et quod non sunt communicata est textus l. 1 § si vir (Dig. 24.3.62). Ibi servi uxoris non sunt servi mariti nec equaliter licet habant unam do-mum, sic non sunt communicata. Ergo de eis potest libere testari cum non inveniatur prohibitum, arg. ff. de test. l. si queramus v. factionem (Dig. 28.1.4 and *gl. ord.* ad id. s.v. *factionem*). Item de dote sua potest mulier testari, C. de iur. dot. l. si mulier (Cod. 5.12.25) et ibi notatur in fine glose. De aliis bonis que communiter obveniunt constante matrimo-nio, si possunt decerni et constet de cuius bonis proveniunt et ex cuius pecunia fuerunt empta vel ex cuius industria fuerunt adquisita tunc ad valorem eorum potest testari, quia soluto matrimonio bona talia debent extrahi, de donat. inter vir. et ux. l. ii in fine (Dig. 24.1.2) et facit nota extra de in inst. rest. c. constitutus verbo communes per B[ernardum] (X 1.41.8 and *gl. ord.* ad id. s.v. utrique). Sed si non constet ex cuius bonis obveniunt nec potest hoc decerni, tunc de hiis non potest testari quia tunc presumuntur quesita ex bonis mariti, ff. de donat. inter virum et uxorum l. quintus (Dig. 24.1.51) et notatur in dicto verbo communes. Sed cum de consuetudine in Anglia obtenta post mortem viri debetur uxori dimidia liberis non existentibus, liberis vero existentibus tercia, et ideo iuxta ratam sibi debitam potest hodie testari. Et quod uxor potest testari constante matrimonio est textus in auth. ut liceat matri et avie § 117 coll. viii (Nov. 117).

NOTES

1. M. M. Sheehan, "The Influence of Canon Law on the Property Rights of Married Women in England," *Mediaeval Studies* 25 (1963): 109–24; *The Will in Medieval England* (Toronto, 1963), 234–39.

2. Two other important studies touching on the subject have come from the pen of one of the contributors to this volume; see Charles Donahue, Jr., "Lynd-wood's Gloss *propriarum uxorum*: Marital Property and the *ius commune* in Fifteenth-Century England," in *Europäisches Rechtsdenken in Geschichte und Gegenwart: Festschrift für Helmut Coing zum 70. Geburtstag*, ed. Norbert Horn (Munich, 1982), 19–37; and "What Causes Fundamental Legal Ideas? Marital Property in England and France in the Thirteenth Century," *Michigan Law Review* 78 (1979): 59–88.

3. Jurisdiction belonged to the Church in England by custom, not by right claimed under the canon law. See William Lyndwood, *Provinciale (seu Constitu-*

tiones Angliae) (Oxford, 1679), 170, s.v. *insinuationem;* and see also Brian Ferme, "The Testamentary Executor in Lyndwood's *Provinciale*," *Jurist* 49 (1989): 632–78. Probate jurisdiction was not finally withdrawn from ecclesiastical jurisdiction until 1857 (20 and 21 Victoria c. 77 § 23), but the extent and effectiveness of the jurisdiction are generally thought to have been curtailed before then. See William Holdsworth, *History of English Law*, 7th ed. (London, 1956), 1:625–30.

4. So stated by one English civilian in a precedent book written c. 1595: Canterbury Cathedral Library, MS. Z.3.27, f. 80v: "Wives in England bee in potestate maritorum. Not that the husband hath vitae et necis potestatem as the Romans had in the old time of their children." For a good discussion of the current *status quaestionis,* together with an abundant bibliography, see Janet Senderowitz Loengard, "'Legal History and the Medieval Englishwoman' Revisited," in *Medieval Women and the Sources of Medieval History,* ed. Joel T. Rosenthal (Athens, Ga., 1990), 210–36. An earlier but still useful survey is Ruth Kittel, "Women under the Law in Medieval England," in *The Women of England,* ed. Barbara Kanner (Hamden, Conn., 1979), 124–37.

5. See Lee Holcombe, *Wives and Property* (Toronto, 1983), 18–36; William Holdsworth, *History of English Law,* 5th ed. (London, 1942), 3:526–27, 542–45; F. Joüon des Longrais, "Le status de la femme en Angleterre," *Recueils de la Société Jean Bodin: La femme* 12 (1962): 135–241, esp. 174–81.

6. *The treatise on the laws and customs of the realm of England commonly called Glanvill,* bk. 7, c. 5, ed. G. D. G. Hall (London, 1965), 80.

7. *Bracton on the Laws and Customs of England,* f. 60b, ed. George Woodbine, trans. S. E. Thorne (Cambridge, Mass., 1968), 178–79.

8. *Fleta,* II c. 57, ed. H. G. Richardson and G. O. Sayles, Selden Society, vol. 72 (1953), 191.

9. E.g., Hostiensis, *Summa Aurea,* vol. 3: *de test. et ult. vol.,* no. 7 (Venice, 1574), col. 1035.

10. C. 23, in *Councils and Synods with other Documents relating to the English Church, vol 2: A.D. 1203–1313,* ed. F. M. Powicke and C. R. Cheney (Oxford, 1964), pt. 1, 682.

11. See *Concilia Magnae Britanniae et Hiberniae,* ed. David Wilkins (London, 1737), 2:705–6.

12. *Provinciale (seu Constitutiones Angliae),* 171–79, esp. 173, s.v. *propriarum uxorum:* "Nam res Paraphernales sunt propriae ipsius mulieris, etiam stante matrimonio, ... de quibus uxor libere testari potest, ut ibi innuitur. Et dicunter bona Paraphernalia quae uxor habet extra dotem."

13. See R. H. Helmholz, "Writs of Prohibition and Ecclesiastical Sanctions in the English Courts Christian," *Minnesota Law Review* 60 (1976): 1011–33; "The Writ of Prohibition to Court Christian before 1500," *Mediaeval Studies* 63 (1981): 297–314; Michael M. Sheehan, "Canon Law and English Institu-

tions: Some Notes on Current Research," in *Proceedings of the Second International Congress of Medieval Canon Law,* ed. Stephan Kuttner and J. J. Ryan (Vatican City, 1965), 391–97.

14. They are contained in *Registrum Hamonis Hethe,* ed. Charles Johnson, Canterbury and York Society, vol. 48 (1948).

15. Sheehan, "The Influence," *supra* n. 1, at 122. See also Doris Mary Stenton, *The English Woman in History* (London, 1957), 30–32, 86–87. See also Mary Carruthers, "The Wife of Bath and the Painting of Lions," *Publications of the Modern Language Association* 94 (1979): 209–18, esp. 210–11.

16. Smythes c. Wowere, Canterbury Cathedral Library, Act bk. Y.1.1. f. 47 (1373). The defendant John Wowere was called "executor testamenti Juliane uxoris sue defuncte."

17. Ex officio c. Soone, West Sussex Record Office, Chichester, Act bk. Ep I/10/1, f. 15 (1509). The defendant was cited "ad probandum testamentum Agnetis uxoris sue."

18. Coche c. Perkyn, Cambridge University Library, Act bk. EDR D/2/1, f. 63 (1376). The defendant was called "executor testamenti Johanne uxoris sue defuncte."

19. E.g., probate of will of wife of John Vryne, Hereford County Record Office, Hereford, Act bk. O/5, p. 3 (1453). Proof was made by John Vryne, the identity of the testatrix was not recorded, however, beyond the notation that she was Vryne's wife.

20. Ex officio c. Hallywell, Guildhall Library, London, Act bk. MS. 9064/6, f. 181v (1496). This was apparently a cause brought to secure a legacy in the will of Isabelle Hallywell; the testimony was that her husband was still alive, although he was not present in court and the claimant sought to charge the son as executor.

21. Probate of will of Joan Gold, Kent Archives Office, Maidstone, Act bk. DRb Pa 3, f. 347 (1458): "Exhibito testamento sive ultima voluntate Johanne Golde per Johannem sponsum suum, probatum est."

22. Ex officio c. Haute (court of the subdean of Salisbury cathedral), Wiltshire Record Office, Trowbridge, Act bk. D1/39/1/1, f. 95 (1478): "Citetur Johannes Haute carnifex parochie sancti Thome ad exhibendum testamentum uxoris sue."

23. Probate of will of Isabelle Walkar, York Minster Library, Act bk. M 2(1)a, f. 14 (1319): "Testamentum Isabelle Walkar probatum fuit viii die iunii et commissa est administracio bonorum ipsius defuncte infra nostram jurisdictionem existencium Willelmo Walkar marito suo de Holgate." See also: Inhabitants of Barnby c. Rynsham, Borthwick Institute of Historical Research, York, CP.F.271 (1489), in which there was testimony that the husband, "licenciavit et permisit Johannam Watkynson uxorem suam pre mortem legare et disponere dictos xxvi s. viii d."

24. Probate of will of Agnes Nassh, Buckinghamshire Record Office, Ay-

lesbury, Act bk. D/A/V/1, f. 10 (1493); administration of the testator's assets was committed to her husband, John.

25. Skipworth c. Cressey, Hertfordshire Record Office, Hertford, f. 3v (1515). Edith Wayte is recorded as having deposed, "quod erat presens et levavit predictum Willelmum Cressey de lecto quo iacebat et portabat eundum ad lectum in quo dicta Johanna iacebat infirma ut audiret ipsam disponere et condere testamentum suum et tunc, ... dicta Johanna peciit licenciam a dicto marito suo ut conderet testamentum; qui quidem Willelmus consensit et dedit ei licenciam."

26. British Library, London, MS. Reg. 11 A XI, fols. 7v– 8, printed below as an app.

27. See Offley c. Barret, British Library, London, Lansd. MS. 135, fols. 81v– 88 (1584), in which the question of the husband's consent was the critical legal question.

28. This raised such a presumption for purposes of securing the writ of consultation, which, according to the common law, permitted proof of the will; see *Year Book 12 Henry VII*, Trin. pl. 2, p. 24 (1497).

29. Canterbury Cathedral Library, Act bk. Y.1.10, f. 43v: "Notatur quod impedivit uxorem suam ad faciendum testamentum de bonis propriis que sibi portavit."

30. Cambridge University Library, Probate Act bk. EDR Liber B, f. 71v: "Rogerus Salter impedit ultimam voluntatem uxoris sue defuncte detinendo a Margaria Tolle de eadem unam cistam, unam togam, duo cooperteria ... et alia vestimenta."

31. Kent Archives Office, Maidstone, Act bk. DRb Pa 2, f. 27v: "Et publice proclamavit quod mulieres non possunt facere aliquod testamentum."

32. Hereford Record Office, Act bk. O/13, p. 204: "Et asseruit uxorem suam nullum condidisse testamentum nec ultimam voluntatem neque debere condere testamentum quia bona uxoris erant sua propria."

33. Ibid., 206: "Et penituit ei ut asseruit de dictis suis." This was in the session assigned "ad exhibendum fidele inventarium omnium bonorum paraphernalium dicte uxoris sue defuncte." The will was nuncupative and was duly probated.

34. See Donahue, "Lyndwood's Gloss," *supra* n. 2. The law relating to paraphernalia is also discussed in Susan Staves, *Married Women's Separate Property in England, 1660–1833* (Cambridge, Mass., 1990), 148–50.

35. E.g., the testament of Margery Milvale, in Kent Archives Office, Maidstone, P.R.C. 3/1, f. 70 (Archdeaconry of Canterbury, 1495), introduced "ut performatur testamentum primi mariti eiusdem defuncti." Two other examples: the testament of Agnes Dod, Canterbury Cathedral Library, Act bk. Y.1.10, f. 50 (1470), and testament of Agnes Soone, West Sussex Record Office, Chichester, Act bk. Ep I/10/1, f. 115 (1509).

36. E.g., ibid., DRb Pa 3, 380v (1467): "Exhibita ultima voluntate Johanne Miller in virginitate sua facta, probata est."

37. E.g., ibid., DRb Pa 3, f. 317 (1467): probate of the testaments of John Hacke and his wife Christina Hacke at the same session. This may also be the explanation for the apparently singular 1519 proceedings recorded in *An Episcopal Court Book for the Diocese of Lincoln, 1514–1520,* ed. Margaret Bowker, Lincoln Record Society, vol. 61 (1967), 86.

38. The courts were also required to record their *acta* by formal canon law. See Decretales Gregorii IX, at X 2.19.11, in *Corpus Juris Canonici,* ed. A. Friedberg (Leipzig, 1879), 2:313.

39. The extent of testation in the adult population is very difficult to gauge. One study put it at 50 percent of the adult male population in the sixteenth century; see Michael Zell, "The Social Parameters of Probate Records in the Sixteenth Century," *Bulletin of the Institute of Historical Research* 57 (1984): 107–13. Another put it closer to 30 percent; see Lloyd Bonfield, "Normative Rules and Property Transmission: Reflections on the Link between Marriage and Inheritance in Early Modern England," in *The World We Have Gained,* ed. L. Bonfield, R. M. Smith, and Keith Wrightson (Oxford, 1986), 165–66.

40. Taken from Kent Archives Office, Maidstone, Rochester Act bk. DRb Pa 3, fols. 308–38.

41. Taken from Canterbury Cathedral Library, Act bk. Y.1.10, fols. 289–329.

42. Taken from Guildhall Library, London, Probate Act bk. MS. 9168/1, fols. 9–26; none of these testaments came from women who were certainly married; their status was not normally given in the record, and no husbands acted as executors. The impression given by these figures is confirmed by Ann J. Kettle, " 'My Wife Shall Have It': Marriage and Property in the Wills and Testaments of Later Mediaeval England," in *Marriage and Property,* ed. Elizabeth M. Craik (Aberdeen, 1984), 96.

43. Taken from Hereford, Act bk. O/5, pp. 81–94. Married women can be identified as such only in cases in which their husbands acted as their executors.

44. Taken from Borthwick Institute of Historical Research, York, Prob. AB.1 (no fol.).

45. Taken from Act bk. Ep I/10/1, fols. 52–87. Forty-two testaments were proved. Of these five were by women, all of whom were stated to be widows.

46. Taken from Probate Act bk., Joint Record Office, Lichfield, B/C/10/2, fols. 1–25. For confirmation of the direction, see P. J. P. Goldberg, "Female Labour, Service and Marriage in the Late Medieval North," *Northern History* 22 (1986): 36.

47. See Nesta Evans, "Inheritance, Women, Religion, and Education in Early Modern Society as Revealed in Wills," in *Probate Records and the Local Community,* ed. Philip Riden (Gloucester, 1985), 67.

48. Norma Basch, *In the Eyes of the Law* (Ithaca, 1982), 51 (citing William Blackstone, *Commentaries on the Laws of England* [Chicago, 1899 ed.], 2:498).

49. See John of Atho (d. 1350), *Constitutiones Legatinae* (Oxford, 1679), tit. 14, p. 108, acknowledging contrary authority under the *ius commune*. For examples, see *Life and Death in Kings Langley: Wills and Inventories, 1498–1659,* ed. Lionel Munby (Herts., Engl., 1981), xix.

50. Well illustrated by a cause from the diocese of Rochester, Hoo c. Fromond, Kent Archives Office, Maidstone, Act bk. DRb Pa 1, f. 74v (1438). The plaintiff's husband initially appeared for her, but the court rejected this, requiring of the woman, "quod veniet et proponat actionem suam in proximo contra dictam Annam si velit."

51. See Henry Swinburne (d. 1624), *Treatise of Testaments and Last Wills* IV § 24, no. 12, 6th ed. (1743), 347. Contrast the Roman Law *Institutes* 2.10.6.

52. See *supra* n. 29–31 and accompanying text.

53. See J. H. Baker, intro., *The Reports of Sir John Spelman,* Selden Society, vol. 94 (1978), 66–70; R. L. Storey, "Clergy and Common Law in the Reign of Henry IV," in *Medieval Legal Records Edited in Memory of C. A. F. Meekings* (London, 1978), 347–51; Ralph Houlbrooke, "The Decline of Ecclesiastical Jurisdiction under the Tudors," in *Continuity and Change: Personnel and Administration of the Church of England, 1500–1642,* ed. Rosemary O'Day and Felicity Heal (Leicester, 1976), 239–57.

54. Canterbury Cathedral Library, Act bk. Y.1.10, f. 88; cited to introduce the testament of Isabelle Parys, with John Kynge the executor named in it, "allegavit quod non habuit unde condere potuit testamentum." The judge took the case under advisement but dismissed it in the next session.

55. Hereford, Act bk. O/13, p. 204; the husband of Agnes Spicer asserting that his wife "neque debere condere testamentum, quia bona uxoris erant sua propria." He was, however, rebuked by the judge for this statement.

56. Other instances in which a married woman was stated or assumed to have no property and consequently no right to bequeath anything: Cause of Isabelle Hallywell, Guildhall Library, London, Act bk. MS. 9064/6, f. 181v (1496); Cause of Katherine Hoke, Hereford, Act bk. O/13, p. 269 (1480); Cause of wife of Robert Gatyard, Cambridge University Library, Ely diocesan records, EDR Liber B, f. 34 (1463). See also *Rotuli parliamentorum* (Record Commission, 1832), 2:149 (complaint of 1344 to the effect that the making of wills by married women was "against reason"); Thyke v. Fraunceys, *Year Book Mich. 5 Edw. II* (1311) (Selden Society, vol. 63 [1947, for 1944], 241) ("A wife cannot claim property, and consequently she cannot make a testament," per Herle).

57. See, generally, Ralph A. Houlbrooke, *The English Family, 1450–1700* (London, 1984), 228–34.

58. See Frederick Pollock and F. W. Maitland, *History of English Law before the Time of Edward I,* 2d ed., (Cambridge, 1968), 2:404–5, 427–34; R. H. Helmholz, *"Legitim* in English Legal History," *Illinois Law Review* 1984: 659–74.

59. See *supra* nn. 6–8, and the civilian's opinion in the app. See also Sheehan, "Influence," *supra* n. 1, at 123, for the connection; and the connection between the goods of both in Bristol (c. 1240), in *Borough Customs,* vol. 2, ed. Mary Bateson, Selden Society, vol. 21 (1906), 108.

60. See, generally, J. M. W. Bean, *The Decline of English Feudalism, 1215– 1540* (Manchester, 1968); J. L. Barton, "The Medieval Use," *Law Quarterly Review* 81 (1965): 562; Amy Erickson, "Common Law versus Common Practice: The Use of Marriage Settlements in Early Modern England," *Economic History Review* 43 (1990): 21–39.

61. E.g., Maria L. Cioni, "The Elizabethan Chancery and Women's Rights," in *Tudor Rule and Revolution: Essays for G. R. Elton from His American Friends,* ed. DeLloyd Guth and John McKenna (Cambridge, 1982), 159, at 161– 62.

62. *Year Book Trin. 7 Edw. IV,* f. 14, pl. 8 (1467); *Year Book Mich. 18 Edw. IV,* f. 11, pl. 4 (1478).

63. E.g., Jay and Saunders c. Clarynbold (1421), Canterbury Cathedral Archives, Y.1.3, f. 172v (trust for support during lifetime of Martha Lord); Estate of Robert Cake (Rochester 1458), Kent Archives Office, Maidstone, DRb Pa 3, f. 357 (gift of goods to executrix *ad sustentationem* for wife and children); Estate of Powynes (Bath and Wells 1533), Somerset Record Office, Taunton, Act bk. D/D/Ca 8, f. 43v (gift "in usum commodum et utilitatem Walthiane filie eius"). On another occasion I hope to be able to deal more fully with the enforcement of trusts in the spiritual courts.

Chapter 8

Female Plaintiffs in Marriage Cases in the Court of York in the Later Middle Ages: What Can We Learn from the Numbers?

Charles Donahue, Jr.

Words, the old saw goes, are a lawyer's stock in tirade. The converse of this proposition is that numbers are not. The same was true, until quite recently, of historians. Small wonder, then, that legal history, the combination of the two disciplines, has traditionally avoided even the simplest forms of statistics. The recent vogue for statistics in historical writing, moreover, has produced a sufficiently large number of questionable results as to warn off all but the most assiduous devotees of the empirical method. Nevertheless, in an essay dedicated to a friend who was the pioneer in the use of quantitative methods to study the records of the English medieval ecclesiastical courts,[1] I want to argue that we can and should use quantitative methods in dealing with certain kinds of medieval material and that the records of the medieval ecclesiastical courts are a prime candidate for such study. I even want to argue that quantitative methods can help us answer that most puzzling of all questions—how do law and society interact?—and to illustrate that argument by examining what those methods can tell us about the role of women as plaintiffs in medieval marriage cases.[2] But I also want to argue that the work has to be done very carefully and that, at least in the case of this body of records, quantitative methods can only be a help to historical imagination; they cannot substitute for it.

First, then, we must use quantitative methods in studying the records

of the medieval ecclesiastical courts because there are so many records
and so few people working on them that the only hope for getting some
idea of the whole is to sample them and to describe them numerically.[3]
Skimming over the material and picking out what seem to be the most
interesting records may yield an answer to certain kinds of questions,
such as when a form or an idea first appeared or when a form or an idea
became part of the regular practice of a court. Even the answers to these
questions, however, may benefit from the greater precision that numbers
can give: When the form or idea first appeared did it begin slowly, or did
it spread rapidly? What do we mean when we say that a form or idea
was the "regular" practice of a court? Underlying both questions is an
implicit quantitative statement, a percentage of total cases, or of total
surviving cases. Words such as *slowly, rapidly,* and *regular* are proxies
for a judgment about what underlying numerical measures indicate.

When we come to ask the question, moreover, what effect the activities of the court had on society and what effect society, as opposed to,
or in addition to, the academic law, had on the behavior of the courts,
the question "how much" becomes even more critical. The essays in this
volume by Janet Loengard, Sue Sheridan Walker, and Barbara Hanawalt
draw attention to the variety of women's responses to litigation in the
civil courts and the essay by Cynthia Neville to the need for extraordi-
nary redress. In a legal system, such as medieval English canon law,
where decisions in individual cases were not meant to set precedents for
the decisions of other cases, the range of possible cases and possible
solutions was wide indeed. One can find in the records of the medieval
English ecclesiastical courts disputes involving a great variety of social
situations and support for a wide range of propositions about the law.
Unless one is simply to list all the possibilities, one must generalize, and
generalization ought to involve a commitment to what was normal and
what was abnormal. Not only must we commit ourselves to what was
normal and what was abnormal; we should also, as historians, try to tell
our readers how what was normal changed over time, how what was
normal became abnormal, and vice versa.

Finally, use of quantitative methods helps us to avoid the fascination
of the "interesting" case. There are many interesting cases in the records
of the medieval English ecclesiastical courts. They are made more interesting by the fact that in many of them the depositions have survived.
We can thus hear ordinary English men and women of the Middle Ages
speaking about their ordinary experiences. The dangers of relying on
such evidence are substantial: Witnesses frequently told lies, and the

process of redacting the testimony into a legal record involved considerable distortions. For historians who cannot resist the temptation to use deposition evidence, quantitative analysis is the penance for succumbing to that temptation. Quantitative evidence allows us to control the deposition evidence, to see which witnesses were telling normal lies and which abnormal and to see whether the way in which the witness tells his or her story was more likely to be a product of the witness or of the clerk who recorded the testimony.

Let me try to illustrate these points by focusing on marriage litigation in the court of York in the fourteenth and fifteenth centuries. Before we reach our social question, however, we must describe our records more broadly. There survive at the Borthwick Institute of Historical Research in York case files (cause papers) from 571 different cases that were heard before the archbishop's consistory court in the period from 1301 through 1499.[4] Two hundred and thirteen of these cases involve marriage, approximately 37 percent of the total.[5] The records are unusually full, and in marked contrast to most records of medieval ecclesiastical courts, they are spread over a relatively long period of time. They would seem, then, to be a good base of data to use in asking the question whether marriage litigation changed over the course of the late Middle Ages. In order to do this I will deal first with the 88 marriage cases that date from the fourteenth century and then with the 125 such cases that date from the fifteenth century.

It is well to sound a note of caution at the start: The York records are good, but they are not a random sample of medieval English marriage litigation.[6] In the first place, the York Consistory heard no criminal cases involving marriage at first instance, and it heard relatively few such cases on appeal.[7] Second, the York court was both the consistory court for a diocese that had many active archdeacons and the appellate court for the province. We would thus expect, and the records confirm this, that there will be a disproportionate number of the wealthy, the powerful, and the persistent among the litigants.[8] Third, although there are records of marriage cases (and of other types of cases) from every decade over our two-hundred-year period, the decades from 1380 to 1440 produced a disproportionate number of surviving files.[9] Fourth, record-keeping practices of the court changed over the course of two hundred years. As it is, the cause papers from the latter portion of the fifteenth century are not so helpful as those from the fourteenth and early fifteenth centuries.[10] A more thorough analysis of the surviving fifteenth-century act books would probably reveal more cases from that century and also provide more information about cases that are only skimpily recorded in the fifteenth-century cause papers.[11] Finally, my own analysis of the fifteenth-century records has not been as thorough as that of the fourteenth-century records.

Despite these difficulties, the work has proceeded to the point at which I can offer at least some preliminary numbers and hypotheses.

The subject matter of the fourteenth-century York marriage cases may be divided according to the type of claim that is being brought, employing a classification of types of claims that is found in the records themselves (table 1). The table shows that the overwhelming majority of actions concerning marriage brought in the York court in the fourteenth century were actions to enforce a marriage (78 percent), while only 19 percent were actions to dissolve or separate a marriage.[12] (The remainder concerned marital property.) Even if we exclude the ten marriage-and-divorce cases and the two marriage-enforcement actions that ended up as actions for separation,[13] the percentage of "straight" marriage-enforcement actions is still high (65 percent). But looking at the cases totally from the point of view of what was sought to be enforced does not tell us what was the crux of the case from a legal point of view, much less from a social point of view. To do this we need to know more. We need to know how the cases were defended (table 2) and what the results were (tables 4 and 5).

When we combine the claims and the defenses, we see that classifying the actions according to the claim frequently obscures what the core legal issue was in the case. For example, the core legal issue in a divorce case brought on the ground of precontract was identical to the core legal issue in a marriage-and-divorce case.[14] The remedy sought was different because the person with whom the precontract was made was not a party to the action, but the core legal issue was the same.[15] The issue in such cases was also identical to that in all the cases involving *competitores* and in the eight two-party marriage enforcement actions that were defended on the ground of precontract. While it is logically possible that cases involving *competitores* could have involved defenses to both marriages, in fact, none did. The fact-pattern that emerges is the same in all four types of cases: A marriage had concededly occurred. The concession might be *sub silentio,* but there was rarely much argument about it. Frequently, though not always, the conceded marriage was a formal one.[16] The issue was whether another marriage claimed or defended as a precontract had also occurred, and if it had occurred whether it had

TABLE 1. York Marriage Cases by Type of Claim

Type of Claim	Fourteenth Century		Fifteenth Century	
	Number	Percentage	Number	Percentage
Causa matrimonialis [a]				
De presenti [b]	28	31	47	38
De futuro [c]	7	8	7	6
Abjuration *sub pena nubendi* [d]	9	10	2	2
Uncertain form of marriage	3	4	9	7
Total	47	53	65	52
Three-party actions				
Causa matrimonialis et divorcii [e]	10	11	17	14
Competitores [f]	10	11	24	19
Total	20	23	41	33
Causa divorcii a vinculo [g]				
Precontract [h]	5	6	5	4
Other [i]	11	13	9	7
Total	16	19	14	11
Causa divorcii quoad mensam et thorum [j]	3	3	3	2
Other [k]	2	2	2	2
Grand Total	88	100	125	100

a. Two-party case to enforce a marriage.

b. Most cases involve informal marriages.

c. Most cases involve promise to marry plus intercourse.

d. Conditional marriage vows exchanged before a judge, normally after the couple has been convicted of fornication: "I take thee to wife/husband if I have carnal knowledge of thee."

e. Plaintiff sues a husband and wife seeking a divorce of their marriage and enforcement of his/her prior marriage with one of the couple.

f. Two men or two women sue a single woman or man, each claiming that the defendant is his/her lawful spouse.

g. Divorce from the bond, annulment.

h. Differs from *causa matrimonialis et divorcii* only in that the person with whom the precontract was made is not a party to the action.

i. Grounds: fourteenth century—affinity (3), force and nonage (2), impotence (2), crime (1), servile condition (1), uncertain (2); fifteenth century—consanguinity (2), force (2), impotence (4), servile condition (1).

j. Divorce from bed and board, separation. Grounds: fourteenth century—adultery and cruelty (2), uncertain (1); fifteenth century—adultery and cruelty (3).

k. Fourteenth century: marital property, *maritagium* (1), dower (1); fifteenth century: action to recover payment for registration of marriage sentence (1), letter certifying freedom from marriage (1).

antedated the conceded one. Normally, the claimed precontract was an informal *de presenti* marriage, although this was not always the case.

Cases raising the issue of precontract occurred more frequently in the fourteenth-century York marriage cases than cases raising any other type of issue (45 percent, table 2),[17] although straight-out denial of the factual validity of the claim occurred in a comparable number of cases (42 percent). This latter type of defense produced a second cluster of legal issues, sometimes found in combination with issues involving precontract. We may have a simple denial of the factual validity of the claim, with no further defense being offered or surviving (9 percent). More often, we have an attack on the witnesses for the other side, alleging that they were unreliable because of their personal characteristics or because they were corrupted or, simply, because they got the story wrong (18 percent).[18] Frequently, an attack on the witnesses was accompanied by an exception of absence, an "alibi" defense: The marriage alleged could not have taken place because one of the parties was someplace else at the time.[19] Exceptions of absence are found in 13 percent of the fourteenth-century York marriage cases. Finally, an unusual defense is found in five of the cases (7 percent), the exception of disparity of wealth. Disparity of wealth was legally irrelevant to the question whether a marriage had been formed. The defense was raised in order to attack the credibility of the claimant's story. The defendant, so the argument ran, could not possibly have married someone whose status was so much below his or hers. The defense was also offered in order to attack the plaintiff's witnesses: The claimant and his or her witnesses were alleged to have fabricated the story in an effort to get the defendant's wealth. Altogether 42 percent of the fourteenth-century York marriage cases raised one or another type of attack on the factual validity of the claimant's story.

All other issues pale in comparison with the defense or claim of precontract and the attack on the factual validity of the claim of the marriage sought to be enforced. The next most common defense was force or nonage (12 percent). Altogether 80 percent of the cases raise one or a combination of these three types of defenses. We occasionally see one of the numerous other issues to which the medieval canon law of marriage could give rise. Cases in the fourteenth century raised issues of consanguinity or affinity (11 percent), unfulfilled condition (7 percent), crime (5 percent), procedure (4 percent), servile condition (3 percent), and impotence (3 percent). Many of these were in divorce actions (11 percent of cases). Altogether, 32 percent of the cases raised one or more

TABLE 2. York Marriage Cases by Type of Defense

Type of Defense	Fourteenth Century		Fifteenth Century	
	Number	Percentage	Number	Percentage
Precontract				
Divorce for precontract	5	7	5	5
Marriage and divorce	10	13	17	17
Competitors	10	13	24	24
Two-party enforcement [a]	9	12	5	5
Subtotal	34	45	51	50
Denial				
"Straight" denial	13	17	10	10
Exceptions to witnesses	14	18	18	18
Absence	10	13	16	16
Disparity of wealth	5	7	6	6
Subtotal [b]	32	42	41	41
Force and/or nonage				
Force [c]	8	11	13	13
Nonage	6	8	4	4
Subtotal [d]	9	12	16	16
Other				
Consanguinity/affinity [e]	8	11	5	5
Unfulfilled condition [f]	5	7	3	3
Crime [g]	4	5	0	0
Procedural objections [h]	3	4	0	0
Servile condition [i]	2	3	1	1
Impotence [j]	2	3	4	4
Vow	0	0	1	1
Orders	0	0	1	1
Mental incapacity (drunkenness)	0	0	1	1
Subtotal	24	32	16	16
Grand Total [k]	76	100	101	100

Notes: Includes claims in annulment cases but excludes defenses in such cases, e.g., dispensation. Excludes separation and "other" cases entirely.

a. Includes one fourteenth-century case of prior bond, i.e., former spouse still living at time of subsequent contract.

b. Cases with more than one defense of this type are counted as one.

c. Includes two fifteenth-century divorce cases.

d. Cases with more than one defense of this type are counted as one.

e. Includes three fourteenth- and two fifteenth-century divorce cases.

f. Includes one fourteenth-century divorce case on ground of precontract.

g. I.e., adultery plus a promise to marry during the lifetime of a former and now-deceased spouse. Includes one divorce case.

h. On appeal to proceedings below; includes two abjuration cases.

i. I.e., unbeknownst to the complaining spouse at the time of the marriage the defending spouse was of servile condition. Includes one fourteenth- and one fifteenth-century divorce case.

j. All divorce cases.

k. Counting as one cases in which more than one type of defense is raised. Seven (14th c.) and nineteen (15th c.) cases reveal no defense. Five separation and "other" cases in each century excluded from table.

of these issues that I have classified as "other." (The reason that 80 percent of the actions involved precontract, denial and/or force, but nonetheless 32 percent of the actions raised an "other" defense is that, in 12 percent of the cases that have defenses, one or more of the "core" defenses was raised and one or more of the "other" defenses.)

Analysis of the claims and defenses alone—even without examining the results or speculating about the social significance of the cases— makes one thing quite clear: What was *legally* significant about marriage litigation in the court of York in the fourteenth century was the principle that present consent freely given between parties capable of marriage, even without solemnity or ceremony, makes an indissoluble marriage. The type of marriage sought to be enforced or claimed as a precontract was most often a *de presenti* informal marriage (table 3). Of the 122 marriages at stake in the fourteenth-century York cases, 95 (78 percent) of them were *de presenti* marriages, 9 (7 percent) *de futuro,* and the type of the remaining 18 (15 percent) cannot be determined.[20] Of the 50 *de presenti* marriages claimed in the first instance, 49 were informal, and only one formal.[21] The proportion of formal marriages raised by way of defense was higher, 14 out of 24 (58 percent). All told, of the 74 *de presenti* marriages raised by way of claim or defense,[22] 59 (80 percent) were informal. When this is coupled with the fact that 68 percent of the cases in which the defense is known (52 out of 76) involved either a defense on the facts or precontract, or both, and another 9 (12 percent) involved force or nonage, the legal significance of the core principle becomes apparent.

How did the court react to these claims and defenses? Marriage cases in fourteenth-century York produced a high proportion of judgments,[23] much higher than in any other type of case. Sixty-four of our eighty-eight cases (73 percent, see table 4) have judgments from one level of court or another. Although in many cases we lack the results on appeal, confirmations were more common than reversals in those cases in which we do have a result on appeal. Thus, any judgment may be taken as a pretty good indication of what the result on appeal is going to be. The first and perhaps most striking characteristic of judgments in marriage cases in fourteenth-century York is the number that are favorable to the plaintiff (51 out of 64 [80 percent]). We should discount this number for the possibilities that some of them would have been reversed on appeal and that plaintiffs abandoned or settled unfavorably some of the cases that have no judgments when it became apparent that judgment would probably go against them. Even if we do discount the number in this way, the court of York in the fourteenth century was still a decidedly pro-plaintiff court in marriage litigation.[24]

Plaintiffs were successful in almost all types of actions. Seventeen of the nineteen (89 percent) two-party actions to enforce a *de presenti* informal marriage that have judgments resulted in judgments for the plaintiff, as did four of the five two-party actions to enforce a *de futuro* promise to marry followed by intercourse and both of the two-party actions to enforce a marriage in which the type of marriage cannot be determined. All ten of the three-party competitor actions have judgments for one plaintiff or the other. Plaintiffs were successful in four of the five actions for divorce on the ground of precontract that have judgments and six of the seven actions for divorce on other grounds that have judgments. Plaintiffs were comparatively less successful in abjuration actions, however, winning six of nine judgments, even less successful in marriage and divorce actions, winning only three of six judgments, and totally unsuccessful in separation actions, losing both of the cases in which a judgment survives.

Obviously, the judgment in each case depends on how successful each of the parties and their witnesses were in persuading the judge, but the pattern of successes and the exceptions to it suggest some places where we might look for clues to what the judges found to be persuasive. One principle that will explain many of the results is that the York court (and many of the lower courts in the province) indulged in a broad presumption in favor of marriage.[25] If the great majority of the cases are marriage-enforcement actions, the great majority of plaintiffs will be successful if the court indulges in that presumption. This principle also explains some of the exceptions to the general rule that plaintiffs usually win. Both two-party *de presenti* enforcement cases that plaintiffs did not win involved a defense of precontract. A presumption in favor of marriage will not help in this type of case; the question must be to which marriage will the presumption attach. Similarly, the relatively low success rate of plaintiffs in marriage-and-divorce actions may be explained by the fact that these were hard cases. However the judge ruled, a marriage, or at least a claimed marriage, was going to be upset. The same is true of the cases involving competitors. All ten of them were won by plaintiffs, but the nature of the action means that in ten such cases plaintiffs lost.[26] The presumption in favor of marriage will also explain the singular lack of success of those seeking a separation.

TABLE 3. York Marriage Cases by Type of Marriage

| | Fourteenth Century | | | | | | | | | Fifteenth Century | | | | | | | | | |
| | Claimed first | | | | | Defense [a] | | | | Claimed first | | | | | Defense | | | | |
Type of Case	DP	IN	FO	DF	UN	DP	IN	FO	UN	DP	IN	FO	DF	UN	DP	IN	FO	DF	UN
Two-party enforcement																			
De presenti	28	28	0	0	0	6	3	3	3	47	37	3	0	0	2	2	0	0	1
De futuro	0	0	0	7	0	0	0	0	0	0	0	0	7	0	0	0	0	0	0
Abjuration	9	0	0	0	0	0	0	0	0	2	0	0	0	0	0	0	0	0	0
Uncertain	0	0	0	0	3	0	0	0	0	0	0	0	0	9	0	0	0	0	0
Three-party actions																			
Marriage and divorce [b]	7	7	0	1	2	6	1	5	4	16	12	2	0	1	12	2	9	0	6
Competitors	9	9	0	1	0	7	5	2	3	24	22	1	0	0	17	15	0	1	6
Annulment																			
Precontract [c]	5	5	0	0	0	5	1	4	0	3	3	0	0	2	4	0	4	0	1
Other [d]	9	2	7	0	2	0	0	0	0	9	0	9	0	0	0	0	0	0	0
Separation [e]	3	0	3	0	0	0	0	0	0	3	0	3	0	0	0	0	0	0	0
Other [f]	1	0	1	0	1	0	0	0	0	1	1	0	0	0	0	0	0	0	0
Total	71	51	11	9	8	24	10	14	10	105	75	18	7	12	35	19	13	1	14
Percent of grand total	81	58	13	10	9	71	29	41	29	85	60	15	6	10	70	38	26	2	28
Total less divorce [h]	59	49	1	9	6	24	10	14	10	93	75	6	7	12	35	19	13	1	14
Percent of total less divorce [i]	78	64	1	12	8	71	29	41	29	83	67	5	6	11	70	38	26	2	28
Cumulative [j]	83	59	15	9	16					136	93	28	8	26					
Percent of cumulative total	75	54	14	8	15					79	58	12	5	16					

Notes: DP = *De presenti* marriage; IN = informal *de presenti* marriage; FO = formal *de presenti* marriage; DF = *de futuro* marriage; UN = uncertain form of marriage. The IN plus FO do not total to the DP in the fifteenth century because a number of the marriages claimed are of uncertain formality.

a. There are no DF marriages claimed as a defense in the fourteenth-century cases.

b. Defense column includes one fifteenth-century case in which two formal marriages were dissolved.

c. Gives first the marriage claimed as precontract, then the marriage from which the divorce is being sought.

d. Gives first the marriage from which the divorce is being sought.

e. Gives first the marriage from which the separation is being sought.

f. One fifteenth-century case omitted.

g. Totals: fourteenth-century first claim, 88; fourteenth-century defense, 34; total fourteenth century 122; fifteenth-century first claim, 124; fifteenth-century defense, 50; total fifteenth century 174.

h. I.e., excluding annulment "other" and separation.

i. Totals: fourteenth-century first claim, 76; fourteenth-century defense, 34; total fourteenth century 110; fifteenth-century first claim, 112; fifteenth-century defense, 50; total fifteenth century 162.

j. I.e., all marriages claimed or defended excluding annulment "other" and separation cases.

The presumption in favor of marriage will not, however, explain the relative lack of success of plaintiffs in abjuration actions. Although plaintiffs ultimately won two-thirds of these actions (six of nine), it took some doing to get there. Two plaintiffs had to appeal to the official from adverse decisions of the commissary general before prevailing. It is hard to escape the sense that the institution of abjuration *sub pena nubendi* was not favored by the York court, particularly at the end of the fourteenth century.[27]

The presumption in favor of marriage will also not explain the success rate of plaintiffs in cases of divorce other than those based on precontract. Here again we must look more deeply at the cases themselves. Suffice it to say that in four of the cases the plaintiff put in a straightforward and compelling case; one does not give the nature of the ground

TABLE 4. York Marriage Cases: Sentences for Female and Male Plaintiffs, Fourteenth Century

Type of Case	FP	MP	% F	SFP	SMP	TO	SFD	SMD	TO	GTO
Two-party *de presenti*	20	8	71	13	4	17	1	1	2	19
Two-party *de futuro*	7	0	100	4	0	4	0	1	1	5
Abjuration	9	0	100	6	0	6	0	3	3	9
Two-party marriage	3	0	100	2	0	2	0	0	0	2
Three-party marriage & div.	9	1	90	3	0	3	0	3	3	6[a]
Three-party competitors	5	5	50	5	5	10	0	0	0	10[b]
Divorce precontract	1	4	20	0	4	4	0	1	1	5
Divorce other	6	5	55	3	2	5	0	1	1	6
Separation	3	0	100	0	0	0	0	2	2	2
Other	1	1	50	0	0	0	0	0	0	0
Total	69	29	70	36	15	51	1	12	13	64

Ratio of sentences to cases: 73% (74/88).
Ratio of female plaintiffs to all plaintiffs: 73% (36/51).
Ratio of successful female plaintiffs to all successful plaintiffs: 71% (64/88).
Female plaintiff success rate: 75% (36 won, 12 lost).
Male plaintiff success rate: 94% (15 won, 1 lost). [c]

Notes: FP = female plaintiff; MP = male plaintiff; % F = ratio of female plaintiffs to total plaintiffs; SFP = sentence for female plaintiff; SMP = sentence for male plaintiff; TO = total sentences for plaintiffs (or defendants); SFD = sentence for female defendant; SMD = sentence for male defendant; GTO = grand total of sentences.

a. In this type of case, a sentence for defendants is automatically a sentence for both a man and a woman. Classifying the case as a sentence for both would throw off the ratios.

b. In this type of case a sentence for one plaintiff is automatically a sentence for the defendant against the other plaintiff. This classification overstates plaintiffs' success, but classifying the case as a sentence for both the winning plaintiff and the defendant obscures the reality. See text and n. 30.

c. See discussion in n. 30.

for the divorce, and the final one is a complicated case involving affinity in the fourth degree.[28]

On the face of it, then, the results all seem quite close to what we have called the core principle of the medieval canon law of marriage: Present consent, even if informally given, will prevail over all else, so long as it is freely given. In almost all the cases in which an alleged marriage did not prevail, a prior marriage was asserted and proved, or it was shown that the consent was not given or that the consent was not free. Occasionally the numerous other issues to which the canon law of marriage could give rise were raised, and occasionally they prevailed, but only occasionally. Take away the core principle, and one cannot explain the bulk of the marriage cases that were litigated in fourteenth-century York.

But what is the social significance of this core legal principle? To put the question another way, why do so many cases raise issues about informal *de presenti* marriage? This is not the type of question about which litigation records give an easy answer, particularly if we are confining ourselves to what can be learned from numbers. It is possible to organize the fact-patterns of the cases into groups and to draw some numerical conclusions from the proportions and changes of proportions in the types of stories that the witnesses told. That procedure, however, involves a substantial amount of interpretation of the records.[29] For our purposes here let us look, rather, at a number that requires no interpretation to derive: the sex ratio of the litigants.

Marriage litigation in the court of York in the fourteenth century was an activity that women initiated. Sixty-four of our eighty-eight four-teenth-century marriage cases (73 percent) have female plaintiffs (table 4). Since a high percentage of the judgments were in favor of the plaintiffs, marriage litigation in the York court in the fourteenth century was not only an activity that women initiated; it was also an activity at which women were successful. In fact, the ratio of successful female plaintiffs to all successful plaintiffs was approximately the same as the ratio of female plaintiffs to all plaintiffs (71 percent vs. 73 percent).

Female plaintiffs did not have as high a success rate, however, as male plaintiffs (71 percent vs. 81 percent).[30] Thus, despite the fact that women win cases in proportion to their proportion in bringing them, the success rate of male plaintiffs is higher. The reason that both statements are true is that fifty-six of the sixty-three female plaintiffs (88 percent) pursued their cases to judgment, whereas only fifteen out of the twenty-four male plaintiffs did (63 percent). The women had to lose more cases than the men in order to get a number of favorable judgments equal to their proportion in the population.

The evidence that we are looking at, then, suggests that female plaintiffs in the York court in the fourteenth century were more persistent than male plaintiffs. As a result, they lost more cases, although ultimately they won proportionally as many as the men did. Now, at least to me, this result is surprising. One has learned that women, at least in our society, tend to compromise more than men do, that they are less interested in winning than men are, more interested in keeping a relationship going than in "scoring points."[31] This does not seem to be characteristic of the female litigants in our sample. There are a number of possible explanations for why this should be the case. One possibility, obviously, is that whatever may be true of women in our society was not true of medieval women in the York province. There are certainly stereotypes of women in medieval literature that might lead us to believe that this was true, but, on balance, I am inclined to discount this suggestion. Another possibility, closer perhaps to the mark, is that female litigants pursued cases that they ought not to have pursued because they misestimated their chances of success. This could be because, despite the high number of successes, the court was biased against women. Even more of them should have won than did win. Or it could be that women did not have access to the advice that men did and so pursued cases that men knew were better dropped or compromised. Finally, it could be that women pursued more cases because they had more to gain by winning or less to lose by losing. Classically "rational" behavior would suggest that someone will pursue a course of conduct even if his or her perception of the odds is the same as another's, if the benefits to be gained from success are greater or the costs of losing are less.

There is some evidence for this last suggestion in the final numerical analysis of this group of cases that I shall undertake. Although women, overall, brought almost three out of four of the marriage cases brought in the York court over the course of the fourteenth century, this ratio was by no means constant over the different types of cases (table 4).

I have already suggested that the legal issues in three-party cases of either type and in cases of divorce on the ground of precontract were identical. But the sex ratios were not. Men hardly ever brought a marriage-and-divorce action, women hardly ever brought an action for divorce on the ground of precontract, and the competitor actions were evenly divided between the sexes. This is hard to explain, but some hint at an explanation may be given by the other types of cases in which there is an imbalance. Except for the competitor actions, the cases in which men were dominant as plaintiffs were all cases in which the result of the action, if successful, would be that the man would get out of a marriage and not get into another one. Women, on the other hand, were dominant in cases in which the result, if the case was successful, would be that the plaintiff would be declared the wife of the defendant.

In four of the eight two-party *de presenti* enforcement actions in which a man was the plaintiff, the defendant is a widow.[32] That suggests that financial considerations were important. In three of the other such cases, the defendant raises a defense of nonage or force.[33] That suggests an arranged marriage and, again, that financial considerations played an important role. In two of the five competitor cases in which men were the plaintiffs, the defendant is also a widow.[34]

The evidence, then, suggests the following: Men sued to enforce a marriage when the financial stakes were high. They dropped cases when the chances of success did not look good. They sued to get out of a marriage more frequently than did women. Women, on the other hand, sued in cases in which the financial advantages to them were less obvious. They sued to enforce a marriage far more often than did men; they sued to dissolve one much less often. They were much more persistent in their suits. They were the only plaintiffs in cases alleging a *de futuro* promise followed by intercourse and in cases of abjuration *sub pena nubendi*.

So summarized, the evidence suggests a tentative hypothesis: Female litigants seem to have valued marriage qua marriage more than did male litigants. This was particularly true in cases in which they had been "compromised" (an allegation that is rarely denied), but it was also true in cases in which it was not alleged, or even suggested, that intercourse had taken place. If we hypothesize that the female litigants valued marriage more than the men did, that would explain why they sued when the financial considerations were not obvious, why they sued more often to enforce a marriage and less often to dissolve one, and why they were more persistent.

Why women should have valued marriage more than men did is only hinted at in our records, and yet the question is fundamental. Marriage in the Middle Ages, as in many societies, seems to have given women more in the way of security and status than it did men. As is well known, the economic opportunities outside of marriage and family were far more limited for most medieval women than they were for most medieval men, even when they were quite limited for most medieval men. This fact meant that relations between the sexes were imbalanced. A man could give a woman more by marrying her than she could give him. That in turn meant that the balance of power in sexual relations lay with the men. The York court in the fourteenth century, with its plaintiff-friendly pattern of judgments, served to some extent to redress this imbalance of power.

So far all we have is a hypothesis, one that I have suggested was at least plausible. To prove that hypothesis, or at least to put it on a firmer footing, one must do more: One must search the depositions and see if there is a difference in the types of stories that women tell and those that men tell that gives credence to the hypothesis suggested by the numbers. That is a large undertaking, and I will not attempt it here. The numbers will not help us with this inquiry. What the numbers have done is help us considerably in framing the question and in answering a number of preliminary questions that help us to identify the problem.

The numbers also help considerably in tracing changes across time. To illustrate this point let us look at another set of York marriage cause papers, those from the fifteenth century. Some commentators have suggested that there were gradual and subtle changes in marriage litigation in England in the fifteenth century.[35] These are just the type of changes that ought to be capturable with numerical indicators.

Table 1 suggests that the pattern of claims brought in the fifteenth century was similar to that in the fourteenth, with one major difference: there were 10 percent more three-party actions (33 percent vs. 23 percent),[36] an increase that was largely made up for by a corresponding reduction in the number of annulment actions (11 percent vs. 19 percent).[37] While both marriage-and-divorce and competitor actions experienced increases, the bulk of the increase was in the competitor actions (19 percent vs. 11 percent).[38] This means that it is even truer of the fifteenth century than it was of the fourteenth that the overwhelming majority of actions (85 percent) were actions to enforce a marriage, while only 13 percent were actions to dissolve or separate a marriage. (In the remainder the basic claim is uncertain.)[39]

As with the fourteenth-century cases, we need to know how the fifteenth century cases were defended and what the results were if we are to discover the crux of each case from a legal point of view and to begin to explore its social implications. Table 2 lays out the defenses in the fifteenth-century cases, and it shows that a somewhat greater percentage of fifteenth-century cases involved a defense that sought to establish another marriage (50 percent vs. 45 percent),[40] while approximately the same number involved a factual denial of the claim (41 percent vs. 42 percent),[41] and somewhat more a claim of force or nonage (16 percent vs. 12 percent).[42] There are fewer cases defended on the grounds of consanguinity and/or affinity, unfulfilled condition, or the impediment of crime. On the other hand, the fifteenth century gives us one example each of defenses that we do not see in the fourteenth century: vow, orders, and drunkenness (indicating mental incapacity to consent).[43] None of these differences is statistically significant and, in any case, are not very great.[44] Overall, we may say that marriage cases were defended in approximately the same way in fifteenth-century York as they were in fourteenth-century York.

Similarly, what was *legally* significant about the rules of medieval canon law about marriage in the York cases of the fifteenth century, as it was in the fourteenth century, is what we have called the core principle: again, that present consent freely given between parties capable of marriage, even without solemnity or ceremony, makes an indissoluble marriage (see table 3). Of the 174 marriages at stake in the fifteenth-century York cases (whether sought to be enforced or claimed as a precontract), 140 (80 percent) were *de presenti* marriages, 8 (5 percent) were *de futuro,* and the type of the remaining 26 (15 percent) cannot be determined. Not only this, but of the 93 *de presenti* marriages claimed at first instance, 75 (81 percent) were informal and six (6 percent) formal.[45] The proportion of formal marriages raised by way of defense is higher, 13 out of 35 (37 percent). All told, of the 134 *de presenti* marriages raised by way of claim or defense,[46] 93 (69 percent) were informal.

While there are slight differences in these proportions when they are compared to those in the fourteenth-century cases, and though more work needs to be done with the fifteenth-century cases in which the type of marriage is uncertain, the results are quite similar to those reported for the fourteenth century. In both cases they confirm the legal significance of the core principle.

As in the fourteenth century, marriage cases in fifteenth-century York produced a high proportion of judgments (56 percent; see table 5). The percentage, however, is not so high as it was in the fourteenth century (73 percent). As a descriptive matter, the reason for this difference is that the decades from 1460 to 1490 produced relatively few cases with judgments, but it is not clear why there should have been fewer judgments in these decades. A combination of different types of record keeping and a general decline of the court probably produced this phenomenon.[47] For our purposes what it means is that, when we speak of judgments in fifteenth-century York cases, we are speaking for the most part about judgments in the first six decades of the century.

The court of York remained a decidedly pro-plaintiff court during the fifteenth century. Fifty-six out of the seventy-two judgments that survive (78 percent) are favorable to the plaintiff (vs. 80 percent in the fourteenth century). As in the fourteenth century, plaintiffs dominated all types of actions, with a couple of exceptions. Plaintiffs won sixteen of the twenty-three (70 percent) two-party actions to enforce *de presenti*

TABLE 5. York Marriage Cases: Sentences for Female and Male Plaintiffs, Fifteenth Century

Type of Case	FP	MP	% F	SFP	SMP	TO	SFD	SMD	TO	GTO
Two-party *de presenti*	26	21	55	8	8	16	4	3	7	23
Two-party *de futuro*	7	0	100	0	0	0	0	2	2	2
Abjuration	1	1	50	1	1	2	0	0	0	2
Two-party marriage	5	4	56	0	0	0	0	2	2	2
Three-party marriage & div.	10	7	59	5	1	6	1	3	4	10[a]
Three-party competitors	15	9	63	13	8	21	0	0	0	21
Divorce precontract	3	2	60	2	1	3	1	0	1	4
Divorce other	7	2	78	6	1	7	0	0	0	7
Separation	2	1	67	1	0	1	0	0	0	1
Other	0	2	0	0	0	0	0	0	0	0
Total	76	49	61	36	20	56	6	10	16	72

Ratio of sentences to cases: 56% (72/125).
Ratio of female plaintiffs to all plaintiffs: 61% (76/125).
Ratio of successful female plaintiffs to all successful plaintiffs: 64% (36/56).
Female plaintiff success rate: 78% (36 won, 10 lost).
Male plaintiff success rate: 77% (20 won, 6 lost). [b]

Notes: FP = female plaintiff; MP = male plaintiff; % F = ratio of female plaintiffs to total plaintiffs; SFP = sentence for female plaintiff; SMP = sentence for male plaintiff; TO = total sentences for plaintiffs (or defendants); SFD = sentence for female defendant; SMD = sentence for male defendant; GTO = grand total of sentences.

a. In this type of case, a sentence for defendants is automatically a sentence for both a man and a woman. Classifying the case as a sentence for both would throw off the ratios.

b. Caution: As noted above (n. 30), this figure is sensitive to the way we characterized the three-party competitor cases. If we include the eight male plaintiffs who lost in those actions, the rate becomes 59 %, but, then again, the women's rate goes down too if we include the thirteen female plaintiffs who lost such actions (61%, 36/59). Again, if we characterize these actions as a total victory for one plaintiff and a half a victory for the defendant, the absolute value of the percentages changes but they remain similar: 67% (male), 67% (female). Ignoring the competitor cases produces a 70% rate for the women and a 67% rate for the men.

marriages. Twenty-one of the twenty-four (88 percent) competitor actions resulted in a judgment for one plaintiff or the other. Plaintiffs were successful in three of the four actions brought on the ground of precontract that have judgments and in all seven of the actions for divorce on grounds other than precontract that have judgments.

By contrast with the results in the fourteenth century, plaintiffs in fifteenth-century York won both the abjuration actions they brought, and the plaintiff won the only separation action in which there was a judgment. In all three cases the plaintiffs had compelling cases.[48] We may speculate that the lack of success of fourteenth-century plaintiffs in such actions led to their being disfavored by plaintiffs. Only plaintiffs who had particularly strong cases would bring them. That would account both for plaintiffs' success in such actions in the fifteenth century and also for the quite small number of such actions.

Finally, as in the fourteenth century, York plaintiffs in the fifteenth century were comparatively less successful in marriage-and-divorce actions, winning only six out of ten judgments.

As in the fourteenth century, the presumption in favor of marriage will explain most of the results in the fifteenth-century York marriage cases.[49] The presumption even explains the relative lack of success of plaintiffs in marriage-and-divorce cases. It will not, of course, explain their success in divorce cases brought on grounds other than precontract. The absolute number of such cases is small, although plaintiffs' success rate is high, and in each case the result may be explained by the fact that the plaintiff put in a convincing case. Again, the disfavored action is brought only by those who have a strong case.

When we come, however, to the sex ratios of the parties, marriage litigation in fifteenth-century York was clearly not the same as it was in the fourteenth century. In the first place, although women still brought more actions than men (61 percent), the disproportion was considerably less than it was in the fourteenth century (73 percent).[50] As it was in fourteenth-century York, the ratio of successful female plaintiffs to total successful plaintiffs was approximately the same as their ratio to total plaintiffs (64 percent vs. 61 percent). In marked contrast to the fourteenth-century cases, however, female plaintiffs' success rate was also approximately the same as male plaintiffs' (78 percent vs. 77 percent, 61 percent vs. 59 percent, 67 percent vs. 67 percent, depending on how you calculate the rate; see table 5).

We thus have two changes to explain: Why the percentage of female plaintiffs went down in fifteenth-century York and why women behaved the same as men in pursuing their cases in the fifteenth century, while in the fourteenth century they seem to have been more persistent than men? I cannot offer definitive answers to these questions, but I would like to close by suggesting some answers as a framework for future research.

I have suggested that fourteenth-century women valued marriage more than did men. I supported this suggestion with evidence that indicated that female plaintiffs sued to enforce a marriage more often than male plaintiffs did, sued less often to dissolve one, and did so in situations in which financial considerations were not obvious. Female plaintiffs were also more persistent than men in pursuing cases that they ultimately lost. None of these characteristics seems as true of the fifteenth century. In the fifteenth century, both men and women sued in cases in which financial considerations seem to have been important, and both men and women sued in cases in which such considerations are not obvious. Further, and perhaps more reliably, the dominance of women in actions to enforce a marriage (as opposed to actions to dissolve one) simply disappeared. Only in the relatively few actions to enforce a *de futuro* promise did women maintain the dominance that they had in the fourteenth century. In abjuration actions, two-party marriage actions of uncertain type, and marriage-and-divorce actions, their proportion approximately equals their overall proportion as plaintiffs. The converse of this proposition is that in the fifteenth century, men no longer dominated certain types of actions. Their proportion in actions for divorce on the ground of precontract and in competitor actions equals their overall proportion as plaintiffs. Women dominated the fifteenth-century actions brought for divorce on grounds other than precontract, whereas in the fourteenth century the percentage of male and female plaintiffs in such actions was approximately equal.

This is not to say that cases do not provide some evidence for the proposition that fifteenth-century women valued marriage more than did men. The overwhelming proportion of fifteenth-century actions are actions to enforce a marriage, and women bring 61 percent of all actions. But we cannot confirm our suspicion that women valued marriage more than men by looking at the different types of actions brought in the fifteenth century.

We are dealing with proportions, not with absolutes. If it is plausible that women in the fourteenth century valued marriage more than men did, the fact that their litigation rate goes down compared to men suggests that the relative valuation by the two sexes of marriage changed over the course of the century. This could have happened either because women valued marriage in the fifteenth century less than they did in the fourteenth, and so brought fewer cases, with the men moving in to fill up the slack, or because men valued marriage more in the fifteenth century than they did in the fourteenth and so brought more cases, thus reducing the percentage of women. The two explanations are not logically inconsistent, and the data are quite consistent with either or both explanations.[51]

Further, and perhaps most troubling, is the fact that some of the changes in proportions may be the result not of changes in the values that plaintiffs placed on winning but, rather, in their perception of their chances of winning. If male plaintiffs were successful in certain kinds of actions in the fourteenth century, female plaintiffs in the fifteenth century may have learned from their experiences and brought more of these types of action. Conversely, male plaintiffs could have learned from the success of female plaintiffs in the types of actions in which women tended to dominate and could have brought more of these types of actions.

While I suspect that some such transfer of knowledge between the two groups of plaintiffs was occurring, such a transfer will not fully explain the differences that we see between the two centuries. It will not, for example, explain the decline in the proportion of female plaintiffs, nor will it explain the larger proportion of women seeking to dissolve a marriage rather than enforce one. We are forced to ask, therefore, if there is any ground for believing that there was either a relative increase in men's valuation of marriage in the fifteenth century over the fourteenth or a relative decrease in women's valuation of marriage over the same two centuries? I have suggested in the case of the fourteenth century that women valued marriage more than men did because marriage gave women more security and status than it gave men. It would be foolish to suggest that the resulting imbalance of power in sexual relations was eliminated in the fifteenth century, and the fact that women continued to bring more cases than men suggests that it was not. On the other hand, if we focus on the last decades of the fourteenth century (from which most of our fourteenth-century cases come) and the middle decades of the fifteenth century (from which most of our fifteenth-century cases come), there are suggestions in the social, and particularly in the economic, history of the two periods that make the notion that women were less dependent on marriage in the latter period at least plausible.

As is well known, the decades following the Black Death saw sharp general increases both in prices of goods and services and in the wages of labor. At the same time population fluctuated radically, as new outbreaks of plague defeated the natural tendency of a population to replenish itself after a disaster. These decades would also seem to be—this is more controversial—a period in which many traditional social networks were breaking down, as laborers migrated in search of high wages and geographical areas adjusted to the differential impact of plague on the population.[52] This combination of circumstances might have been peculiarly unfavorable to single women. Obviously, there would be substantial differences among such women depending on their class, wealth, and skills, but as a general matter, a single adult woman in a society in which prices were fluctuating radically but generally rising and wages were rising as well would be worse off than a single adult woman in a society in which prices were steady and labor cheap. Unable to be self-sustaining both because of her supposed physical inability to do certain kinds of work (e.g., ploughing) and because of the social barriers that prevented her from doing other kinds of work (e.g., many trades), the single woman with some capital (be it land, goods, or skills) would be better off in a society in which she need not expend much of her capital to obtain basic necessities and in which she could easily hire others to do what she could not do herself.[53] When prices and wages went up, particularly when they fluctuated on an upward trend, single women during the late fourteenth century had more need of the economic potential of a husband to give them some measure of economic security. This would be all the more important if social networks were breaking down, since that could have meant that there were fewer stable households in which single women could work as servants or live as "paying guests" or as members of an extended family.

In the fifteenth century prices stabilized at a level higher than they were before the plague but lower than they had been during the fourteenth-century peaks. Wage rates also stabilized at a relatively high level—sufficiently high that most students of the subject believe that there was a substantial transfer of wealth from the upper economic classes to the working population. Population, on the other hand, took a sharp drop, and then began a slow process of increasing. Social networks may well have become more stable. This combination of circumstances might have been less unfavorable to single women than the circumstances at the end of the fourteenth century. The greater economic stability of the early decades of the fifteenth century would have allowed a greater amount of wealth to be stored and transferred to women by way of inheritance or dowry and thus would have made women less dependent on the wages of their husbands. There may have been more stable households in which single women could have lived. Particularly, among lower-level merchants and artisans and the upper levels of the peasantry (classes that seem to have formed the bulk of the litigating population at York), greater wealth and greater stability overall could have meant that women would have had an easier time living without a husband. If they were wealthy, they could have brought more into a marriage than they could have in the latter decades of the fourteenth century. The economic contribution that each partner made to a marriage would thus have tended to equalize. Under these circumstances, we would expect to find more men and fewer women seeking to enforce marriages in the fifteenth century than in the fourteenth. And that is just what we find.

Obviously, this argument needs more spelling out and refinement than can be done within the confines of this chapter.[54] It is offered as a suggestion, a way to deal with what seems to be a long-term trend in litigation rates in the York court. If the suggestion is correct, however, it means that the high proportion of female plaintiffs that we see in the York court in the fourteenth century is not an indication of a high status for women, as might be assumed, but, rather, quite the reverse and that their relative absence as plaintiffs in the fifteenth century suggests some improvement in status.

Finally, what of the court and its effect on these social patterns? I suggested above that the pro-plaintiff pattern of judgments of the court served, to some extent, to redress the imbalance of power between the sexes in late fourteenth-century York. With the appearance of more male plaintiffs and more female defendants in the fifteenth century, the court's pattern of sentencing did not change. Indeed, the decades from 1460 to 1490, which have the lowest proportion of female plaintiffs, have the highest rate of pro-plaintiff judgments (67 percent, 100 percent, and 100 percent). In individual cases one can detect a particular sympathy of the court with the story that a woman is telling. On a statistical basis, which is all that I have undertaken in this chapter, the

York court appears as a pro-plaintiff court, whether the plaintiff is a man or a woman.

NOTES

1. Michael M. Sheehan, "The Formation and Stability of Marriage in Fourteenth-Century England: Evidence of an Ely Register," *Mediaeval Studies* 33 (1971): 228–63.

2. Technically, there were no "plaintiffs" in the medieval ecclesiastical courts; there was a *pars actrix* and a *pars rea*. In civil litigation, however, the two terms were sufficiently close to the modern *plaintiff* and *defendant* that it seems precious to use the Romano-canonic terms.

3. For a sense of the extent of the records, see Charles Donahue, ed., *The Records of the Medieval Ecclesiastical Courts, pt. 1: The Continent,* Comparative Studies in Continental and Anglo-American Legal History, vol. 6 (Berlin, 1989). A similar description of the surviving English records will take another whole volume in the series.

4. For the archive and its general classes, see David M. Smith, *A Guide to the Archive Collections in the Borthwick Institute of Historical Research,* Borthwick Texts and Calendars, vol. 1 (York, 1973); David M. Smith, *A Supplementary Guide to the Archive Collections in the Borthwick Institute of Historical Research,* Borthwick Texts and Calendars, vol. 7 (York, 1980). The fourteenth-century files under discussion here are classed as CP.E. and are calendared in David M. Smith, *Ecclesiastical Cause Papers at York: The Court of York, 1301–1399,* Borthwick Texts and Calendars, vol. 14 (York, 1988). The fifteenth-century files are classed as CP.F. and are described in an older handlist available at the institute. For statistical purposes I have grouped some cases that are in separate files and separated some cases that are in the same file, but the references offered in the notes are all to existing file numbers in the two series.

5. The percentage of the total is slightly different in the two centuries (34 percent in the fourteenth century; 40 percent in the fifteenth century), but since the confidence intervals overlap, it is better to combine them. (For confidence intervals, see Charles Donahue, Jr., "Roman Canon Law in the Medieval English Church," *Michigan Law Review* 72 [1974]: 712–13, and sources cited, and my n. 6.)

6. I have argued elsewhere that they may be a random sample, or at least an unbiased sample of litigation in the court of York (Donahue, "Roman Canon Law," 708–12). I am convinced enough of the validity of those arguments that we will employ some kinds of simple statistical tests with this data (confidence intervals and chi^2 tests). Of course, there is no reason for believing that the York

cases are an unbiased sample of all medieval marriage cases, far less an unbiased sample of all medieval marriages.

7. E.g., CP.E. 82/[8d] (1339); CP.F. 123 (1434).

8. E.g., Alexander de Percy, kt. c. Robert de Colville, kt., CP.E. 12 (1323); William Hagarston c. Mary, widow of Robert, baron of Hilton, CP.F. 314, 310/[2] (1467). Let me record an impression for which I do not yet have, and may never have, numbers to support: As the distance from the city of York increases, so does the wealth of the litigants. Within a radius of about twenty or thirty miles from the city the litigants in the court of York are quite ordinary people, ranging from citizens of York to village tradespeople and the wealthier peasants. Such people probably make up at least two-thirds of the litigants. The remaining one-third is heavily biased in the direction of the wealthy, though normally not rising above the class of simple knights. The very poor are almost, but not entirely, absent.

9. This may be seen most clearly in the following list, which gives by twenty-year period the number of marriage cases (MM), the number of all cases (TO), the ratio of marriage cases to total cases in the period (percentM), the expected number of marriage cases (assuming that they were evenly spread over the 200-year period), and their expected percentage (XM, Xpercent), and the expected total number of cases and the expected percentage of the grand total (XT, Xpercent):

York Cases, Actual vs. Expected Percentages

	MM	TO	%M	XM	X%	XT	X%
1300–1319	3	14	21	21	37	57	10
1320–39	12	29	41	21	37	57	10
1340–59	15	47	32	21	37	57	10
1360–79	20	52	38	21	37	57	10
1380–99	38	115	33	21	37	57	10
1400–1419	30	109	28	21	37	57	10
1420–39	40	80	50	21	37	57	10
1440–59	22	40	55	21	37	57	10
1460–79	21	37	57	21	37	57	10
1480–99	12	48	25	21	37	57	10
Total	213	571	37				

Three points stand out from this data: (1) Both the total number of cases and the number of marriage cases peaks in the years from 1380 to 1440, but the peak in the number of marriage cases comes later than that in other kinds of cases, and the decline in the number of marriage cases in the latter part of the fifteenth century is not so sharp as it is in other types of cases. The overall decline in the latter part of the fifteenth century may be more apparent than real. As we note in the text, the York court seems to have made more use of act books for record-keeping purposes in the fifteenth century than it did in the fourteenth. Nonetheless, it is hard not to see a connection between this decline and the overall decline in York's economy in the latter part of the fifteenth century. See E. Miller, "Medieval York," in *A History of Yorkshire: The City of York,* ed. P. M. Tillott, Victoria History of the Counties of England (London, 1961), 84–106. If this is correct, the gentler decline in marriage litigation may be an indication that medieval marriage litigation was less subject to economic fluctuations than were other kinds of litigation, although I will argue at the end of the chapter that some aspects of marriage litigation may be related to economic trends. (2) The total number of cases increases at the very end of the fifteenth century. Although analysis of the sixteenth-century cause papers at York is still in its infancy, it is clear that their numbers are of a different order of magnitude from those of the fifteenth century. (Over three thousand file numbers are in use.) It has been suggested (see, e.g., R. H. Helmholz, *Marriage Litigation in Medieval England* [Cambridge, 1974], 165–68) that marriage litigation did not participate fully in this increase, and the results from the last two decades of the fifteenth century suggest that this phenomenon was already occurring. (3) Assiduous devotees of the literature on the court of York will note that having published two analyses of the subject matter of the surviving fourteenth-century York cause papers, I have once more changed my mind (Donahue, "Roman Canon Law," 659; "Institutional History from Archival History," in *The Weightier Matters of the Law,* ed. John Witte and Frank S. Alexander, Essays on Law and Religion, vol. 51 [Atlanta, 1988], 43). I now believe that the number of cases is best described as 257. This recalculation slightly changes the overall percentages but not enough to warrant a republication of the entire table.

10. Cause papers from the second half of the fourteenth century and the first decades of the fifteenth century tend to be carefully endorsed with the names of the proctors and the date, sometimes also with *acta.* Where the case can also be found in the act books (see n. 11), the act book rarely gives much more information than could have been learned from the cause papers themselves. Sometime in the middle of the fifteenth century endorsement practice changed radically; relatively little is found on the dorse of the documents from this period onward. There are also relatively few sentences from this period. This may be because more reliance was being placed on act books that are now lost, or it may be because the personnel of the court were losing their grip. What has not yet been done is to correlate the surviving cause papers from the last two decades of the fifteenth century with the two act books that survive from this period. It is here that the hope for recovery of more information is greatest. See n. 47.

11. Two fragments of act books with entries bearing dates from 1371 to 1375 survive in the archives of York Minster (York Minster Archives and Library, M2/1b and M2/1c). These fragments are interesting, but they contain little of relevance to the subject of marriage litigation. The main series of Consistory Court Act Books is at the Borthwick. There are five of them for the fifteenth century: Cons.AB.1 (1417–20), Cons.AB.2 (1424– 27), Cons.AB.3 (1428–30), Cons.AB.4 (1484–89), and Cons.AB.5 (1497–1508). Thus, the middle decades of the fifteenth century, which are relatively poor in cause papers, also have no surviving act books.

12. For the reader who is convinced (as I am; see n. 6) that the surviving York marriage cases are an unbiased sample of all York marriage litigation in the relevant period, I can offer the following guidance for proceeding from these sample statistics to estimates of the overall population: Confidence intervals for proportions are broader in the middle of the distribution than they are in the tails. Thus, at a confidence coefficient of .9, the 78 percent figure given in the text is valid within approximately plus or minus four percentage points (and the same is true of its opposite, 22 percent). As we approach 50/50, the interval widens to plus or minus five or six percentage points; as we go toward 90/10, or vice versa, the interval narrows to about three percentage points. With a sample of this size we should be reluctant to say much at all about any proportion more extreme than 90/10, except that it is large (or small).

13. CP.E. 257 (1349); CP.E. 274 (1395).

14. It is logically possible that a marriage-and-divorce action could be brought on the ground not of precontract but of postcontract, with the prior marriage being attacked because of another impediment to it. There is one fifteenth-century case in which such an issue is raised (CP.F. 101 [1431]). Even here, however, the ground for the invalidity of the concededly prior marriage is a precontract with a person other than the plaintiff.

15. For similar reasons all the divorce cases that raise issues that might also be raised in a marriage enforcement action (e.g., consanguinity) may be said to involve the same legal issue as the corresponding marriage enforcement actions.

16. I have used the terms *formal* and *informal* in order to avoid that most difficult of terms, *clandestine marriage*. I define a "formal" marriage as one that takes place publicly at a church in the presence of a priest. (Banns should have been promulgated for such a marriage, and many cases mention them, but some do not.) All other marriages are classified as "informal."

17. Note that the percentages in table 2 are calculated on the basis of those cases in which the defense (or, in the case of divorce, the claim) is known.

18. For a summary of the types of issues that could be raised in such exceptions with references to York cases, see Charles Donahue, Jr., "Proof by Witnesses in the Church Courts of Medieval England," in *On the Laws and Customs of England,* ed. Morris S. Arnold et al. (Chapel Hill, N.C., 1981), 127–58.

19. On exceptions of absence, see Donahue, "Roman Canon Law," 693–95; "Witnesses," 144, and sources cited.

20. If we classify the abjurations as de futuro marriages, as technically they are not (see literature cited in n. 27), the figures become 86 (70 percent), 18 (15 percent) and 18 (15 percent).

21. I have excluded from this calculation the abjuration cases and the divorce cases brought on grounds other than precontract. Ten of the twelve marriages involved in the divorce cases were formal. By its very nature the exchange of consent in an abjuration case is formal, but the fulfillment of the condition was normally highly informal.

22. Again, excluding the abjuration cases and the cases of divorce on grounds other than precontract.

23. The records avoid using the word *judgment* (*judicium*), perhaps because judgment is reserved for God. They use, instead, the word *sentence* (*sententia*, and its verbal forms). Unfortunately, *sentence* has become associated with criminal cases in modern English, and we have preferred the less literal *judgment*.

24. Even if we assume, e.g., that *every* case that has no judgment was abandoned or compromised by the plaintiff because the case was going badly for him or her (something that strikes me as highly unlikely, given the vagaries of the survival of the records), plaintiffs still received favorable judgments in 58 percent (51/88) of all actions brought.

25. Such a presumption has support in the academic law. See L. de Naurois, "Matrimonium gaudet favore iuris," *Revue de droit canonique* 29 (1979): 54–73.

26. It is rare that the defendant in a competitor action contests both actions. Normally, the defendant concedes one of the actions and contests the other. This leads to the suspicion that in some of these cases one of the plaintiffs is "friendly" to the defendant. In six of the ten competitor actions the plaintiff who won was the plaintiff whom the defendant seems to have favored.

27. This impression, of course, is formed by more than just the numbers, and its confirmation must await another occasion. See Helmholz, *Marriage Litigation,* 172–81; Sheehan, "Formation and Stability," 245–55; Rudolf Weigand, "Die Rechtsprechung des Regensburger Gerichts in Ehesachen unter besonderer Berücksichtung der bedingten Eheschliessung nach Gerichtsbüchern aus dem Ende des 15. Jahrhunderts," *Archiv für katholisches Kirchenrecht* 107 (1968): 403–63.

28. "Straightforward": CP.E. 26 (1334) (force); CP.E. 259 (1348) (impotence); CP.E. 76 (1375) (nonage); CP.E. 105 (1370) (impotence). Uncertain: CP.E. 158 (1395). Affinity: CP.E. 140 (1372).

29. I hope to be able to do this in a forthcoming book.

30. Caution: this figure is very sensitive to the way we characterize the three-party competitor cases. If we characterize them as we did in table 4, as a victory for the plaintiff who won, ignoring the plaintiff who lost, the success rate of

male plaintiffs is 94 percent and that of female 75 percent. (Chi^2 = 3.000; this is significant at a level between .9 and .95, i.e., a difference this size can be produced "by the luck of the draw" between one in ten and one in twenty. On the use of chi^2, see Donahue, "Roman Canon Law," 713–14, and literature cited. There are more sophisticated measures of significance, but chi^2 is easy to calculate, and I will use it throughout this chapter.) If we include the five male plaintiffs who lost competitor actions, their success rate becomes 71 percent, the same as the women, but the women's rate goes down too if we include the five female plaintiffs who lost such actions (68 percent, 36/53), but not so much because there are many other kinds of women's actions. (This difference is not significant; chi^2 = .113.) The first rate overemphasizes plaintiffs' success, because it ignores the failure of the other plaintiff; the second rate overemphasizes defendants' success both because it gives undue weight to this type of case (it makes it seem like two cases, whereas it is in fact only one) and because it suggests that the victory for the plaintiff who won was also a victory for the defendant, which is not always the case. The rate given in the text compromises by counting plaintiffs' victory in such cases as one and plaintiffs' loss in such case as one-half a victory for defendants (female: 36/14.5; male: 15/3.5). (Chi^2 = 1.951, significant at approximately .7.) Ignoring the competitor cases, the female plaintiff success rate is 72 percent (31 won, 12 lost), and the male plaintiff success rate is 91 percent (10 won, 1 lost). (Chi^2 = 6.779, significant at approximately .9.)

31. Of a large recent literature on this topic, one might cite Carol Gilligan, *In a Different Voice* (Cambridge, Mass., 1982). Judith M. Bennett, *Women in the Medieval English Countryside* (Oxford, 1987), 31, notes a similar quality of persistence among the female litigants in Brigstock manor court before the plague and suggests some of the same explanations for it that I offer here.

32. CP.E. 241I (1345); CP.E. 61 (1348); CP.E. 62 (1348); CP.E. 179 (1390).

33. CP.E. 85 (1362); CP.E. 89 (1365); CP.E. 97 (1368).

34. CP.E. 188 (1391); CP.E. 245 (1391).

35. Helmholz, *Marriage Litigation,* 165–83.

36. Chi^2 = 6.779, significant at approximately .99.

37. Chi^2 = 4.941, significant between .95 and .99.

38. Chi^2 = 8.585, significant beyond .995.

39. There is one other difference in the types of cases that may be significant. While the overall proportion of two-party marriage enforcement actions was approximately the same over the two centuries (53 percent vs. 52 percent), there were substantially more *de presenti* actions in the fifteenth century (38 percent vs. 31 percent) and substantially fewer abjuration actions (10 percent vs. 2 percent). The first difference is significant at just under the .9 level (chi^2 = 2.546), the second well beyond the .995 level (chi^2 = 9.800). While chi^2 is unreliable for samples as small as the one that we have for abjuration cases, the

decline in abjuration cases is confirmed in the literature (see n. 21). The increase in *de presenti* cases is not confirmed in the literature, and I would want to look further both at the records and at other statistical measures before I made much of this.

40. Chi^2 = 1.232, significant between .7 and .8.

41. Chi^2 = .082, not significant.

42. Chi^2 = 1.411, significant between .7 and .8.

43. We also find, as we do not in the fourteenth century, one instance each of condonation and ratification as defenses in divorce cases.

44. See nn. 40–42. The difference in precontract and force/nonage cases is significant if we are willing to be wrong approximately one out of four times. One might rely on this if there were other reasons for believing that there was a real difference, but, as it is, it seems better to ignore the difference.

45. There were two abjuration cases, and the degree of formality of the remaining ten cannot be determined. For the exclusion of the abjuration cases, see n. 21.

46. Excluding the abjuration cases and the cases of divorce on grounds other than precontract.

47. See n. 10. The decades that have the lowest percentage of surviving marriage cause papers are the 1470s (7 percent), 1480s (4 percent), and 1490s (6 percent), while the decades that have the lowest percentage of judgments in the cause papers are the 1460s (25 percent), 1470s (22 percent), and 1480s (40 percent).

48. CP.F. 56 (1410) (adultery); CP.F. 78 (1418) (abjuration); CP.F. 123 (1434) (abjuration).

49. In marked contrast to the fourteenth-century cases, the presumption will not explain the two-party cases that defendants won. There are seven of these, five defended on the ground of absence (with one adding a defense of disparity of wealth and another a more general attack on the witnesses) and two defended on the ground of force.

50. Chi^2 = 9.439, significant beyond .995.

51. If we could arrive at a plausible estimate of the overall litigation rate in the relevant population, we could make a start on a hypothesis about which is at stake. Such a number may be calculable; Michael Sheehan calculated one for Ely in the fourteenth century ("Formation and Stability," 231–34), with considerable diffidence, given the uncertainties about the population figures and the possibility of overlapping jurisdictions. These same difficulties are multiplied when it comes to trying to calculate such a number for the York province in the fourteenth and fifteenth centuries. The time frame is much wider, the area much larger, and the competing jurisdictions more complicated.

52. The social and economic generalizations in this and the succeeding paragraph can be pursued in any of the standard books: e.g., J. L. Bolton, *The*

Medieval English Economy, 1150–1500 (London, 1981); Edmund King, *England, 1175–1425* (London, 1979). I do not recall having seen elsewhere the argument made here about the differential effects of these changes on women and men, but the literature is large, and I may simply have missed it.

53. The situation of the single woman without capital is more complicated. Her comparative situation depends on whether the wage of "women's work" rises comparably to that of men's. My impression is, however, that the typical female plaintiff in the court of York is not one without capital, however small that capital may have been.

54. In particular, there are many assumptions about life cycles buried in the argument. This is a complicated topic, though I believe that what I have said here can be reconciled with the more recent work on the topic. See, e.g., Richard M. Smith, ed., *Land, Kinship and Life-Cycle* (Cambridge, 1984).

Contributors

James A. Brundage, Ahmanson-Murphy Distinguished Professor of History at the University of Kansas, specializes in the history of medieval European law. His recent books include *Law, Sex, and Christian Society in Medieval Europe* (1987) and *The Crusades, Holy War and Canon Law* (1991). He is currently at work on a study of the emergence of canon lawyers as a professional elite.

Charles Donahue, Jr., currently a professor of law at Harvard, received his B.A. at Harvard University and his LL.B. at Yale University. His publications include *Select Cases from the Ecclesiastical Courts of the Province of Canterbury c. 1200–1301* (1981); *Records of the Medieval Ecclesiastical Courts, pt. 1: The Continent.* Comparative Studies in Continental and Anglo-American Studies in Continental and Anglo-American Legal History, vol. 6 (1989); and, with others, *Cases and Materials on Property: An Introduction to the Concept and the Institution,* 3d ed. (1992). He is the author of articles in the fields of medieval canon law, English legal history, and modern property. He is working on a book on the intersection of marriage and society in the Middle Ages.

Barbara A. Hanawalt, professor of medieval history at the University of Minnesota, received her Ph.D. from the University of Michigan. Her publications include *Crime and Conflict in English Communities, 1300–1348* (1979), *The Ties That Bound: Peasant Families in Medieval England* (1986), and *Growing Up in Medieval London: The Experience of Childhood in History* (1993). She has also edited several collections of essays, including *Women and Work in Preindustrial Europe* (1986) and *Chaucer's England: Literature in Historical Context* (1992).

Richard H. Helmholz, currently Ruth Wyatt Rosenson Professor of Law at the University of Chicago, is a graduate of Princeton University and Harvard Law School and received his Ph.D. in medieval history from the University of California–Berkeley. Like Michael Sheehan, he has interested himself in the workings of the ecclesiastical courts in medieval England, trying to show the relevance of canon and Roman laws in the historical development of English and American law. Among his publications are *Marriage Litigation in Medieval England* (1974), and his most recent book, *Roman Canon Law in Reformation England,* was published in 1990.

Janet Senderowitz Loengard is a professor of history at Moravian College and a lecturer in law at Rutgers School of Law–Newark. She is the author of a number of articles on topics in medieval and sixteenth-century English legal history, and her volume *English Viewers and Their Certificates, 1508–1558* was published in 1989. She received her B.A. from Cornell University, her LL.B. from Harvard, and her Ph.D. from Columbia.

Cynthia J. Neville is currently an associate professor of history at Dalhousie University in Halifax. She completed her M.A. in medieval history at Carleton University, Ottawa, under the supervision of John J. Bellamy, and her Ph.D. at the University of Aberdeen, where she worked with Grant G. Simpson. She held a Social Sciences and Humanities Research Council (SSHRC) of Canada Postdoctoral Fellowship in the Department of History at Dalhousie University from 1987 to 1989 and after that was a SSHRC Canada Research Fellow there. She is the author of several articles on the laws and customs of the Anglo-Scottish borderlands in the later medieval period and is currently working on a book on the subject.

Joel T. Rosenthal has his Ph.D. and other degrees from the University of Chicago and is a professor of history at SUNY–Stony Brook. He has published on Anglo-Saxon England and the social history of late medieval England. Recent publications include (editor) *Medieval Women and the Sources of Medieval History* (1990) and *Patriarchy and Families of Privilege in Fifteenth-Century England* (1991).

Sue Sheridan Walker, professor of history at Northeastern Illinois University, holds a Ph.D. from the University of Chicago. She edited *The Wakefield Court Roll for 1331–33* (1982). Most of her research and writing is based on plea rolls and related materials in the Public Record Office; her articles explore the law relating to widows and wards. A 1990–91 Newberry Library / National Endowment for the Humanities Fellow, she is presently working on a book about the legal and social context of dower litigation in the royal courts of late medieval England.

Index